Neutralization

The function of language is to transmit information from speakers to listeners. This book investigates an aspect of linguistic sound patterning that has traditionally been assumed to interfere with this function – neutralization, a conditioned limitation on the distribution of a language's contrastive values. The book provides in-depth, nuanced, and critical analyses of many theoretical approaches to neutralization in phonology, and argues for a strictly functional characterization of the term: neutralizing alternations are only function-negative to the extent that they derive homophones, and, most surprisingly, neutralization is often function-positive, by serving as an aid to parsing. Daniel Silverman encourages the reader to challenge received notions by carefully considering these functional consequences of neutralization. The book includes a glossary, discussion points, and lists of further reading to help advanced phonology students consolidate the main ideas and findings on neutralization.

DANIEL SILVERMAN is Associate Professor in the Department of Linguistics and Language Development at San José State University, California.

KEY TOPICS IN PHONOLOGY

'Key Topics in Phonology' focuses on the main topics of study in phonology today. It consists of accessible yet challenging accounts of the most important issues, concepts and phenomena to consider when examining the sound structure of language. Some topics have been the subject of phonological study for many years, and are re-examined in this series in the light of new developments in the field; others are issues of growing importance that have not so far been given a sustained treatment. Written by leading experts and designed to bridge the gap between textbooks and primary literature, the books in this series can either be used on courses and seminars, or as one-stop, succinct guides to a particular topic for individual students and researchers. Each book includes useful suggestions for further reading, discussion questions, and a helpful glossary.

Forthcoming titles:

Underlying Representations by Martin Kraemer

Variation in Phonology by Marc Van Oostendorp

Modularity in Phonology by Thomas Purnell, Eric Raimy and Joseph Salmons

Intonation and Prosody by Caroline Féry

Phonological Markedness by Elizabeth Hume

Distinctive Features Christian Uffmann

Neutralization

DANIEL SILVERMAN

CAMBRIDGE UNIVERSITY PRESS
Cambridge, New York, Melbourne, Madrid, Cape Town,
Singapore, São Paulo, Delhi, Mexico City

Cambridge University Press
The Edinburgh Building, Cambridge CB2 8RU, UK

Published in the United States of America by
Cambridge University Press, New York

www.cambridge.org
Information on this title: www.cambridge.org/9780521145015

First published 2012

Printed and bound in the United Kingdom by the MPG Books Group

A catalogue record for this publication is available from the British Library

Library of Congress Cataloging-in-Publication Data

Silverman, Daniel Doron, 1963–
   Neutralization / Daniel Silverman.
      p.   cm.
   ISBN 978-0-521-19671-0 (Hardback) – ISBN 978-0-521-14501-5 (Paperback)
   1. Neutralization (Linguistics)   2. Grammar, Comparative and general–Phonology.
3. Phonetics. I. Title.
   P299.N48S53 2012
   414–dc23

                                                                            2012001738

ISBN 978-0-521-19671-0 Hardback
ISBN 978-0-521-14501-5 Paperback

"If singing birds must sing, with no question of choice
Then living is our song, indeed our voice ... "   Paddy McAloon

Contents

List of figures		*page ix*
Preface		*xi*
Acknowledgments		*xiv*
1.	The rhyme and the reason of neutralization	1

Part I: Rhyme   13

Section A: Observation and description

2.	Topology	15
3.	Taxonomy	31
4.	Typology	42

Section B: False positives

5.	Partial phonemic overlap	53
6.	Near-neutralization	62

Section C: Explanation

7.	Ease of production	78
8.	Ease of perception	86
9.	Phonetic misperception	101
10.	Semantic misperception: early proposals	110
11.	Semantic misperception: recent proposals	119

Section D: Exemplification

12.	Case study	130
13.	Domains of application	140
14.	"Distinctions are drawn that matter"	149

Part II: Reason   159

15. Cement   161

16. Boundary signals   165

17. Prosodies   .   174

18. Transitional probabilities   188

19. The power of Babelese   194

Glossary   200
References   204
Language index   218
Subject index   220

Figures

2.1: Russian *ta* and *ti*
(Based on Mikolaj Kruszewski, Očerk Nauki O Jazyke
[An outline of linguistic science]. In Konrad Koerner,
ed. 1995. *Writings in General Linguistics*, 1995. Amsterdam:
John Benjamins. 35–178. With kind permission by John
Benjamins Publishing Company, Amsterdam/Philadelphia.
www.benjamins.com.)   17

2.2: Articulation as multiple paths through a cylinder
(Reprinted with permission from Kenneth L. Pike, 1952.
Operational phonemics in reference to linguistic relativity.
Journal of the Acoustical Society of America **24**: 618–625.
Copyright ©1952, Acoustical Society of America.)   20

2.3: An "orchestral score" in Nootka
(Charles F. Hockett. 1955. *A Manual of Phonology*.
Indiana University Publications in Anthropology and
Linguistics 11.)   21

2.4: A superficial breakdown of orchestral "voices"
(Reproduced with permission from MIT and
John A. Goldsmith.)   22

2.5: Distinctive patterns of nasality's distribution within the
syllable in Songkhla
(Eugenie J. A. Henderson. 1985. Feature shuffling in
Southeast Asian languages. In Suriya Ratanakul,
David D. Thomas, and Suwilai Premsrirat, eds., *Southeast
Asian Linguistic Studies Presented to André-G. Haudricourt*.
Institute of Language and Culture for Rural Development,
Mahidol University. 1–22.)   23

2.6: A "gestural score" of "palm"
(Catherine P. Browman and Louis Goldstein. 1986.
Towards an articulatory phonology. *Phonology Yearbook 3*.
Cambridge University Press. 219–252.)   24

2.7:   Movement of the articulators during "good morning"
       (John Kelly and John Local. 1989. *Doing Phonology*. Manchester
       University Press. Permission granted by Paul Tench.)   25
2.8:   The articulatory spans and acoustic cues of a canonical
       voiceless nasal
       (Daniel Silverman. 1995 (1997). *Phasing and Recoverability.*
       Doctoral dissertation, University of California, Los Angeles.
       Outstanding Dissertations in Linguistics series. New York:
       Garland.)   26
2.9:   The "genuinely balletic" character of articulation
       during the production of "loony"
       (Daniel Silverman. 2006. *A Critical Introduction to
       Phonology: Of Sound, Mind, and Body*. London/New York:
       Continuum Books.)   27

Preface

"OVERARCH"

"Neutralization" is a conditioned limitation on the distribution of a language's contrastive values.

The theses explored herein:

(1) Most cases of neutralizing alternation are heterophone-maintaining, and are consequently function-neutral in the sense that lexical semantic distinctness remains stable.

(2) Only in those rare instances when a neutralizing alternation is homophone-deriving might it be function-negative, in terms of potentially rendering lexical semantic content non-distinct.

(3) Indeed, neutralization is often function-positive, as it may serve as an aid to parsing the speech stream into its functional (morphemic and lexical) components.

In all, it is proposed that neutralization may proceed largely unchecked (thus increasing what I term phonological RHYME), until encountering a passive, usage-based pressure inhibiting excessive derived homophony (that is, until phonological REASON would be breached).

"UNDERGIRD"

The book considers neutralization from many different theoretical vantage points and schools of linguistic thought, from Kazan, to Prague, to London, to Boston, to Los Angeles, and beyond.

The book is divided into two parts. For the bulk of the book – RHYME – I observe, describe, and explain neutralization from many different theoretical perspectives, all the while building towards a discussion of neutralization's minor function-negative role. The shorter second part – REASON – also surveys approaches to neutralization, but from a very different perspective, emphasizing its function-positive role.

Throughout, special emphasis is placed on theoretical approaches that do *not* typically get thorough airings in today's classrooms. My reasons for this special emphasis are at least threefold:

(1) Students should have knowledge of their intellectual forebears' scholarship. By placing a strong emphasis on scholarship that young researchers might rarely have the time or the inclination to pursue, I hope to pique their intellectual curiosity.

(2) Students and others who read this volume are probably well versed in generative (rule-based, constraint-based) approaches to the issues, and thus my delving into depth therein would be largely redundant.

(3) The emphasis herein accords better with my own research interests, in particular with respect to searching for phonetic (formal) and semantic (functional) explanations for phonological patterns.

"BRICK AND MORTAR"

This is not a book for beginners. It assumes fairly extensive exposure to phonological theory, and it challenges readers to consider unfamiliar ways – both old and new – of analyzing phonological data. I don't hold back from presenting the "new"; less advanced readers may prefer to skip the Preamble until having gotten further into the book.

Regarding the discussion questions at the end of each chapter, loosely, these come in three varieties:

(1) Questions that are rather brazenly designed to lead readers towards answers consistent with the proposals advanced herein.

(2) Questions that are indeed open-ended, in the sense that I am unsure how to go about answering them myself, and for which I would greatly appreciate reader feedback.

(3) Questions that offer possibilities for research projects, including papers, theses, and even dissertations.

There is certainly overlap among these three categories.

The IPA (International Phonetic Alphabet) is used throughout, and always appears in bold. It is used for phonetic transcriptions, and for representing *normative*, *typical*, or (perhaps) *idealized* pronunciations. Neither square brackets nor virgules are ever used.

For corrections, updates, info on buying book rights for the inevitable Hollywood blockbuster (Steve baby? Marty my man?), and
any other news related to the form or content of this book, please
visit my website (www.seedyroad.com). You can also email me
from there.

Acknowledgments

This book was written in Santa Cruz over three summers: 2009, 2010, and 2011. At the time of my writing the words you are reading now, no one except me has read through the entire volume, and so here comes the scary part: sending it off to Cambridge University Press with who knows how many galling errors, gaping omissions, and glaring inconsistencies remaining. Still, many friends have read bits and pieces, and I wish to extend my sincere thanks to them. Really, there are so many people to thank: Michelle Arden for her inspiring scholarship, Jonathan Barnes for generously sharing his great book with me, Helen Barton for giving me this opportunity to write for Cambridge, Dan Everett for his warm friendship and his help with the Pirahã, Chris Golston for his hospitality and gener(ative)osity, Naomi Gurevich for her pioneering scholarship and her ability to make me laugh no matter the travail, Jongho Jun for his own scholarship and his insights into mine, Abby Kaplan for doing her best to make things simple for little me, Bob King for his gracious correspondence on functional load and I. B. Singer, Hahn Koo for his razor-sharp eye and astute level-headedness, Jean Léo Léonard for his enthusiastic moral support, Ken Lodge for so much I wouldn't know where to begin, Bruce Lyon for helping me hone the evolutionary metaphor, Jean-François Mondon for his homophonic erudition, Leendert Plug for the Firthian assist, Glyne Piggott for bringing me back to life after nine long years of ... death, Péter Rácz for his lively commentary and killer questions, Girard Ramsay for his trans-oceanic telescopic vision, Koen Sebregts for his scintillating intellect and his forcing me to think inside the box, Donca Steriade for *still* being my teacher and allowing me free access to "Doncapedia", Patrycja Strycharczuk for great help with near-neutralization, Rory Turnbull for his very challenging and thoughtful commentary, Suzanne Urbanczyk for getting to the root of the problem (or, rather, the problem of the root), Andy Wedel for his steadfast partisanship, and Paul Willis for all his wonderful insights and all the great marathon geek sessions we've enjoyed.

And, oh yeah, John Allen for *thirty* years of friendship, He Jie for two continents' worth of memories, Jonathan Karpf for his flawless moral compass, Lois Leardi for always helping me "make words", Jamie Reinstein for being there during life's ups and downs across *three* continents, Aviva Shimelman for helping me find a bit of humor in a humorless situation, Paul Silverman for his unconditional support, and Zhang Jie for his remarkable sechel.

And of course, my family: Bob (ז״ל), Phyl, Jer, Eth.

Nanuet, NY

1 The rhyme and the reason of neutralization

Consider a language – we'll call it Babelese – with the following nine values:

p	t	k	i		u
m	n	ŋ		a	

If all roots in Babelese contain either four, five, or six of these values in sequence, then, logically, the largest possible number of phonetically unique roots in Babelese is $9^4+9^5+9^6$, or 597,051. That is, the free commutation of the nine values, in sequences of four, five, or six, produces 597,051 unique phonetic forms.

Of course, Babelese won't have this many phonetically unique roots. Instead, there will surely be a number of systematic limitations on its roots' phonetic content.

First, not every value will freely occupy every "slot"; there will be gaps. For example, if Babelese roots are exclusively of the form **CVCV**, **CVCVC**, **CVCCV**, and **CVCCVC** (where C=consonant and V=vowel), then only six of the values may be commuted in the first position of a root (**p t k m n ŋ**), and only three of the values may be commuted in the second position of a root (**i u a**), and so on. That is, roots in Babelese consist of a number of sequenced *paradigms*, some with more members that might be substituted for one another, some with fewer. These are *paradigmatic* limitations on root structure.

Second, not every value will be found next to every other value. For example, let's say root-internal **CC** sequences in Babelese involve only homorganic nasal–stop sequences. Thus, the only consonant clusters found morpheme-internally are of the form **NP** (where N=nasal, P=plosive). Such limitations clearly reduce the number of phonetic root types. For example, due to its context, there are only three phonetic values that commute in the relevant **N** paradigm: **m(p) n(t) ŋ(k)**. This is a *syntagmatic* limitation on root structure.

As our root-internal **CC** sequencing limitation demonstrates, the distinction between paradigmatic systems and syntagmatic systems is not clear-cut: paradigmatic limitations are directly affected by syntagmatic ones. Still, it is clear that, far from possessing free combinatoric possibilities, roots in Babelese – and also, roots in every real language – involve systematic limitations on the distribution of their values that may be characterized in both paradigmatic and syntagmatic terms.

The morpheme-internal **CC** sequencing limitation is a *static* property of the Babelese root inventory: it is *always* the case that root-internal consonantal sequences in Babelese are one of three *fixed* homorganic nasal–stop sequences (**mp nt ŋk**). However, words in Babelese – and again, words in almost all real languages – are often polymorphemic. Let's suppose that Babelese words are maximally bimorphemic. Moreover, let's suppose that cross-morpheme **N+C** sequences are necessarily homorganic as well. Derived **C+C** clusters may thus take twenty-four different forms:

p+p	p+t	p+k	t+p	t+t	t+k	k+p	k+t	k+k
p+m	p+n	p+ŋ	t+m	t+n	t+ŋ	k+m	k+n	k+ŋ
m+p				n+t				ŋ+k
m+m				n+n				ŋ+ŋ

Due to this morpheme boundary condition, some nasal consonants that come to immediately precede a heteromorphemic consonant *alternate* with values that differ with respect to their oral configuration. For example, if a morpheme that is **n**-final when at the end of a word finds itself in a word-internal context where a **k**-initial morpheme immediately follows, the **n** will alternate with **ŋ**: n# – ŋ+k (where underlined symbols indicate values in alternation). This sort of alternation pattern serves to reduce the number of configurations in the relevant context. Consequently, Babelese words have only three **NP** configurations, though they each come in two rather different varieties: **mp nt ŋk** and **m+p n+t ŋ+k**.

Unlike those observed within morphemes, distributional limitations due to morpheme concatenation are not static in nature. Rather, they are *dynamic*; in Babelese, for example, as we have just observed, one such dynamically imposed limitation involves one nasal consonant alternating with another just in case it comes to immediately precede another consonant; such assimilatory patterns are extremely common, in fact.

Babelese now looks quite different from our naive first approximation. Although we initially characterized Babelese as possessing nine values, these values do not combine freely. There are both paradigmatic and syntagmatic limitations on these values' distribution, and there are both statically imposed and dynamically imposed limitations on these values' distribution.

We might say that the limitations on values and their sequencing increase phonological RHYME, in the sense that, due exactly to these observed limitations, distinct words necessarily end up sounding more similar to each other than they would if there were no such combinatory limitations. Indeed, due in particular to dynamically imposed limitations (due to alternation), there are *synchronically active* increases in phonological RHYME.

But despite this inevitable increase in phonological RHYME, phonological REASON is rarely adversely affected. Many's the time that alternations locally reduce the number of distinct configurations – that is, the syntagmatic context involves a reduction in the number of commutable values in the paradigm – but such reductions are typically inconsequential from the point of view of keeping elements phonetically distinct that differ in *meaning*. Phonological REASON, then, refers to the successful conveyance of lexical *meaning* from speaker to listener.

Take one example: consider again a nasal–plosive sequence in Babelese. Nasal alternations in the context **N+C** result in a smaller number of contrastive values here, but this reduction in *phonetic* distinctness (this increase in RHYME) does not necessarily entail a reduction in *semantic* distinctness (a decrease in REASON), simply because, in most cases, there will be other contrastive values that function to keep morphemes phonetically distinct from each other. For example, we may observe **taŋkan# – taŋkam+p – taŋkan+t – taŋkaŋ+k** versus **tiŋkaŋ# – tiŋkam+p – tiŋkan+t – tiŋkaŋ+k**. For the two words **taŋkan#** versus **tiŋkaŋ#**, despite the dynamically imposed phonetic identity (or, more precisely, near-identity) of the nasal–stop sequences in particular morphologically complex contexts, the morphemes maintain phonetic distinctness due to V_1 differences, **a** versus **i**. Rather, only in those comparatively rare instances when morphemes are otherwise identical are increases in phonological RHYME accompanied by a decrease in phonological REASON: **taŋkan# – taŋkam+p – taŋkan+t – taŋkaŋ+k** versus **taŋkaŋ# – taŋkam+p – taŋkan+t – taŋkaŋ+k**. Stated more succinctly, most alternations do not involve minimal pairs such that particular alternations derive homophones. Consequently, most such alternations are heterophone-maintaining and thus not function-negative; crucial phonetic differences are maintained despite increases in phonological RHYME.

In fact, rather remarkably, an increase in phonological RHYME oftentimes correlates positively with an increase in phonological REASON. Consider how this is so in Babelese. Recall that morpheme-internal CC sequences always consist of homorganic nasal–stop sequences. Consequently, whenever a sequence of consonants is encountered in the speech stream that takes any other phonetic shape, a listener may safely conclude that the two consonants do not belong to the same morpheme. Here, an overall increase in phonological RHYME correlates positively with an increase in phonological REASON: systematic sequential limitations at the morpheme level provide important clues to listeners about the morphological structure of the speech stream.

Oftentimes then, limitations on the distribution of contrastive values increase phonological RHYME, *and* increase phonological REASON. As stated, reductions in phonological REASON are limited to those rare cases in which an alternation derives homophones.

All these systematic limitations on morpheme structure – be they paradigmatic or syntagmatic, be they static within morphemes, or dynamic due to morpheme concatenation, be they homophone-deriving or heterophone-maintaining – fall under the general rubric of "neutralization". Broadly interpreted then, neutralization is a conditioned limitation on the distribution of a system's contrastive values. *It is these sorts of patterns that are the focus of the present study.*

And although I will continue to discuss all these sorts of systematic limitations on morphological and phonological structure as neutralizing in nature, I ultimately refrain from suggesting a definition of neutralization in these terms. Rather, in this study I move towards a strictly *functional* – more specifically, *function-negative* – definition of neutralization, one of NEUTRALIZATION as derived homophony. (When used in this formal sense, the term appears in small capitals.)

It bears repeating: throughout, I use the term "neutralization" when discussing any and all systematic limitations on morpheme structure, both lexical and derived. Nonetheless, I ultimately define the term with respect to its sole genuinely function-negative consequence: NEUTRALIZATION results from an alternation that derives homophones.

It is not (or, rather, not *only*) for polemical reasons that I limit the formal definition of NEUTRALIZATION to this strictly function-negative sense. Rather, strange as it may initially seem, this definition of NEUTRALIZATION requires the fewest assumptions to be made about the nature of phonological structure; defining NEUTRALIZATION as derived homophony is maximally theory-neutral, despite (or, I'd like to think, exactly because of) its strictly functional orientation.

To see how this works, let's now return to our discussion of Babelese, considering in a bit more detail how we might phonologically characterize the observation that its morpheme-internal **NP** sequences are always homorganic.

First, we could say that nasals do not contrast in place-of-articulation when a stop follows. That is, the oral properties of the nasal can be "read off" the oral properties of the following plosive. This is an especially common characterization, because it is often the case that nasal–plosive sequences that occur *across* morpheme boundaries induce the neutralizing alternation of the nasal itself (just as in Babelese), and so it feels right to group the two patterns – **NP** and **N+P** – into one, claiming that the nasal's oral properties are always a consequence of the following plosive's, and consequently, such nasals' oral properties need not be lexically specified.

Second, we could say that plosives do not contrast for place-of-articulation when a nasal precedes. That is, the oral properties of the plosive can be "read off" the oral properties of the preceding nasal. Although evidence from both alternation and from sound change are discrepant with this characterization (since it is typically nasals that assimilate to following plosives, and not plosives to preceding nasals), it must be emphasized that patterns of (dynamic) assimilation (for example, **m̲+p, n̲+t, ŋ̲+k**) are irrelevant to the analysis of (static) morpheme-internal sound structure (for example, **mp nt ŋk**), regardless of their phonetic comparability.

Third, we could say that **NP** sequences possess oral place contrasts at a paradigmatic level of analysis, but not at a syntagmatic level of analysis. That is, we could characterize one **NP** span (say, **nt**) as engaging in oral contrast with other **NP** spans (say, **mp ŋk**).

Regarding the first and second alternatives, it must be emphasized that, due to the strict non-alternating quality of morpheme-internal **NP** sequences, there is no motivation for either value to be "read off" the other. For any given morpheme-internal **NP** sequence (**mp nt ŋk**), oral qualities strictly co-vary with each other, and so "reading off" one oral quality from the other is wholly arbitrary from both the language analyst's perspective, and from the language user's perspective.

The third alternative is more plausible. There is indeed something fundamentally correct in asserting that the observed morpheme-internal limitation involves a commutation of oral values across a span of the speech stream involving a change from nasal-channeled airflow to a complete cessation of airflow (giving us **mp nt ŋk**). The motivation, again, is the fixed status of the various phonetic states within this span such that no one phonetic subcomponent of the complex is different in status from any other phonetic component: as all components are necessarily fixed throughout the span, there is every reason to treat the complex as a whole, a *Gestalt*. (Note that, by "fixed", I don't mean static or unmoving – indeed, the soft palate is in a state of motion, from open to closed, across this span – but rather, by "fixed", I refer to any phonetic content that co-varies over an expanse of the speech stream: <labial nasal – labial stop>, <alveolar nasal – alveolar stop>, <velar nasal – velar stop>.)

At this point then, I need to emphasize that the IPA symbols we have been using (and will continue to use) should be interpreted as cover terms, or shortcuts, for the constellation of motor routines and their attendant acoustic cues – *whatever their shape or size* – that possess genuine linguistic status, readily encompassing more – or less – of the temporal span represented by a single IPA symbol. Thus, IPA symbols are not isomorphic with *Gestalten*. Rather, they are mere visual expedients.

Now, once we acknowledge the fact that particular expanses of the speech stream may be fixed with respect to their phonetic properties, the next step is to see how far we can push the idea. Clearly, *any* stretch of the speech stream that possesses fixed phonetic content (again, in the sense that the phonetic content co-varies for an expanse of the speech stream) is amenable to this sort of analysis.

What elements of the speech stream meet this criterion for *Gestalt* status? We might first consider those elements of the speech stream that are cycled and recycled in a phonetically stable manner, due to their serving a single linguistic function: morphemes, and collocations of morphemes that tend to recur together in their patterning (words, and perhaps rote phrases). As a first approximation then, we might propose that morphemes, exactly because of their fixed phonetic properties, should be regarded as *Gestalten*.

Obviously, this won't do. Morphemes are not always phonetically fixed, of course. Rather, there may be systematic changes that morphemes undergo, depending on their context. These are the synchronic alternations that result in allomorphy that we have already discussed. So, we must retreat from the claim that morphemes are indivisible, fixed wholes. Rather, it is only those components of morphemes that are not subject to alternation for which phonetic properties are strictly fixed. For example, in Babelese, we have allomorphic patterns like taŋkan – taŋkam+p – taŋkaŋ+k. Here, part of the morpheme is phonetically fixed, but also, there is a systematic pattern of alternation that is not fixed with respect to other elements of the morpheme. This part of the morpheme co-varies (is fixed) with respect to elements *outside* the domain of the morpheme (specifically, the following plosive). Indeed, since nasals at different places of articulation differently coarticulate with preceding vocalism, the alternation here no doubt encompasses more of the speech stream than is implied by the mere change in IPA symbol, incorporating at least a sizable portion of the preceding vowel: **taŋkan** – **taŋkam**+**p** – **taŋkaŋ**+**k**.

Consequently, in general, we may indeed treat non-alternating components of morphemes – whatever their shape or size – as wholes, as *Gestalten*, and further recognize that components in alternation – again, whatever their shape or size – are *Gestalten* as well, ones that are set in high relief against their phonetically fixed morpheme-internal backgrounds. *These* are the proposed elements of phonological contrast. Indeed, as I write in my 2006 book, "there is no reason to assume that language users subdivide the words they learn into distinct sound-components unless there is evidence from alternation to do so" (2006a:50).

We now see just how wrong-headed our first proposals regarding Babelese root structure were. Phonetic events that function as elements of contrast in one context may not serve this same function in other contexts, and so, even as a theoretic straw man, it is downright silly to consider their free commutation and their free combination. The spans of speech within morphemes – despite phonetic appearances to the contrary, and however "recyclable" their attendant motor routines – are *not* necessarily built out of smaller linguistically significant units that combine in various ways. Rather, the spans of the speech stream underlain by a specific linguistic *function* – morphemes, words, and perhaps certain rote phrases – are the genuine building blocks of linguistic structure, blocks that may only be partitioned into smaller units if there is evidence from alternation to do so.

Let's back up for a moment. I have been belaboring the assertion that morphemes might only be analyzed into smaller components when there is evidence from alternation to do so, because I am moving towards a purely function-negative definition of NEUTRALIZATION as the product of derived homophony. How do my assertions about morpheme structure relate to this proposed definition of NEUTRALIZATION? Well, once we (permanently) rid the morpheme of extraneous submorphemic structure (distinctive features, segments, syllables, etc.), there remains no way to relate components of the speech stream to each other by any other than *semantic* means. Consequently, instances of non-alternating morphemes are obviously non-distinct, but morphemes in alternation are typically functionally non-distinct as well, since they do not induce a semantic change. This is the result we want, because, apart from their mere *extrinsic phonetic similarity*, there is no reason to group any disparate components of the speech stream together into a functional set unless there is linguistic evidence that they do indeed possess some sort of *intrinsic functional non-distinctness*. In phonology, the *only* instance in which physical dissimilarity is regularly overridden by functional identity comes from alternation: components of the speech stream that substitute for one another, and yet morpheme meaning remains the same, share an *intrinsic functional identity*.

This establishes the functional link among allomorphs that we're looking for, ridding phonology of its emphasis on positing functional links among mere phonetic correspondents (the hypothetical segment, the hypothetical distinctive feature). The result is that, for example, morpheme-internal ŋk bears no intrinsic phonological relationship to any other ŋk in Babelese, be the sequence found in another morpheme-internal context (ŋk), or at a morpheme boundary (ŋ+k), or across a word boundary (ŋ#k). Rather, functional links may be established solely by semantic criteria; allomorphs are functionally – semantically – non-distinct.

There is, of course, one – and *only* one – exception to the assertion that alternation maintains morpheme identity, and that is when the alternation derives homophony. Here – and *only* here – the allomorphs in alternation do not share a unique functional identity. Rather, in just this instance, identity is forfeited – indeed it is shared, or overlapped, with another morpheme – due to the absence of phonetic evidence for these morphemes' distinctness in meaning.

NEUTRALIZATION, then, involves an *extrinsic phonetic similarity* – indeed, a derived *phonetic (near-)identity* – among items, but it is the consequent *intrinsic functional non-distinctness* of the alternant forms that establishes the phenomenon's linguistic relevance: any phonetic evidence for these items' difference in meaning is washed away. The result? Alternations that eliminate the *phonetic* distinctness among morphemes also eliminate phonetic evidence for the *semantic* distinctness among morphemes. By contrast, any definition of neutralization that relies on the mere phonetic similarity among elements of the speech stream relies on fallacious assumptions about the functional relevance of sub-morphemic content.

Let's now return to Babelese. Let's suppose that suffixation is a pervasive process in the language. In Babelese, suffixes are monosyllabic (**CV** or **CVC**), and are subject to vowel harmony, such that their vowel is identical to the final vowel of the root, for example, **taŋkan+tak**, but **kupit+tik**.

Patterns like this exemplify a number of trends that we observe in morpho-phonological systems. First, affixes are usually shorter than roots, and also are often subject to assimilatory phenomena such as vowel harmony. The functional origin of these tendencies is well understood: since there are always fewer affixes than there are roots, and since their distribution is so predictable, there is less functional pressure for affixes to consist of the many and varied values found in roots. So, as a natural evolutionary consequence, affixes are often shorter, and are more readily subject to root-controlled assimilatory alternations.

Second, the vocalic alternation observed in Babelese suffixes is almost surely not localized to one individual vowel. Indeed, the alternation in evidence likely encompasses any consonant(s) that intervene between the root-final vowel and the suffix vowel (**taŋkan+tak**, but **kupit+tik**). That is, due to its syntagmatic context, the paradigm subject to alternation consists of the entire span from the second root vowel up to and including the suffix vowel, and not only suffix vocalism itself. Even though we might transcribe the allomorphs with the same consonant symbols, in actuality these consonants are implemented differently from each other, due to their differing vocalic contexts.

Third, although affixes are more readily subject to assimilatory alternations, still, exactly because they are members of a small set, NEUTRALIZATION is rarely an issue here. This is not just a fortuitous or coincidental result. Rather, there are constant pressures on the sound pattern – some quite superficial and proximal, others extremely deep and distal – that are responsible for the slow-going shaping of the system such that function-negative phenomena like NEUTRALIZATION are kept at bay.

For example, as our discussion of Babelese suffixes has suggested, certain assimilatory tendencies may go largely unchecked in just those cases where NEUTRALIZATION is not likely to be an issue. Since such assimilations may be seen as the diachronic "end-state" along a gradient scale of coarticulation, it might be wise to back up for a moment and consider the sorts of pressures that oftentimes act on coarticulation.

In Babelese, we can readily imagine that vowel-to-vowel (transconsonantal) coarticulation within roots is somewhat circumscribed, exactly because root vowels function contrastively: too much vowel-to-vowel coarticulation might jeopardize the distinctiveness of one or both vowels. In the limiting case, such coarticulation leads to vowel-to-vowel assimilation, or vowel harmony. To the extent that distinctions in root vocalism are responsible for minimal pairing, complete vowel assimilation would result in a decrease in phonological REASON: some roots would be rendered non-distinct from each other.

We can, in fact, imagine several possible scenarios that might play themselves out over time, depending on the "initial conditions" (or at least "preceding conditions") established by the structure of the Babelese lexicon.

First, as just noted, if many Babelese roots are crucially dependent on vocalism for their phonetic distinctness, vowel-to-vowel coarticulation may indeed be passively curtailed: since distinctions in vocalism embody the crucial phonetic distinctions among many roots, coarticulation is rather likely to be significantly inhibited.

Second, if many Babelese roots are *not* crucially dependent on vocalism (and instead rely more heavily on their consonantism), we might expect vowel coarticulation to proceed relatively freely, perhaps culminating in fully harmonized root-internal vocalism.

Third, again, if many Babelese roots are *not* crucially dependent on vowel distinctions, we might see an interaction with the Babelese stress system such that vowel paradigms have fewer members in unstressed contexts.

Fourth, we might imagine a scenario in which these unstressed syllables attrit completely, culminating in a system that possesses only monosyllabic roots. This would surely result in a significant reduction in the number of root shapes, and the phonology might be bereft of options to countervail the threat of NEUTRALIZATION. Morphology, however, may come to the rescue: the increase in RHYME among roots may be offset by the co-evolution of a root-compounding process, and thus REASON is never jeopardized.

Readers versed in the phonological patterning of linguistic systems will be able to summon actual examples comparable to each of these scenarios.

The overarching proposal, then, is that phonological RHYME may increase until encountering a counter-pressure that inhibits undue decreases in phonological REASON. More specifically, the inventory of motor routines that a language deploys is likely to be influenced by lexical semantic factors: coarticulation and assimilatory alternations may conceivably evolve rather freely, provided the transmission of *meaning* between speaker and listener is not adversely affected. Indeed, as a passive consequence of communicative success – of effective transmission of lexical semantic content – speech with curtailed coarticulation (as opposed to uncurtailed coarticulation) may emerge as the conventionalized norm. Articulatory details put in service to failed communication – as when the meaning associated with overly coarticulated or assimilated speech tokens is not effectively communicated to listeners, due to consequent derived homophony – are less likely to be reproduced as listeners become speakers (since, due to derived homophony, such speech may be misunderstood), and thus are less likely to become conventionalized motor routines.

Thus, so-called "phonetic" or "low-level" effects (such as patterns of coarticulation) are likely the result of deep historical and systemic pressures many times removed from the physical systems that proximally underlie speech; the emergent result of persistent, slow-going, interlocutionary tendencies that shape and change speech conventions.

CONCLUSION

I began this discussion by claiming that Babelese possessed nine contrastive values. We now see that this was incorrect. Babelese possesses as many contrastive values as there are components of the speech stream that either alternate or are stable within morphemes. These values consist of motor routines and acoustic complexes of varying shapes and sizes, involving few if any of the neat, organized, phonetic "slices" – be these slices temporal (loosely, segments), or spectral (loosely, distinctive features) – that linguists typically manipulate. For language users, these phonetically complex values emerge when links are established between sound and meaning.

Indeed, almost all alternations, in fact, maintain heterophony, and are thus function-neutral; only those alternations that result in ambiguity in meaning – by deriving homophony – have function-negative consequences. This is NEUTRALIZATION. Still, phonological RHYME may increase – and may even be function-positive to the extent that it assists in parsing – until encountering a counter-pressure that inhibits undue decreases in phonological REASON.

Now, despite all the admittedly speculative discussion I have been engaging in (indulging in?) in this Preamble, I'd like to reassure the reader that the bulk of this book is dedicated to elucidating various approaches to neutralization that have been discussed at length in the literature, though, to be sure, we will be slowly building towards a new definition of neutralization, one of neutralization as derived homophony, that is, NEUTRALIZATION.

In Part I, RHYME, in Section A I make *observations* about, and provide *descriptions* of, patterns of neutralization, considering the "topology" (Chapter 2), the "taxonomy" (Chapter 3), and the "typology" (Chapter 4) of neutralization. In Section B I take a detour to discuss a few "false positives": "partial phonemic overlap" (Chapter 5) and "near-neutralization" (Chapter 6). In Section C I move on to consider various proposed *explanations* for neutralization, considering, in turn, "speaker-based" (Chapters 7 and 8) and "listener-based" approaches (Chapters 9 through 11). Section D includes a case study of NEUTRALIZATION in Korean (Chapter 12), then a survey of the *domains* over which anti-homophony may passively exert its pressure (Chapter 13). I conclude Part I by asserting that "distinctions are drawn that matter" (Chapter 14).

In Part II, REASON, I discuss the functional value of neutralization in terms of Kruszewski's "cement" (Chapter 15), Trubetzkoy's "boundary signals" (Chapter 16), Firth's "prosodies" (Chapter 17), and Saffran's "transitional probabilities" (Chapter 18).

Finally, as a postscript, I summarize our results, and very briefly revisit Babelese (Chapter 19).

PART I
Rhyme

2   Topology

In the broadest sense of the term, neutralization involves the dynamic reduction and/or the static limitation of contrastive values within a lexical form. Segmentally speaking ("segment" being a theoretical construct we will abandon), these reductions and/or limitations result in a speech signal that is not temporally uniform with respect to the amount of phonologically significant material it encodes. Rather, the speech signal consists of time periods with *more* phonologically significant information (contrastive cues) interwoven with time periods of *less* phonologically significant information (the suspension or loss of contrastive cues). The informational output across the temporal duration of a spoken lexical form thus rises and falls as a consequence of cue expression and cue neutralization. We may characterize this ever-changing rate of information-encoding in any number of ways, but in this chapter we focus on one characterization in particular. Specifically, we consider the topological malleability of informational content with respect to its temporal encoding within lexical forms. Thus, reductions in informational content may be characterized with respect to what temporal components of the lexical form they affect. These include (1) *spans*, (2) *edges*, and (3) *points*. As discussed in subsequent chapters, in most instances, topological constancy is indeed maintained despite this malleability, in the sense that lexical semantic content almost always remains unchanged.

Neutralization affecting *spans* includes any and all patterns of cue reduction that manifest themselves across some expanse within the lexical form, typically falling under the rubric of assimilation. These include vowel and nasal harmony systems, for example, but also more local forms of assimilation, such as nasal place assimilation and other sorts of word-internal place and laryngeal assimilations.

Neutralization affecting *edges* is limited to word edges, and more particularly – since neutralization very rarely affects word-initial values – word-final edges. Word-final laryngeal neutralization is a case *par excellence*.

Finally, neutralization affecting *points* includes patterns that effect a word-internal local reduction in the number of contrastive values, where "local" refers to a domain in which only single contrastive values may commute with other single values. Both *centrifugal* and *centripetal* vowel contrast reductions under stresslessness thus fall under the rubric of *point* effects, for example, where centrifugal systems reduce the vowel inventory to "corner" values (as in Portuguese or Russian), and where centripetal systems reduce the vowel inventory to "center" values, typically, a schwa-like element (as in Dutch or English).

In this chapter, we consider, in turn, these three sorts of topological deformation with respect to lexical phonological content.

SPANS

Certain contrastive features may be either singularly present or singularly absent within some domain, such that particular spans of the speech stream involve a reduction in the number of the system's contrastive configurations, be these spans *statically present* (within-morphemes; non-alternating), or *dynamically derived* (between-morphemes; alternating). Such spans may be analyzed as neutralized with respect to the suspended feature. Neutralization that involves speech spans especially includes patterns of assimilation, whether these patterns involve consonant-to-consonant spans (consonant assimilations, including transvocalic consonant harmony), vowel-to-vowel spans (vowel harmony), or vowel–consonant/consonant–vowel spans (for example, consonant palatalization in the context of a following front vowel).

Indeed, the proposal that phonological structure is built from stretches of speech that are greater in length than individual speech sounds ("segments") is hardly new. Let's then consider a number of comparable proposals that have been made since the latter part of the nineteenth century.

Kruszewski (1883)

Kruszewski was one of the first linguists to propose that the coarticulatory and/or assimilatory patterns we observe over and over again in speech may be analyzed as a gestural span across a domain. Observe his graphic characterization of the coarticulation inherent to alveolar-vowel sequences in (for example) Russian. Notice especially that the tongue postures for the distinct vowels are implemented during the preceding consonants.

The complex *ta*:

First moment: *t*   Second moment: *a*

mouth opens enough to pronounce *a*	remains open
uvula rises	remains raised
tip of tongue rests against the alveoli	
tip of tongue breaks contact stream of air is released from lungs	stream of air continues
tip of tongue arrives at position required for *a*	remains in this position
	vocal cords vibrate

The complex *ti*:

First moment: *t*   Second moment: *i*

mouth opens enough to pronounce *i*	remains open
uvula rises	remains raised
tip of tongue rests against alveoli mid-portion of tongue approaches palate	remains near the palate
tip of tongue breaks contact stream of air is released from lungs	stream of air continues
tip of tongue approaches position necessary for *i*	remains in this position
	vocal cords vibrate

Figure 2.1 Russian *ta* and *ti* (Kruszewski 1883)

Kruszewski writes (1883:21ff.):

> In these two tables [Figure 2.1] we see the onset of the operations
> of the second sound at the moment of the first. In the second set, i.e.,
> the Russian complex **ti** ... this onset is accompanied by an acoustic
> effect which anyone can notice; the softness or the palatality of the
> consonant ... [T]here is *uniformity in* [such] *sound complexes*: just as in
> any language only certain sounds are possible, so, likewise, only
> certain specific complexes of these sounds are possible ... [F]rom
> the physiological point of view the word is a series of groups of
> physiological operations ... [I]ndividual operations can go outside
> their own group and join with the operations of the adjacent group.
> Hence, we are justified in saying that when sounds are combined,
> a *reintegration of the groups of physiological operations* takes place.

Harris (1944, 1951)

Harris also considers the role of spans in phonology, especially with
respect to the characterization of long segments. He characterizes these
"long components" as "defective distributions" of the relevant contrastive elements, or phonemes. Unlike Kruszewski, who is largely silent on
whether such spans are ultimately delimited in their distribution to a
specifically (multi-)segmental domain, Harris (1944:181ff.) indeed proposes that spans are ultimately affiliated with segment-size elements:

> [T]he various limitations of phonemic distribution, including
> defective distributions of phonemes, can be compactly expressed by
> means of ... analyzing the utterance of a language into simultaneous
> components ... [T]his operation ... breaks all or most of the phonemes
> into new sub-elements (components). Each of the old phonemes will be
> a particular simultaneous combination of one or more of these new
> elements; and the total number of different components will be
> much smaller than the previous number of different phonemes. It
> will be possible to select and symbolize the components in such a
> way as to show immediately the limitations of distribution, and in
> many cases the phonetic composition, of the phonemes in which they
> occur ... [S]ome components ... have the length of more than one
> phoneme ... When phonemes are written with such long components,
> we shall be able to know the limitations of distributions of any
> phoneme by looking at the components of which it is composed ...
> English ... /ŋt/ ... does not occur, nor does /nk/ because the component
> of mouth position always extends over both phoneme places. If we
> mark <u>n</u> for nasal without regard to mouth position, and <u>s</u> for stop
> without regard for mouth position, and $\overline{}$ for alveolar and $\overline{\overline{}}$ for
> velar position, then we say that the latter two marks always have
> two-phoneme length when beginning with /<u>n</u>/. Thus /$\overline{\underline{\mathbf{n\,s}}}$/ = /nt/ and
> /$\overline{\overline{\underline{ns}}}$/ = /ŋk/; there is no way to write /nk/, since $\overline{}$ is so defined that

> it cannot be stopped after the /n̲/ ... The technique of using these components to express limited distribution may [also] simplify the description of morphophonemic alternation.

Harris thus overtly establishes a link between spans and "defective distribution", or limitations on contrast, both within morphemes and between morphemes; in a word, neutralization. (Note that Harris does not invoke the theoretical construct "syllable" in his character-ization of his "long components". This precludes the possibility of establishing generalizations about neutralization affecting syllable-final elements, including both word-internal and word-final positions.)

Firth (1948)

Among the most sophisticated approaches to spans – due in great part to observations made about their functional significance as parsing aids – is Firth's (1948) "prosodic analysis" approach. While a full investi-gation of Firth's ideas awaits our discussion of neutralization and phono-logical REASON in Chapter 17, I here provide Robins' (1957a:192–193) explication of so-called "prosodies" and their relevance to spans:

> Broadly speaking [prosodies] come about in two ways. In the first case a feature may be spread or realized phonetically over a structure, such as a syllable, as a whole ... In the second case may be mentioned features which are not realized phonetically over the whole or large part of a structure, but which nevertheless serve to delimit it, wholly or partly, from preceding or following structures, thus entering into syntagmatic relations with what goes before or after in the stream of speech. By virtue of their syntagmatic relations in structures, such features may be treated as prosodies of the structures they help to mark or delimit ...

Consider Robins' first sort of prosody, in which "a feature may be spread or realized phonetically over a structure ... ". His characteriza-tion of Sanskrit retroflexion – a feature that is limited in its distribu-tion within some domain or span – is graphically characterized in a manner that calls attention to its neutralizing nature. Crucially, values within the span do not contrast for retroflexion. Rather, the entirety of the span is retroflexed ("**R**"), including the intervening vocalism.

$$\overset{\textbf{R}}{\overbrace{\text{niṣaṇ-ṇa-}}} \; = \; \text{nisanna-} \quad \overset{\textbf{R}}{\overbrace{\text{aːɽabʲa-maːɳa-}}} \; = \; \text{aːrabʲamaːna-}$$

But note further than any role for Robin's second sort of prosody – "features ... not realized phonetically over the whole or large part of a

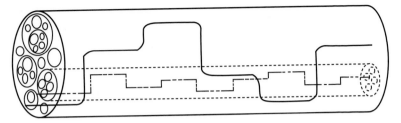

Figure 2.2 Articulation as multiple paths through a cylinder (Pike 1952)

structure, but which nevertheless serve to delimit it, wholly or partly, from preceding or following structures" – is predicated on the notion of neutralization as well: if the *presence* of a locally realized feature serves to demarcate a span of the speech stream, then the remainder of this span is characterized by this feature's *absence*, that is, its neutralization.

Pike (1952)

Pike comes to similar conclusions, and also comes quite close to characterizing the phonetic content of the speech stream in genuinely topological terms:

> The articulatory movements producing two sounds in sequence tend to slur into one another or tend to anticipate one another ... If ... we conceive of speech as a long cylinder which simultaneously contains the potentials of the consonant, vowel, and pitch subsystems, and so on, [see Figure 2.2] we can then by dotted lines suggest dimly the way in which the actual speech is a composite of several simultaneous paths selected from the various sets of contrastive subsystem potentials always present ... At each moment a segment of speech represents a complex choice from many subsystems. The two paths through the cylinder suggest that numerous types of choices within each subsystem are made simultaneously – e.g., tonal and consonantal or vocalic.

Again, the observation being made is that contrastive configurations cannot freely combine, but are instead limited with respect to the domains within which they are expressed.

Hockett (1955)

Hockett (1955:135ff.) proposes an "orchestral score"-like model of speech production, further allowing for time signatures other than a strict military 4/4 beat, that is, allowing for a non- (supra- or sub-)segmental realization of the elements of contrast.

	/qʷ	a	m'	a·/	/q	a	č	c'	a/	/ʔ	a	ƛ	p	u/
lips	w		k										k	w
tongue		a		a·		a			a		a			u
tip								ks						
blade							ks						kl	
fd														
bd	k				k									
velic			o											
pharynx														
glottis		v	kv	v		v		k	v		k	v		v

Figure 2.3 An "orchestral score" in Nootka (Hockett 1955)

It is not too difficult to reanalyze [a segment inventory] in order to
achieve a "full [orchestral] score" notation more directly comparable
to that in music ... We must have a staff for each of the following
instruments; the lower lip; the apex of the tongue; the blade of the
tongue; the tongue as a whole; the front part of the dorsum; the back
part of the dorsum; the velic; the pharynx; and the glottis ... All these
"instruments" are like percussion instruments in an orchestra in that
they are individually capable of very few distinct roles. In an orchestral
score an instrument which is confined ... to either making a sound
or not ... is scored not on a full staff of five lines but on a staff of a
single line ... The essential difference between [segmental notation
and "orchestral score" notation] ... lies in this: in one, positions and
manners of articulation are alike regarded as features ... [i]n the
other, positions of articulation (or, rather, actively functioning
articulators) are regarded as items individually capable of two or
more differentiated functions, some of those functions being the
same for two or more organs, some of them not.

As his notation makes clear, the suspension of speech gestures is
manifested across spans, rather than being fixed in an active or inactive
posture for any given "beat". Consider then his "orchestral score" for
the three short phrases "thus much", "three", and "seven" in Nootka in
Figure 2.3.

Goldsmith (1976)

Like Harris, Goldsmith's (1976) "autosegmental" phonology treads
something of a middle ground between acknowledging the role of
spans in phonology, and maintaining the segment as a phonological
primitive. Employing distinctive feature theory, he proposes that
certain phonological patterns are best treated as the "spreading" of

Lips	.... Close up .... Open ....
Tongue	.... High and front .... touch the palate
Velum	...... Raise .... Lower ....
Larynx	...... High Pitch .... Low Pitch ....

Figure 2.4 A superficial breakdown of orchestral "voices"
(Goldsmith 1976)

a feature across a domain that is longer than a single segment, that is,
a span. Nonetheless, he adheres to a segmental analysis in the sense
that he assumes these so-called "autosegments" are ultimately affiliated to standard segmental structure, asserting that such segments, or
phonemes, are "psychologically real" (in the sense of Sapir 1933):

> [T]he act of speech [is likened to] an orchestral production, a
> harmonized score of several independent musical "voices." These
> "voices" of the analogy correspond to the distinctive features of
> phonology. At the most superficial level, the speech signal is broken
> down into a large number of independent linear parts – autosegmental
> tiers – with at least as many of these tiers as there are independent
> articulators. Thus there will minimally be such a tier for the velum,
> for the laryngeal gesture corresponding to pitch, and so forth ...
> Yet even if [this display; see Figure 2.4] is an adequate sketch of the
> phonetic representation, it is unquestionably the wrong picture for
> the more abstract – that is, psychologically real – level, where there
> are atomic units like /p/, /i/, and so forth – in a word, phonemes.

Henderson (1985)

Henderson (1985) notes the remarkable degree of interaction among
consonants and vowels in certain Southeast Asian languages, assimilatory behaviors that often obviate the need for positing segmental
structure, and instead point to the role of spans in characterizing these
systems' inventories of contrast. She asserts the following:

> [T]he popular phonological models of the time, with their
> preoccupation with segment-based matrices of features ... [do] not
> provide a convincing or even an adequate framework of description
> for [certain] processes ... For many languages it may be helpful at
> times to think of certain of the phonological features of syllables
> as being dealt out in "hands" of "playing cards", so to speak, to the
> syllable as a whole rather than as firmly attached to any one segment
> in it, or even to any one place ... ([F]or example,) [n]asalization is
> [a] feature which may sometimes profitably be regarded as pertaining
> to the syllable or to parts of syllables, rather than as confined to a
> single segment matrix. It is ... a matter of ... timing ... of the raising
> or lowering of the soft palate.

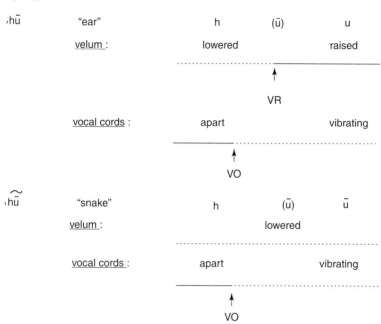

Figure 2.5 Distinctive patterns of nasality's distribution within the syllable in Songkhla (Henderson 1985)

Her graphic notation (see Figure 2.5) clearly explicates her proposed role for spans: speech gestures are not limited in their scope to particular segment-sized slots, but instead, may slip and slide with respect to their extrinsic timing relationships. Thus, for example, in a lexical distinction between **hũ:ꓸ** ("ear") and **h̃ũ:ꓶ** ("snake") in Songkhla, the timing of velic rising is comparatively untethered with respect to the onset or offset of other speech gestures.

Browman and Goldstein (1986)

In Browman and Goldstein's "articulatory phonology" approach to phonological structure, individual speech gestures are modeled as 360° cycles of movement from (1) a resting or starting point, to (2) a point of maximal displacement, to (3) a return to the starting or resting point. These speech gestures are not assumed to be organized along segmental lines, but instead may be of varying lengths, and configured in varying degrees of overlap with respect to each other. Thus, a single gesture may indeed be realized over a span of speech during which other gestures may or may not be implemented.

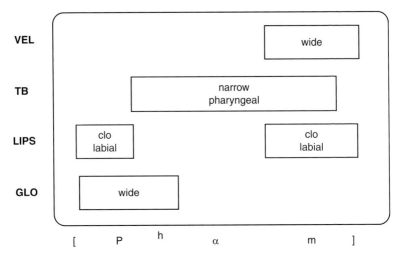

Figure 2.6 A "gestural score" of "palm" (Browman and Goldstein 1986)

Employing Hockett's "orchestral score" analogy, Browman and Goldstein (1989:206ff.) characterize their model thus:

> [A] gesture is an abstract characterization of coordinated task-directed movement of the articulators within the vocal tract ... the gestures for a given utterance are ... organized into a larger coordinated structure, or constellation, that is represented in a *gestural score*. The score specifies the sets of values of the dynamic parameters for each gesture, and the temporal intervals during which each gesture is active ... [G]estures are posited to be the atoms of phonological structure ... A gestural score for the word *palm* (pronounced **pɑm** [sic]) is displayed [in Figure 2.6] ... As can be seen in the figure, the tiers in a gestural score, on the vertical axis, represent the set of articulators (or the relevant subset thereof) employed by the gestures, while the horizontal dimension codes time.

Kelly and Local (1989)

In their discussion of the graphic representation of speech, Kelly and Local consider both alphabetic and non-alphabetic transcription systems. For present purposes, their discussion of non-alphabetic notation is most relevant, as it acknowledges a role for spans (termed "stretches") in the speech stream:

> [W]e might choose to concentrate on a mode of recording [transcribing –D.S.] which selects and emphasizes the continuous variation present in speech. For instance, we might highlight the

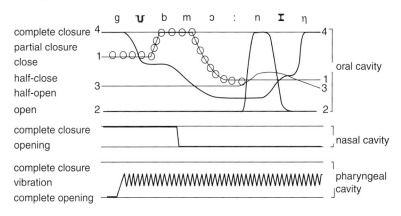

Figure 2.7 Movement of the articulators during "good morning" (Kelly and Local 1989)

movement aspect of utterance (movement of articulatory organs, laryngeal and pulmonic activities, etc.) or the corresponding auditory aspect (such as sensations that we label "falling pitch" or "rising pitch" or "friction"). If in our written records we concentrate on this continuous, dynamic aspect and try to deal independently but simultaneously with, for instance, the movement of tongue parts, lips, or nasal sphincter, we will have a parametric record. (p. 56)

Kelly and Local's emphasis on the dynamic components of the speech stream necessitates a role for spans. Simply put, those sub-systems that are not in a state of dynamism persist (as spans) until dynamism is (re-)introduced. The authors provide a parametric display of articulatory action during a production of "good morning" (see Figure 2.7) that exemplifies the role of both dynamism and spans (stretches).

Silverman (1995, 2006a)

Inspired by the pioneering work of Mattingly (1981) and Bladon (1986), in my 1995 dissertation I propose that speech gestures are orchestrated in order to enhance the auditory salience of the acoustic cues to lexical distinctions (see also Chitoran, Goldstein, and Byrd 2002). Eschewing a standard segmental approach, I typologize the extrinsic timing relationships among speech gestures as either (1) gestural sequencing, (2) gestural expansion, (3) gestural truncation, or (4) parallel production of gestures. Depending on the gestures involved – their degree of stricture, their oral, nasal, or laryngeal origin – particular timing

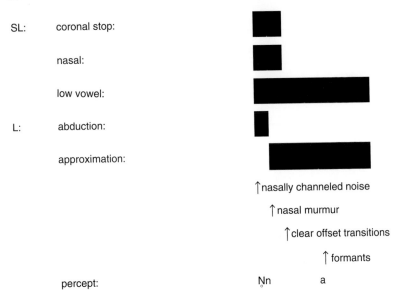

SL: coronal stop:

           nasal:

           low vowel:

L: abduction:

           approximation:

                                        ↑nasally channeled noise

                                          ↑ nasal murmur

                                            ↑clear offset transitions

                                              ↑ formants

           percept: N̥n   a

Figure 2.8 The articulatory spans and acoustic cues of a canonical voiceless nasal (Silverman 1995)

configurations may give rise to a more (or less) salient percept of the attendant acoustic cues. Spans, then, are part and parcel of the approach, simply because acoustic cues are not limited in their distribution to traditional slot-by-slot segmental positions, but are timed such that they achieve particular efficacious auditory results:

> The primary function of a phonological system is to keep meaningful elements distinct. Realizing this function involves optimizing the [auditory] salience among contrastive values. [Timing] relationships among gestures are organized to maximize [cue] recoverability. These relationships involve temporal sequencing, temporal expansion, temporal truncation, and parallel production. The achievement or non-achievement of auditory salience involves the complex interdependence among articulatory phonetics, aerodynamics, acoustic phonetics, auditory phonetics, and the systems of contrasts and morphology. (Silverman 1995 [1997]:32)

The notation I employ – a pre-theoretical variant of Browman and Goldstein's "articulatory score" (see Figure 2.8) – makes clear both the role of gestural spans, and the role of acoustic cueing.

In this graphic display of a canonical voiceless alveolar nasal followed by a low vowel, the laryngeal abduction is implemented for

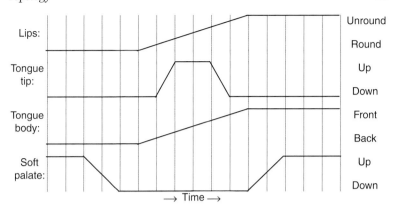

Figure 2.9 The "genuinely balletic" character of articulation during the production of "loony" (Silverman 2006a)

only a sub-span of the nasal – its initial portion – in order to optimize the auditory salience of all attendant contrastive cues. Meanwhile, the vowel gesture is present throughout. The presence of spans – their sustain across an expanse – invites the topological characterization of neutralization that is the subject of this section.

A brief illustration of the role of spans – especially with respect to their function-positive role in adding redundancy to the acoustic signal – is also provided in my 2006 book (2006a:54):

> It is clear that phonology does not consist of the speech-segment by speech-segment chunks implied by an alphabetic writing system. Just consider what's going on when we make a nasal sound between vowels. The various gestures are choreographed in a genuinely balletic fashion, overlapping each other to produce many and varied acoustic cues for each of the linguistically relevant components of the speech stream. Indeed, since sound substitution is the defining mechanism of phonology, it shouldn't be surprising that languages have evolved a property that multiplies the opportunities for listeners to receive the intended message from speakers ... [Consider] [t]he overlapped movements of the articulators for the word "loony", minus the initial "l" [see Figure 2.9]. Overlapping of the articulatory gestures gives rise to multiple and varied acoustic cues, thus better serving the communicative function of language.

EDGES

As noted in the introduction to this chapter, neutralization at the edge of a (lexical) domain is almost exclusively found word-finally, and almost never word-initially. There are well-understood phonetic reasons for this edge-asymmetry, perhaps first noted by Kruszewski (1883). Kruszewski observes that morpheme-initial sounds are far more prominent than morpheme-final ones in at least three ways: (1) initials are more resistant to loss than finals; (2) initials are more stable in terms of their phonetic properties than finals; and (3) morpheme-initial elements are more resistant to morpheme re-integration than are morpheme-final elements (that is, initials lack a tendency to re-affiliate with preceding morphological structure whereas final elements possess a tendency to re-affiliate with following morphological structure). He presciently ascribes the privileged status of such elements to phonetic pressures on sound change: initial position is typically immediately followed by a vowel, whereas final position is typically followed by a consonant. Though perhaps unconfirmed at the time of Kruszewski's writing, consonant releases possess aerodynamic, acoustic, and auditory advantages that make them more resistant to the pressures of change and attrition (Bladon 1986, Silverman 1995, Wright 2004).

A full century after Kruszewski, certain of these and related observations were re-introduced by Nooteboom (1981), and have even more recently been considered by Beckman (1997, 2004), who notes the "privileged" status of initials, expressing their character with the machinery of the "optimality" approach (Prince and Smolensky 2004).

As stated, while neutralization rarely affects the initial edge of a word, final-edge neutralization is very common indeed, especially when laryngeal features are involved. Thus, final devoicing – whether dynamic (as in German or Polish), or static (as in Cantonese or Thai) – is a very prevalent pattern. Neutralization of aspiration is also common at this edge. Now, recall that word-initial neutralization is infrequent exactly because initial-edge consonants are typically followed by a vowel. It follows that final-edge consonants are often subject to neutralization exactly because they are typically followed by a (word-initial) consonant. Thus the "privileged" status of initial edges and the prohibitive status of final edges largely reduce to these straightforward phonetic pressures. Note finally that a comparable phonetic pressure goes quite far in explaining neutralized consonantal *spans* (for example, nasal place assimilation): it is exactly because one consonant is followed by another consonant and not a vowel (here, within the word) – and thus lacks audible release – that it is especially susceptible to cue loss, thus precipitating its assimilatory neutralization.

POINTS

Point neutralization typically affects stressless vowels. In particular, in many languages, stresslessness is accompanied by a reduction in the number of vowel distinctions. These systems can be centripetal or centrifugal in their configuration. Centripetal systems involve vowel reduction towards the center of the vowel space (oftentimes ə or ɐ); centrifugal systems involve vowel reduction towards the corners of the vowel space (for example, i u ɐ).

Barnes (2006) discusses many cases of both centrifugal and centripetal vowel reduction in stressless contexts. Central Eastern Catalan, for example, displays a centrifugal pattern (as in many Romance languages). There are seven vowels in stressed contexts, but only three in unstressed ones. Here, e ɛ a reduce to ə under stresslessness, while u o ɔ reduce to u; i remains i. Thus, for example, we see ˈnɛw ("snow") – nəˈwɛte ("snow-DIM"); ˈpalə ("shovel") – pəˈlɛtə ("shovel-DIM").

SUMMARY

This brief exploration of the topology of neutralization focused specifically on the malleability of the phonological content of the speech stream; how the flow of phonologically significant information may rise or fall, may be statically suspended or dynamically reduced, across spans, or at edges or points. Still, recall that in most instances, topological constancy is indeed maintained despite this malleability, in the sense that lexical semantic content almost always remains unchanged. But of course, neutralization may be characterized in any number of ways. In the next chapter we approach neutralization from a specifically taxonomical perspective, outlining both prevalent and rare patterns of neutralization, primarily from an acoustic cue-based perspective.

DISCUSSION QUESTIONS AND FURTHER READING

(1) We've discussed several ways linguists have characterized phonological "spans", including the proposals of **Kruszewski (1883)**, **Harris (1944)**, **Firth (1948)**, **Robins (1957a)**, **Pike (1952)**, **Hockett (1955)**, **Goldsmith (1976)**, **Henderson (1985)**, **Browman and Goldstein (1986)**, **Kelly and Local (1989)**, and **Silverman (1995, 2006a)**. Read up on these approaches, and compare and

contrast some or all of these researchers' proposals on how to handle spans in phonological theory. Some issues to consider are: (1) Is the traditional segment a necessary component to the model, or might reference to the segment be extraneous in whole or in part? (2) Does the model refer to linguistic levels beyond the purely phonological (for example the morphological, the semantic), and do you regard such "cross-referencing" a desirable component of our phonological theories? Why or why not? (3) Relatedly, are the researchers' hypotheses motivated by the implications for neutralization and/or contrast expression, or rather, are their attempts merely to model speech patterns without considering the functional consequences for contrastive cue expression?

(2) Consider both generative (**Nooteboom 1981, Beckman 1997, 2004**) and phonetic (**Kruszewski 1883, Bladon 1986, Wright 2004**) approaches to the "privileged" status of word-initial consonantal elements. What are some of the arguments in favor of one or another account of these "privileged" positions? Might a compelling account of this patterning reference *both* phonetics and generative modeling, à la approach to phonology considered in quite a few of the papers in the **Hayes, Kirchner, and Steriade (2004)** volume?

3   Taxonomy

Having now briefly considered patterns of neutralization from a topological perspective, in this chapter we move on to consider the taxonomy of neutralization, where taxonomy refers to the inventorying of both common and uncommon patterns of neutralization, and also any implicational hierarchies that might be established (though these await detailed discussion in Chapter 8). Our point of reference herein is the work of Jun (1995, 2004, 2010), who taxonomizes patterns of neutralization into positions that typically *resist* and/or *trigger* neutralization, and positions that typically *undergo* neutralization. Resisting and/or triggering elements include (1) prevocalic consonants, (2) stressed elements, (3) initial elements, and (4) roots. Undergoers include the flips of these positions: (1) non-prevocalic consonants, (2) unstressed elements, (3) non-initial elements, and (4) affixes. In this chapter we consider these contexts, concluding with Jun that values in resistor/trigger positions tend to possess more robust acoustic cues, while values in positions that undergo neutralization tend to possess weaker cues. Regarding consonants in particular, positions of cue robustness/ stability display a strong tendency to be *lexically prevocalic*, whereas positions of neutralization/assimilation tend to be *lexically non-prevocalic*.

JUN (2010): LEXICAL PREVOCALIC VERSUS LEXICAL NON-PREVOCALIC CONSONANTS

Jun (2010) focuses primarily on the asymmetry between lexically prevocalic consonants (as stated, typical resistors and triggers of neutralization) and lexically non-prevocalic consonants (recall, typical undergoers of neutralization). He considers, in turn, patterns of neutralization involving (1) oral and (2) laryngeal features, further observing a distinction between (1) assimilatory and (2) non-assimilatory patterns of neutralization. Keep in mind our working definition of neutralization: *neutralization is a conditioned limitation on the distribution of a language's contrastive values*. Consequently, such patterns are neutralizing *only* if the relevant values are contrastive in some other context. Thus, for example, consider a language that possesses both voiced and voiceless stops in prevocalic contexts (say, **p t k b d g**). Here, the presence of only a voice-assimilated version of these values in certain contexts may be characterized as a case of neutralization (specifically, an assimilatory laryngeal neutralization). However, if a language has only one series of stops, then these stops' voicing assimilation is not an instance of neutralization. With this caveat in mind, we might expect (at least):

(1) Assimilatory oral neutralization
(2) Assimilatory laryngeal neutralization
(3) Non-assimilatory oral neutralization
(4) Non-assimilatory laryngeal neutralization
(5) Assimilatory oral and assimilatory laryngeal neutralization
(6) Assimilatory oral and non-assimilatory laryngeal neutralization
(7) Non-assimilatory oral and assimilatory laryngeal neutralization
(8) Non-assimilatory oral and non-assimilatory laryngeal neutralization.

Let's consider – and, to the extent possible, exemplify – these eight patterns in turn.

(1) *Assimilatory oral neutralization* is, quite simply, canonical regressive place assimilation, in which the place-of-articulation of C_1 is identical to that of C_2. This identity may be lexical (static) or derived (dynamic). In Diola Fogny, for example, nasals orally assimilate to following stops (throughout, transcriptions are taken from Jun): **gam** – **ni+gaŋ+gam** ("I judge"). In Yakut, coronals orally assimilate to a following consonant: **at** – **ak+ka** ("to a horse"). Indeed, cross-linguistically we observe that both nasals and coronals are especially susceptible to such oral assimilations.

(2) *Assimilatory laryngeal neutralization* is usually limited to the common pattern of regressive voicing assimilation. Jun mentions Dutch, Yiddish, Sanskrit, Romanian, Serbo-Croatian, Ukrainian, Hungarian, Egyptian Arabic, and Lithuanian as examples, though this list may be extended with ease. Jun provides examples from Catalan – **gat+ə** ("cat, f.") – **gad+dulen** ("bad cat"), **pɔk+ə** ("little, f."), **pɔg+du** ("a little hard") – and Polish – **żaba** ("frog") – **żap+ka** ("small frog"), **woda** – **wot+ka** ("vodka").

Assimilatory aspiration or glottalization is unattested, almost certainly because such patterns would require the release of C_1 in order to saliently encode the assimilated laryngeal value. Consonantal release in this context is exceedingly rare, and would mitigate the likelihood of assimilation anyway. Moreover, interconsonantal context is a poor site for saliently encoding the acoustic cues associated with aspiration or glottalization.

(3) *Non-assimilatory oral neutralization* is typically limited to word-final position. This pattern involves the collapse of place distinctions towards a single value. Jun considers several cases, among them Ancient Greek, Spanish, Japanese, Slave, and Kelantan Malay. For example, in standard varieties of Spanish, nasal contrasts found elsewhere collapse to **n** in final position: "e**n** Chile", "ta**n** frio", "u**n** elefante"; this is a static (non-alternating) pattern. In Kelantan Malay, all oral place distinctions collapse to the glottal stop in final position: **ikat+V … – ika?** ("tie"), **səsak+V … – səsa?** ("crowded"); this is a dynamic (alternating) pattern. (Though the glottal stop is a laryngeal, the neutralization itself involves oral values.)

(4) *Non-assimilatory laryngeal neutralization* is a common pattern in which laryngeal distinctions – voicing, aspiration, glottalization – collapse to a single value, typically, in non-prevocalic position, for example, Dutch final devoicing: **bɛtə** ("(we) dab") – **bɛt** ("(I) dab"), **bɛdən** ("beds") – **bɛt** ("bed"); Greek non-prevocalic laryngeal neutralization: **laryng+os** ("larynx, gen.sg.") – **larynk+si** ("larynx, dat.pl."), **trikʰ+os** ("hair, gen.sg.") – **trik+si** ("hair, dat. pl."). Additionally, many languages suspend laryngeal distinctions in word-final position (by definition a lexically non-prevocalic context), for example, Cantonese.

(5) *Assimilatory oral and assimilatory laryngeal neutralization*: some languages neutralize both oral and laryngeal contrasts in pre-consonantal contexts, at least at certain places of articulation. For example, we have already seen that Catalan displays across-the-board voicing assimilation, but it also displays place assimilation of its pre-consonantal coronal nasals: so**n** amics ("they are friends") – so**m** pocs ("they are few") – so**n** dos ("they are two") – so**ŋ** grans ("they are big"). It follows that coronals assimilate both in terms of their oral values and their laryngeal values.

It is less clear whether there are cases of particular values that neutralize *both* their oral and laryngeal values in this fashion. Such a pattern would involve, for example, **p t k b d g** always geminating with a following stop, whether voiced or voiceless, such as **d+t → tt, p+g → gg**. Indeed, the absence of this pattern is not terribly surprising: for well-understood aerodynamic reasons, voiced geminates are quite rare, as a prolonged oral closure makes it difficult to maintain the trans-glottal airflow necessary for vocal fold vibration. Consequently, we don't expect a surplus of systems that actually derive voiced geminates from morphologically ordered sequences that possess a voiceless element, especially to the exclusion of allowing *heterorganic* voiced clusters, which need not involve as prolonged an oral closure as do geminates; heterorganic sequences rely far less on their closure duration than they do on their formant transitions, whereas, by contrast, would-be-derived voiced geminates rely far more crucially on maintaining a long-duration closure in order to maintain their contrastive status with their singleton counterparts.

(6) *Assimilatory oral and non-assimilatory laryngeal neutralization*: in some languages, pre-consonantal consonants are necessarily assimilated with respect to their oral features, and their laryngeal distinctions collapse towards a single value. For example, both German and Korean display certain place assimilations, as well as word-final (non-assimilatory) laryngeal neutralization.

(7) *Non-assimilatory oral and assimilatory laryngeal neutralization*: here, oral distinctions among pre-consonantal obstruents would collapse towards a single value, and furthermore, these obstruents take on the voicing value of the following consonant: in a system with **p t k b d g**, the first element in morphologically ordered obstruent sequences might collapse towards, for example, alveolarity: p̱+**g** → d̲**g**, g̲+**p** → t̲**p**. I am unaware of any such system, however.

(8) *Non-assimilatory oral and non-assimilatory laryngeal neutralization*: here, there is a collapse towards a single value of both oral and laryngeal contrasts in some context or other. For example, in Slave, all non-prevocalic obstruents go to **h**, thus neutralizing both oral and laryngeal contrasts in a non-assimilatory fashion: **ts'ah̲** – **ts'ade** ("hat"), **tl'uh̲** – **tl'uɬe** ("rope"). A comparable pattern is present in Toba Batak, in which all stops reduce to **ʔ** before another stop, be this second stop voiced or voiceless.

Before moving on it should be noted that, while not terribly prevalent, manner of articulation may neutralize in both assimilatory and non-assimilatory fashion. For example, in Korean, lateral–coronal nasal sequences, lateral–tap sequences, and coronal nasal–tap sequences, are all realized as long laterals: l+n, l+ɾ, n+ɾ → l:, for example, tʃʰal+na → tʃʰal:a ("a moment"), il+ɾju → il:ju ("peculiarity"), hwan+ɾo → hwal:o ("file"). This is both an assimilatory (l+n → l:, l+ɾ → l:) and a non-assimilatory (n+ɾ → l:) pattern. Non-assimilatory manner neutralization may be found in, for example, Ponapean: in certain morphological contexts, would-be obstruent sequences become nasal–obstruent sequences, for example, **kik-kik** → **kiŋkik** ("kicking"), **did-did** → **dindid** ("build a wall"), **sas-sas** → **sansas** ("stagger"). As nasals are otherwise contrastive, this non-assimilatory "nasal substitution" pattern is indeed neutralizing in nature.

BARNES (2006): STRESSED ELEMENTS VERSUS UNSTRESSED ELEMENTS

Recall that vowel systems may undergo either centripetal or centrifugal reconfiguration under de-stressing, centripetal systems involving vowel reduction towards the center of the vowel space (oftentimes ə or ɐ); centrifugal systems involving vowel reduction towards the corners of the vowel space (for example, i u ɐ).

Barnes (2006) makes several astute observations about the cross-linguistic patterning of unstressed vowel reduction, for which he proposes a compelling unifying explanation:

(1) Centrifugal reduction almost always reduces the number of vowel height contrasts, rather than reducing the number of contrasts involving other vowel quality features, such as labiality, palatality, and pharyngeality.

(2) Upon centrifugal reduction, the acoustic vowel space still avails itself of maximal distinctness on the second formant dimension (correlating with backness and roundness), while first formant distinctions are reduced, and typically skewed downwards, (correlating with vowel rising).

(3) Reductive tendencies in the number of vowel height distinctions under stresslessness may induce complete neutralization (termed "phonological vowel reduction" by Barnes), or may induce near-neutralization (his "phonetic vowel neutralization").

(4) Non-reducing features (labiality, palatality, pharyngeality) are those that typically engage in vowel harmony, whereas the reducing feature (height) typically does not.

Barnes (2006:29): "Generally speaking, [unstressed vowel reduction] appears in languages with a large durational asymmetry between stressed and unstressed syllables, such that unstressed syllables undergo significant durational contraction relative to a substantially longer stressed syllable . . . ." Following an earlier proposal of Lindblom's, Barnes observes that such shorter vowels may tend to rise, since, quite simply, it takes more time to significantly lower the jaw than to keep it comparatively raised. In time (that is, over generations of language use), the shorter duration and concomitant rising of unstressed vowels of differing qualities may induce perceptual confusion among them, perhaps eventually culminating in their neutralization.

Note, then, that Barnes' proposals regarding the phonetic and diachronic origins of these unstressed vowel neutralizations nicely accounts for his four observations:

(1) Centrifugal reduction almost always reduces the number of vowel height contrasts, rather than reducing the number of contrasts involving other vowel quality features, because durational shortening under stresslessness has its greatest articulatory effect on (a curtailment of) jaw lowering.

(2) Upon centrifugal reduction, the acoustic vowel space still avails itself of maximal distinctness on the second formant dimension, while first formant distinctions are reduced, and typically skewed downwards, again, because reduced jaw lowering limits the degree of vowels' F1 distinctiveness, while having little effect on their F2 distinctiveness.

(3) Reductive tendencies in the number of vowel height distinctions under stresslessness may induce complete neutralization, or may induce near-neutralization, because such vowel reductions have their origins in slow diachronic pressures on the system, and thus a vowel system may alight at any stop – however transitorily – along this decidedly continuous diachronic/phonetic track towards complete neutralization.

(4) Non-reducing features (labiality, palatality, pharyngeality) are those that typically engage in vowel harmony, whereas the reducing feature (height) typically does not, because vowel height limitations under stresslessness have local phonetic origins that are unlikely to propagate to neighboring regions not subject to these local phonetic pressures, whereas those features that do propagate remain largely unaffected by the durational truncation induced by stresslessness.

And while languages display remarkable variation with respect to the specifics of unstressed vowel reduction (investigated in thoroughgoing detail by Barnes), the overall pattern emerges remarkably clearly.

INITIAL ELEMENTS VERSUS NON-INITIAL ELEMENTS

These straightforward "edge effects" have already been considered in Chapter 2, and need not be repeated here.

URBANCZYK (2011): ROOTS VERSUS AFFIXES

Urbanczyk (2011) provides a fine overview of cross-linguistic structural asymmetries between roots and affixes. She cites Jakobson (1965:29), who notes that "affixes [as opposed to roots] illustrate a selective use of phonemes and their combinations". The primary distinction that Urbanczyk attends to is that between the expression of contrast in some morphological context (root or affix), versus its suspension. Her overall findings may be inventoried thus:

(1) Roots tend to possess more contrastive values; affixes fewer. Bybee (2005) reports that labials, alveo-palatals, and laterals are sometimes restricted to roots, never appearing in affixes. For example, roots in Abipon, Kanuri, and Tohono-O'odam may possess alveo-palatals, but affixes never do. Comparably, glottal distinctions in the form of ejectives and implosives show a marked preference for appearing in roots over affixes, as in Cuzco Quechua, Amharic, Salishan. Long vowels and nasal vowels are also commonly limited to roots.

(2) A superset–subset relationship is typically observed with respect to the inventory of contrastive values in roots versus affixes. Urbanczyk makes the interesting point that the larger set of phonetic values found in roots, as compared to the smaller set of values found in affixes, may, in theory, be in a relationship of only partial overlap, or even complete disjunction. In fact, she emphasizes that this is *not* what is observed: root and affix values engage in a superset–subset relationship, such that affixes do not typically possess phonetic values – whether stable or alternating – that are not also found in roots.

(3) Root values tend to be non-alternating, while affixes are more often the locus of neutralizing alternations. The superset–subset relationship between roots and affixes follows logically from the fact that affixes tend to be subject to alternations that are specifically neutralizing in character.

Actually, it is a bit more complicated than this, in that it's not completely correct to characterize these alternations as neutralizing in nature. Let's take an example of Urbanczyk's to understand why. Akan possesses "root-controlled" vowel harmony, a common type of system in which affixal values of the harmonic feature (here, ATR; advanced tongue root) are determined by the root to which these affixes attach, never the other way around (that is, affix values never affect roots).

So, for example, [+ATR] root /E+√bu+O/ → **ebuo** ("nest"); [−ATR] root /E+√bʊ+O/ → **ɛbʊɔ** ("stone"). Here, ATR values of affixes are determined by the root, and thus alternation in affix vocalism never introduces new phonetic values into the inventory. But still, it might be premature to regard this as a specifically *neutralizing* alternation, simply because, in the relevant – affixal – domain, there is no ATR distinction to be neutralized in the first place. In other words, we are dealing with something of a middle ground between a (dynamic) neutralizing alternation and a (static) suspension of contrast: there is indeed both alternation and contrast suspension in the relevant domain, but there is no lexical contrast that is being actively eliminated, since the affixes do not contrast for ATR. Moreover, the alternating character of affixes may be functionally linked to the fact that they are a small, closed class. As such, these grammatical formatives are under less functional pressure to resist assimilatory influences from their associated roots, since such assimilations are less likely to induce neutralization. Indeed, even if such assimilations *do* neutralize contrasts in such domains, the counter-functional consequences are mitigated by the simple fact that the set of affixes is small.

We return to such domain-specific factors as they relate to the character – and the definition – of neutralization in Chapters 4, 16, and 17.

(4) Roots tend to be phonotactically more complex, affixes less so. In some languages – Sanskrit being a well-known example – consonant clusters may be found in roots, but not affixes (Whitney 1889, Steriade 1988). In others (Salish, Bantu), prevocalic consonants are limited to roots, and are never found in suffixes.

(5) Roots tend to be longer, affixes shorter. This is an oft-noted pattern that should require no explication.

The overall conclusion we may draw from Urbanczyk's investigation is that phonetic variety is greater in roots than in affixes. This makes perfect functional sense: every language requires many more roots that it does affixes, and, consequently, every language passively evolves such that lexical distinctions among its many roots may be saliently encoded in the speech signal. Bybee (2005), for example, suggests just such an account of her observed asymmetries in this area. Urbanczyk: "Under [Bybee's] view, affixes are reduced forms of lexical morphemes, which start off with a full inventory of sounds. As morphemes are grammaticized, they tend to get reduced phonologically, thus eliminating some of the complex articulations." This, it seems to me, is the right conclusion, but we still need both phonetic and functional reasons *why* grammatical formatives may be subject to phonetic simplification in the form of "phonological reduction". As forms become grammaticized, their articulatory complexity may slowly reduce due exactly to their newly acquired function: functors are frequently encountered in the speech stream, and their morpho-syntactic patterning with respect to the lexical categories thus becomes increasingly predictable. Due to both their increased frequency and the increased predictability of their distribution in the speech stream, even speech tokens that are somewhat simplified in their phonetic properties may yet effectively play their semantic (that is, their grammatical) role, in the sense of being conveyed successfully to listeners by unambiguously encoding their meaning. As listeners recover the semantic content of these simplified tokens, they are more likely to produce them in kind. As this process is iterated, grammatical markers may, over time, become phonetically simpler.

Urbanczyk calls special attention to systems in which the root–affix distinction is not so clear-cut, as in non-concatenative systems such as those found in Salishan, Semitic, and also ablaut sub-systems, for example; we could add stem-modifying systems like Nilotic and Otomanguean to this list, among others. This interesting area of exceptionality is not considered in detail herein. Indeed, Urbanczyk laudably investigates a number of these "problem cases", ones that do not fit neatly into the overall patterns she observes; the reader is strongly encouraged to seek out her work on this topic, also including Urbanczyk (2006, 2007).

Urbanczyk further considers generative approaches to her documented asymmetries. For example, in autosegmental phonology (Leben 1973, Goldsmith 1976), the observed asymmetries may be an epiphenomenal consequence of the so-called "directionality parameter". If lexical values are, by default, associated "one-to-one" and "left-to-right", the alternating values found at the ends of words may be accounted for. Whether or not this approach may characterize the behavior of prefixes remains an unanswered question, however.

An alternative generative characterization involves the establishment of morpheme structure constraints (MSCs) (Halle 1959, Stanley 1967), an approach which recapitulates observed recurrent phonological paradigmatic and syntagmatic patterns in morpheme structure in the form of statements about what patterns are allowed (that is, are recurrent) or disallowed (that is, are absent).

Several generative researchers working within the optimality framework have also addressed the issue at hand. For example, McCarthy and Prince (1995) propose that a candidate surface form's "faithfulness" to underlying root structure is more highly valued than is a candidate surface form's "faithfulness" to affix structure. This approach, like Halle's and Stanley's, recapitulates observed patterns in terms of iron-clad statements ("constraints" again) about synchronic patterning. However, on a language-specific basis, these statements may be falsified due to a greater importance being placed on other, potentially contradicting statements. For example, as discussed by Urbanczyk, Sanskrit may be characterized as possessing a constraint that bans complex onsets altogether (thus accounting for their absence in affixes), though it also possesses an even stronger constraint (a "higher-ranked" constraint) that requires complex onsets to surface if they are underlyingly present in roots (thus accounting for their presence in roots). That is, faithfulness to root structure outranks the ban on complex onsets. It's certainly a neat trick, but one may wonder whether it captures anything genuinely insightful about the pressures that are ultimately responsible for the pattern.

SUMMARY

In this chapter we have considered – in decidedly non-exhaustive detail – patterns of neutralization from a taxonomical perspective by documenting common versus uncommon patterns of neutralization, and considering certain implicational hierarchies that emerge from this documentation. Overall, it may be stated with certitude that positions in which cues may be robustly encoded in the speech stream tend to be resistant to neutralization, whereas positions of neutralization tend to be those with fewer opportunities for cue expression. Expressed in raw lexical phonotactic terms, positions of consonantal contrast maintenance, for example, display a strong tendency to be *lexically prevocalic*, whereas positions of consonantal neutralization tend to be *lexically non-prevocalic*.

DISCUSSION QUESTIONS AND FURTHER READING

(1) "Implicational hierarchies" are often expressed with reference to markedness. For varying opinions on this and other proposals on what, exactly, markedness should and/or should not encompass, consider **Zipf (1949), Vennemann (1972), Battistella (1990, 1996), Rice (1999), Gurevich (2001), Blevins (2004), Haspelmath (2006), Hume (2011, 2012)**. Discuss how these authors' proposals

are either wedded or unwedded to the phonetic motivation for the patterns documented by **Jun (1995, 2004, 2010)**. That is, should markedness proposals make reference to phonetic factors, or, instead, should they be viewed as determined by other means? Indeed should markedness, in whatever guise, be a genuine object of theoretic pursuit?

(2) Syllable-based approaches to phonotactic generalizations – for example, **Fischer-Jørgensen (1952)**, **Kahn (1976)**, the papers in **Bell and Hooper (1978)**, **Vennemann (1988)**, **Ito (1989)**, **Blevins (1995)**, **Goldsmith (2011)**, **Szigetvari (2011)** – often make critical use of proposed syllable-internal components. For example, onsets tend to resist neutralization, while codas tend to be undergoers. Consider the explanatory value of some of these proposals, and compare them to phonetically based accounts of the observed patterns – for example, **Steriade (1999)** – and the relevance of "lexical prevocalic" and "lexical non-prevocalic" contexts. What are some arguments in favor of and/or against the extra phonological "layer" that syllables involve, in comparison to the "rawer" phonetic/phonotactic account of Steriade and that considered herein?

4   Typology

Far and away, the most thorough – and most thoroughly compelling – investigation into the typology of neutralization is that of Trubetzkoy. In his landmark work *Principles of Phonology*, posthumously published in 1939, Trubetzkoy is primarily concerned with inventorying the logical classifications of phonological oppositions and phonological processes. While much of the book is devoted to the typology of phonological oppositions (contrast), and sequential combinations (phonotactics), he also devotes some discussion to the typology of neutralization.

TRUBETZKOY (1939)

Neutralization is characterized by Trubetzkoy as a static distributional restriction on the phonological units that possess contrastive status in a particular language, that is, as the positional suspension of contrast, and not as the product of (dynamic) synchronic alternations. These latter forms are called *morphonemes*, and fall under the rubric of *morphonology*.

In order to understand the details of Trubetzkoy's typology of neutralization, it is first necessary to have at least a partial understanding of his typology of phonemic distinctions, or the *logical classification of distinctive oppositions*. This is because, according to Trubetzkoy (1939), not every logical type of distinctive opposition is neutralizable. Rather, the extent to which neutralizing phonemes possess features in common is of paramount relevance. Those features that distinguish a set of neutralizing phonemes are referred to as *marks*, while the remainder – those features that are common to the neutralizing phonemes – are referred to as *archiphonemes*. The archiphoneme, therefore, is "the sum of distinctive properties that the two phonemes have in common" (p. 79); archiphonemes appear in positions of neutralization. (By convention, archiphonemes are written in upper-case letters;

typically, the upper-case version of the Roman symbol approximating their phonetic value. For example, a nasal archiphoneme may be written "**N**".)

Trubetzkoy (1939) asserts that only certain types of phonological oppositions are susceptible to neutralization. Specifically, only *bilateral oppositions* might neutralize, where a bilateral opposition is defined as an opposition for which "the sum of the properties common to both opposition members is common to these two opposition members alone" (p. 68). Trubetzkoy employs a clever orthographically based illustration of a bilateral opposition. In the Roman alphabet, the letters **E** and **F** constitute a bilateral opposition, because the features they share – the vertical line and the upper and middle horizontal lines – are not possessed by any other letters in the alphabet (the bottom horizontal line thus constitutes the mark). By contrast **P** and **R** do not constitute a bilateral opposition (rather, they constitute a *multilateral opposition*), because the elements they share are not exclusive to them, since **B** possesses these elements as well.

Now recall that, according to Trubetzkoy, only bilateral oppositions may neutralize. For example, **E** and **F** may neutralize, but **P** and **R** cannot, due to the presence of **B**. This follows logically according to Trubetzkoy, because in the absence of marks, the remaining features – the archiphoneme – are the sum of common elements for these phonemes, and these phonemes alone. Removing the marks from a multilateral opposition does not result in an archiphoneme however, because the shared elements are necessarily found in some other phoneme(s) as well. For example, in German, **t–d** is a bilateral opposition, because removing the voicing mark results in a set of features that is not possessed by any other element of the German system, and indeed, **t–d** is neutralizable in German: in the position of neutralization, the phonological value is neither a voiced stop nor a voiceless stop, but an archiphoneme, "a non-nasal dental occlusive". In short, the phonemic contrast is suspended in the position of neutralization, and instead, the archiphoneme is found. (While all neutralizing oppositions are bilateral, it is not the case that all bilateral oppositions are neutralized.) By contrast, the German **b–d** opposition is multilateral in nature, because removing the mark does not result in a set that consists of these two members only: if we remove the mark, we are left with "a voiced stop in general", which includes **g** as well. As a consequence, according to Trubetzkoy, the **b–d** opposition is non-neutralizable in German.

Trubetzkoy observes that certain oppositions are *constant* in the sense that they function contrastively in all plausible contexts. Thus, for example, in Danish, æ and e may play a contrastive role in any plausible segmental or prosodic context (that is, wherever a vowel might be found). In French, however, vowels e and ɛ may only contrast in open final syllables, for example *lait* le, *les* lɛ. Elsewhere in French, the distribution of these two vowels is completely predictable: e occurs in open syllables, while ɛ occurs in closed syllables. This opposition is thus not constant, but is instead *neutralizable*. For Trubetzkoy, French e and ɛ are regarded as phonologically distinct only in final syllables. This is the *position of relevance*. In non-final position, the vowels are not contrastive. These are *positions of neutralization*, in which archiphonemes are found (in the case of French e–ɛ, since each appears in a position of neutralization, additional criteria must be employed in order to determine the archiphoneme; more on this momentarily). He characterizes the system of phonemes in positions of neutralization as *partial systems*.

Having now considered certain of the rudimentary properties of phonological oppositions, let's move on to our main concern, that is, neutralization. Trubetzkoy divides his investigation here into two parts: (1) relationships between opposition members and archiphonemes (discussed in his Chapter 3, Section 2, Part C) and (2) relationships between archiphonemes and their conditioning environments (discussed in his Chapter 5). Following his lead, we consider each of these in turn.

(1) Relationships between opposition members and archiphonemes

Consider four types of neutralization that differ in terms of the phonetic relationship between the opposition members and the archiphoneme.

(1a) In the first case, in the position of neutralization the archiphoneme is phonetically distinct from both members as they appear in their positions of relevance. For example, Russian possesses both palatalized and non-palatalized labials. This opposition is neutralized before palatal dentals. However, the archiphoneme is neither purely palatalized, nor purely non-palatalized. Rather it is "semipalatalized", a phonetic attribute that is part-way between the values found in positions of relevance. A comparable pattern is found in English, which possesses an opposition traditionally called *fortis* versus *lenis* that is neutralized after s. In this position of neutralization we find neither fortis nor lenis values, but instead a "special type" of lenis value that is phonetically distinct from both the fortis and lenis values found in their positions of relevance.

(1b) A slight variation of this sort of neutralization involves an archi-phoneme that, instead of being phonetically intermediate between the opposition members, has phonetic qualities that are possessed by neither of the opposition members. In such cases, the unique properties of the archiphoneme may be deter-mined by assimilation to a neighboring value. For example, in Mandarin, the **k–ts** opposition is neutralized before high front vowels **i** and **y**, being realized as **tɕ**. Here, the archiphoneme possesses qualities that are absent from both of the contrastive values, and instead are determined by assimilation to a following high front vowel.

 (2) The second pattern involves archiphonemes that are identical to one of the opposition members. For example, in many languages obstruent voicing is neutralized before other obstruents: voice-less values are found before voiceless obstruents, and voiced values are found before voiced obstruents. In this particular case, the archiphoneme is determined *externally*, that is, as a conse-quence of its phonetic context. However, it probably should not be concluded that this second class of neutralization is always externally conditioned.

(3a) External conditioning may be contrasted with archiphonemes that are *internally* conditioned. In such cases, the value of the archiphoneme is not influenced by its phonetic context. Rather the archiphoneme consists of the unmarked member of the opposition, irrespective of its phonetic context. This presupposes that the opposition (in positions of relevance) is *privative* in nature, that is, the opposition consists of one member whose featural make-up is a unique subset of the other member. For example, a voiceless value possesses a unique featural subset of its voiced counterpart (assuming that voicing is featurally speci-fied, whereas voicelessness is not, voicing is the mark). Similarly, a non-nasalized value possesses a unique featural subset of its nasalized counterpart (again, assuming that nasality is featurally specified, whereas orality is not).

(3b) By contrast, if the opposition is not privative in nature, but is instead *gradual* (that is, the opposition is characterized by various degrees or gradations of the same property, for example, vowel aperture), Trubetzkoy asserts that it is always the *minimally extreme* opposition member that is found in the position of neu-tralization (thus prefiguring the observations of Barnes 2006). For example, in Bulgarian and Modern Greek, **u–o** and **i–e** are neutralized in unstressed syllables. Given the gradual nature of this opposition (since low vowels are contrastive as well), the position of neutralization possesses the high vowels, never the mid vowels; the extreme close vowels thus represent the archiphonemes. Trubetzkoy proposes that the extreme members of such gradual oppositions are in fact the "minimum" degree of the relevant property. Using our same example, high vowels possess the minimum degree of vocalic aperture, and are thus the only candidates for the archiphoneme, since vowels possessing non-minimal degrees of aperture are not proper subsets of the high vowels.

(4) Finally, both opposition members may represent the archiphoneme, one in one environment, the other in another environment (this is our French **e–ɛ** example from a moment ago). In German, to consider another example, the **s–z** opposition is neutralized both root-initially and root-finally. Root-initially we find **z**, and root-finally we find **s**. In such cases, additional criteria must be considered when determining the unmarked member. Trubetzkoy suggests that the archiphoneme that is present in the context that allows for the greater number of contrastive values be the unmarked member. In the German case, the archiphoneme is thus **z**, because root-initial position possesses more contrastive values than does root-final position.

Overall, Trubetzkoy employs neutralization as the major criterion for the determination of markedness. In short, archiphonemes are unmarked quite literally, in the sense that they lack the mark that distinguishes them from their marked counterpart.

(2) Relationships between archiphonemes and their conditioning environments

Moving away from the relationship that archiphonemes bear to their opposition members, Trubetzkoy further considers the relationship between archiphonemes and their conditioning environments. The following outline will help us navigate this complex discussion.

(1) Contextually conditioned neutralization
  (a) Dissimilative neutralization
    (i) Conditioned by both members of an opposition
    (ii) Conditioned by the marked member of an opposition
    (iii) Conditioned by both members of a related opposition
    (iv) Conditioned by the marked member of a related opposition
  (b) Assimilative neutralization, conditioned by the absence of a mark
  (c) Combined (dissimilative/assimilative) neutralization

(2) Structurally conditioned neutralization
    (a) Centrifugally conditioned
    (b) Reductively conditioned
        (i) Free tonic
            (α) Bidirectional
            (β) Unidirectional
        (ii) Bound tonic
    (c) Combined (centrifugal/reductive) neutralization

Some neutralizations are contextually conditioned while others are structurally conditioned. Neutralization is *contextually conditioned* if the opposition is neutralized in the environment of specific phonemes; neutralization is *structurally conditioned* if the opposition is neutralized in particular prosodic contexts, that is, in specific positions in the word. Let's first consider contextually conditioned neutralizations.

(1) Contextually conditioned neutralizations may be either dissimilative or assimilative

Dissimilative neutralization (1a) involves the loss of a distinction in the context of a *contextual phoneme*. Such contextual phonemes either possess the feature that is being neutralized, or possesses a "phonologically related" property. Moreover, the dissimilative neutralization may be due to the contextual phoneme possessing a marked feature, or due to the contextual phoneme lacking the mark. Such neutralizations are (perhaps counter-intuitively) regarded as dissimilative because the feature that is neutralized is exactly the contextual feature that is responsible for the neutralization. That is, a contrastive feature is neutralized due to the neighboring presence of just that contrastive feature. In this sense, an opposition dissimilates (that is, is lost) due to the presence of a neighboring phoneme that is contrastive for that very feature. Schematically then, a language may possess a contrastive feature of the form **x** versus **y** that is present on segments **a** and **b** where, for our purposes, **b** is always the contextual phoneme, and **x** is always the mark. Thus the language has segments a^x, a^y, b^x, b^y. However, when **a** is in the vicinity of **b**, the a^x–a^y opposition is neutralized, and only the archiphoneme is found: Ab^x or Ab^y (where, for our purposes **A** – the archiphoneme – is phonetically equivalent to a^y). In this sense, the neutralization is dissimilative, since the contrast **x**–**y** on **a** is eliminated when **a** is in the vicinity of b^x or b^y.

We can go through the resulting matrix of possibilities to see what Trubetzkoy actually means.

A dissimilative neutralization may take place in the context of both members of an opposition (1ai). For example, in many Slavic languages, obstruent voicing is neutralized in the context of a following obstruent: obstruents are voiceless before voiceless obstruents, and are voiced before voiced obstruents. In Serbo-Croatian, we have *srb* (Serb, masc.), *srpski* (Serbian), *srpkinja* (Serb, fem.). Employing our schematic notation, a^x, a^y, b^x, b^y are contrastive, but in the relevant contexts we find $a^x b^x$ or Ab^y.

A dissimilative neutralization may take place only in the context of the marked member of an opposition (1aii). Again, if we assume feature value x is the mark, we may consequently find Ab^x, $a^x b^y$, $a^y b^y$. For example, in Slovak, a vocalic length distinction is neutralized after a long vowel. Here, the long vowel is assumed to be the marked value, and thus the archiphoneme – the short vowel – appears in the position of neutralization.

A dissimilative neutralization may take place in the vicinity of both members of a "related" opposition (1aiii). Here, the feature that neutralizes does so when in the vicinity of a comparable feature, though not an identical feature. Let's call **w** and **z** the two values of the related feature. We consequently may find Ab^w, Ab^z. Trubetzkoy discusses a pattern from Lezghian, one in which the opposition between plain and labialized consonants is neutralized when adjacent to a high vowel (**u y i**). Trubetzkoy regards high vowels as related to consonant labialization in Lezghian, since rounding is a contrastive feature for both; the non-high vowels, for which rounding is non-contrastive (**a e**), do not induce neutralization.

Finally, a dissimilative neutralization may take place in the context of the marked member of a related opposition (1aiv), but not in the context of the unmarked member. If we assume **w** is the marked value, then we expect to find Ab^w, $a^x b^z$, $a^y b^z$. An example: in the Eastern Caucasian languages Ch'ak'ur, Rutulian, Artshi, Aghul, Darghinian, and Kubachi, the contrast between plain and labialized consonants is neutralized when a round vowel follows, where labialization is a privative feature, that is, a mark.

Regarding *assimilative neutralization* (1b), a particular opposition will lose its mark only in the vicinity of phonemes that do not have that particular mark. In a language that possesses a^x, a^y, **b** (**b** does not contrast for **x–y**), we find Ab. For example, in Eastern Cheremis, plain stops and voiced fricatives are contrastive, but the contrast is neutralized in the context of a preceding nasal (this is post-nasal occlusivization). The archiphonemes are voiced stops in this context of neutralization, or, more properly, simply obstruents (since the only property uniquely shared by the plain stops and the voiced fricatives is their status as obstruents). The neutralization is assimilative because the mark that distinguishes the (neutralized) opposition is not relevant to the contextual phoneme: neither voicing nor occlusivization is contrastive in the nasals, and thus the non-contrastive features of the contextual phoneme are shared by the archiphoneme.

A third type of neutralization combines elements of dissimilative and assimilative neutralization (1c). For example, the Bulgarian contrast between palatalized and non-palatalized consonants is neutralized whenever a consonant immediately follows. This neutralization is both dissimilative and assimilative, because palatalization is contrastive on some of the contextual phonemes (thus dissimilative), but not others (thus assimilative).

(2) Structurally conditioned neutralizations may be centrifugal or reductive

Centrifugal neutralization (2a) (not to be confused with our previous discussion of so-called centrifugal vowel neutralization) occurs at a word or morpheme boundary. For example, many Slavic languages (Russian, Polish, Czech, etc.) neutralize obstruent voicing contrasts in final position (the archiphoneme is voiceless).

Reductive neutralization (2b) occurs in non-tonic syllables (that is, syllables that lack primary stress).

The tonic may be *free* (2bi) (or in some cases, genuinely contrastive) in terms of its placement in the word. For example, in Slovenian, the long–short vowel contrast is only present in stressed syllables.

Elsewhere, a length contrast may be reduced to the (short) archiphoneme. Such reduction occurs both before and after the tonic, and thus neutralization is *bidirectional* (2biα).

In other such cases reduction is *unidirectional* (2biβ). For example, in Serbo-Croatian, only syllables that precede the tonic are reduced.

Alternatively, the non-reductive domain may be *fixed*, or *bound* (2bii), at a word edge (or in word-penultimate syllables). In Barra Gaelic, for example, both the vocalic e–æ opposition, as well as the consonantal plain–aspiration correlation, are reduced in all syllables other than the initial. Trubetzkoy characterizes Mongolian vowel harmony in comparable terms: certain vocalic contrasts are relevant only in word-initial position, and are neutralized non-initially.

It is further true that in some cases of bound reductive structurally conditioned neutralizations, the tonic itself is free, and thus certain contrasts that are present at word edges are in fact neutralized in word-internal stressed domains. For example, in most Turkic languages, vowel harmony reduces contrasts in non-initial syllables, but stress is word-final.

In fact, centrifugal and reductive neutralization may co-occur (2c). For example, in Chemeris, obstruent voicing is neutralized word-initially, while vowels achieve their full contrastive status in word-initial syllables only (post-initial syllables are subject to vowel harmony).

Trubetzkoy notes finally that various types of neutralization may be so pervasive in a particular language that certain oppositions may be realized only under very circumscribed conditions. For example, in certain Slavic languages, the consonantal palatalization opposition is only manifested before back vowels. In all other contexts ("before consonants by a combined contextually conditioned neutralization; before front vowels by a dissimilative structurally conditioned neutralization … and in final position"), the contrast is neutralized. In Bulgarian, extensive neutralization sets up a situation such that there is, in fact, no position that allows all oppositions to be manifested. In other words, Bulgarian is completely lacking in constant oppositions.

DISCUSSION

Recall that the archiphoneme – the value that appears in positions of neutralization – is not an allophone of either of the opposition members. Instead, it is another phonological entity altogether: the value found in positions of neutralization does not belong to any of the phonemes with which it might contrast in positions of relevance. Thus, if a^x and a^y contrast before b^x but not before b^y – thus $a^x b^x$, $a^y b^x$, and Ab^y are found – A is an archiphoneme belonging to neither a^x or a^y, regardless of its phonetic properties.

Further recall that Trubetzkoy treats neutralization not as the product of (dynamic) synchronic alternations, but rather, as the (static) suspension of contrast in particular positions (though, to be sure, Trubetzkoy does indeed sometimes exemplify archiphonemics with values in alternation). Recall that alternation (neutralizing or otherwise) is subsumed under the label *morphonology* (a broad – and very relevant – topic that, owing to his early death, was never satisfactorily explicated by Trubetzkoy in his 1939 volume). Thus, we cannot conflate the archiphoneme with the morphoneme: archiphonemes are present in contexts where contrast is (statically) suspended; morphonemes are present in contexts of (dynamic) neutralizing alternation. Indeed, no matter how we define the phoneme (be it in psychological terms or functional terms), there are important differences in the linguistic status of lexically static distributional restrictions (Trubetzkoy's archiphoneme) and dynamically imposed neutralizations (Trubetzkoy's morphonemes). Some of these differences have already been hinted at in Chapter 1 of the present volume.

Let's move on to consider a couple of minor internal inconsistencies in Trubetzkoy's discussion, some of which I have already alluded to.

First, recall that, according to Trubetzkoy, only bilateral oppositions may neutralize. However, he discusses cases of *multilateral oppositions* for which a subset of their members neutralize. Recall that in Bulgarian and Modern Greek, **u–o** and **i–e** are neutralized in unstressed syllables, though these systems also possess the low vowel. Within the context of Trubetzkoy's typology, this pattern is not predicted to exist. One may argue that this contradiction could be remedied if Trubetzkoy were to abandon his proposal that gradual oppositions actually exist, and in their place substitute an exploded array of binary features (à la Jakobson, Fant, and Halle 1952). Thus, the Bulgarian and Greek patterns may be accounted for by positing, for example, a binary feature [High]. High and mid vowels are distinguished by their different values for this one feature, while low vowels are distinguished by another feature, [Low]. While such an analysis might salvage Trubetzkoy's assertions regarding the non-existence of neutralization among gradual oppositions, it begs a more fundamental question: Why bother? It is not clear what is to be gained by Trubetzkoy's original assertion, especially since it is patently incorrect: neutralization (employing virtually any definition other than Trubetzkoy's) is not limited to binary oppositions.

Related to this matter is the subset relationship that an archiphoneme presumably bears to its opposition members. Trubetzkoy proposes that the archiphoneme possesses only those features common to the neutralizing phonemes. But once we accept that gradual oppositions may neutralize (which we must do), this definition fails in identifying the proper criteria for archiphoneme status.

CONCLUSION

Trubetzkoy's is – far and away – the most thorough (and most thoroughly compelling) investigation into the typology of (static, contrast-suspending) neutralization of which I am aware. It thus provides a fitting culmination of our brief investigation of the phenomenon from the perspective of *observation* and *description*. In this chapter we have thus completed our inventory of the various ways neutralization may be characterized: topological, taxonomical, and herein, typological. The next two chapters investigate phonological patterns which bear certain similarities to neutralization, but which are most emphatically *non*-neutralizing in character: partial phonemic overlap, and near-neutralization.

DISCUSSION QUESTIONS AND FURTHER READING

(1) Trubetzkoy makes little effort to evaluate the cognitive status or relevance (if any) of the generalizations he makes regarding neutralization. Do you view this as a shortcoming of Trubetzkoy's discussion, or, rather, do you think it a wise, even principled move on his part? Consider, for example, relevant discussion by **Bloomfield (1933)**, **Twaddell (1935)**, **Bloch and Trager (1942)**, **Harris (1951)**, and **Malmberg (1963)**.

(2) Trubetzkoy makes a clear distinction between archiphonemes and morphonemes. Consider other approaches that address this distinction from various theoretical vantage points, for example those of **Akamatsu (1988)**, **Stampe (1969, 1973a, 1973b)**, **Kisseberth (1970)**, **Clayton (1976)**, **Kenstowicz and Kisseberth (1977)**, **Davidsen-Nielson (1978)**, **McCarthy (1998)**. How compelling do you find the arguments considered therein?

5   Partial phonemic overlap

"Partial phonemic overlap" earned its name from Bernard Bloch, who discussed the phenomenon in a paper published in 1941. As discussed by Bloch, partial phonemic overlap, though bearing some superficial similarities to neutralization, is most emphatically contrast-preserving: a single phonetic value may be unambiguously assigned to either one phoneme or another phoneme, due to the different contexts in which this phonetic value is present. We first consider a very clear example of partial phonemic overlap – the interaction of tapping and raising in Canadian English – and then move on to consider the three cases discussed by Bloch. We'll see that, actually, none of Bloch's examples provide unambiguous evidence for the existence of phonemic overlap. We then continue with Gurevich's (2004) detailed typology of the phenomenon. We conclude by reiterating the fact that, although partial phonemic overlap bears some superficial – that is, phonetic – resemblance to neutralization, the phenomenon is most emphatically non-neutralizing because, despite their phonetic non-distinctness, the values in question remain phonologically distinct.

Let's first consider a clear case in order to elucidate what exactly is meant by partial phonemic overlap. Whereas many American English dialects possess the ɐɪ diphthong when a voiceless obstruent follows, as in "write" ɹɐɪt and "bite" bɐɪt, certain dialects of Canada (and also of the northern US) possess ʌɪ (ɹʌɪt, bʌɪt) though retain ɐɪ when a voiced obstruent follows, as in "ride" ɹɐɪd and "bide" bɐɪd. This distribution is complicated by the presence of tapping: both t and d alternate with ɾ when a stressless syllable follows, but the raised diphthong is still present before those taps that alternate with t, for example, "write"–"writer" ˈɹʌɪt̚–ˈɹʌɪɾɹ̩, "ride"–"rider" ˈɹɐɪd̚–ˈɹɐɪɾɹ̩. Notice that, considered in isolation, the tapping of both t and d might be regarded as a neutralizing alternation, since both values alternate with the same phonetic value. Nonetheless, due to the presence of the vowel quality differences preceding the taps, the distinction between the two values is recoverable: the tap that alternates with the voiceless value is necessarily preceded by the higher diphthong, and the tap that alternates with the voiced value is necessarily preceded by the lower diphthong. The distinct contexts of the taps thus serve a disambiguating function, and so the two values should not be regarded as neutralized. Bloch (1941:279): "The intersection or overlapping of phonemes will be called partial if a given sound x occurring under one set of phonetic conditions is assigned to phoneme a, while the same x under a different set of conditions is assigned to phoneme b." In our example, x is ɾ, a is t, and b is d. We find phoneme a (t) when x is preceded by the higher diphthong (ʌɪ__), and we find phoneme b (d) when x is preceded by the lower diphthong (ɐɪ__).

Take note of the main point here: a single phonetic value, considered in complete isolation, is of ambiguous affiliation. However, disambiguation is provided by the different contexts in which this single phonetic value is present. In this sense then, partial phonemic overlap should not be viewed as an instance of neutralization, simply because no opposition has been neutralized.

Let's now turn to the three cases discussed by Bloch. Recall: we will see that Bloch's definition of the phenomenon is fine, but his examples do not provide unambiguous evidence for its existence.

BLOCH (1941)

(1) Bloch's first example also involves tapping (he calls it "flapping"). At the time of his writing, in certain American English dialects the so-called "[r] phoneme" could reportedly be flapped when an interdental fricative immediately precedes, for example, "three" θɾi, "throw" θɾoʊ. Meanwhile, as we know, the flap (tap) may also be found intervocalically when a stressless syllable immediately follows, though for the dialects in question, ɾ is apparently an alternant of t, never d. According to Bloch, the context serves to cue which phoneme – t or ɹ – the flap/tap is affiliated with: "Every flap between vowels belongs to the [t] phoneme, every flap after a dental spirant belongs to the [ɹ] phoneme" (1941:279f.) For Bloch then, a is t, b is ɹ, and x is ɾ. We find phoneme a (t) when x is flanked by vowels, the second one stressless ('V__V), and we find phoneme b (ɹ) when x is preceded by an interdental fricative (θ__). (There are lexical exceptions, such as "today" tʰəˈreɪ, "obesity" oʊˈbisəɾi, etc.)

The flaw: according to Bloch, there are contextual cues that indicate which phoneme – t or ɹ – the flap/tap is affiliated with (recall: "Every flap between vowels belongs to the [t] phoneme, every flap after a dental spirant belongs to the [ɹ] phoneme"). The problem in Bloch's logic is that there is no compelling evidence that the post-spirant tap is indeed affiliated with the so-called "[r] phoneme", since it never alternates with any other value; its behavior is static. It is thus an unmotivated assumption (rooted, apparently, in orthographic convention) to group these taps with ɹ; such post-spirant taps could just as readily – and just as arbitrarily – be grouped with t (or with any other value, for that matter), though such a conclusion is no better motivated than concluding that they are grouped with ɹ. Rather, we are dealing with a case of contrast suspension. Simply stated, in the dialects under consideration, contoids do not contrast after interdental fricatives.

So, the proper statement concerning the distribution of taps in these dialects is that "every flap between vowels belongs to the [t] phoneme" (this is a direct quote from Bloch), and after a dental spirant, all consonant contrasts are suspended; only ɾ may be present. We thus conclude that Bloch's first case does not, in fact, exemplify partial phonemic overlap at all, because there is no evidence – either by alternation or by context – that the tap in the context θ__ may be unambiguously grouped with t or with ɹ. This is, instead, a case of (static) contrast suspension.

(2) Bloch's next example involves contextual versus contrastive labialization of consonants in English. For words like "tool" and "cool", the initial consonants are claimed to be contextually labialized as a consequence of the round vowels that immediately follow: $t^w u ł$, $k^w u ł$. Meanwhile, words like "twin" and "queen" are contrastively labialized: $t^w ɪn$, $k^w ɪn$. In fast speech, according to Bloch, the contrastive labialization here is phonetically comparable to the contextual sort. But despite this phonetic comparability, "[t]he intersection is obvious, but only partial; for the character of the following vowel always distinguishes the two values of lip-rounding" (1941:280). Employing Bloch's formulation of partial overlap, in this case, the values in partial overlap are t and t^w (or perhaps a sequence, tw, though nothing crucial hinges on this). Considering only u for the present, x is t^w, a is t, and b is t^w. We find phoneme a (t) when x is immediately followed by u (__u), and we find phoneme b (t^w) when x is immediately followed by vowel of any other quality (__∼u).

The flaw: even assuming that Bloch's phonetic characterization is correct, there is, again, no evidence – either by alternation or by context – for Bloch's conclusion that the underlined values in $\underline{t^w u}ł$

and t̪ʷɪn are phonemically distinct; he is, again, relying on orthographic conventions (one is spelled with a "w", the other is not).
Consequently, we are again dealing with a static contrast suspension:
apart from a few words (for example, "swoon"), labiality is not contrastive on consonants that precede round vowels.

(3) Bloch's third example (due to discussion with Charles Hockett)
involves what has subsequently been called the "excrescent" or
"intrusive" stop that may be found between a nasal and a fricative; a consequence of raising the velum before releasing an oral
closure: "[A]t the end of a stressed syllable after a nasal, there is
free variation between a spirant and a cluster of stop plus spirant
(the stop being homorganic with the nasal but voiced or voiceless
like the spirant)" (1941:281). Thus, we may find wɔɹmθ ∼
wɔɹmpθ "warmth", leŋθ ∼ leŋkθ "length", "feɪnz ∼ feɪndz
"finds", but also "fines". In cases involving palato-alveolars,
things get a bit dodgy, since the excrescent stop results in sound
sequences that are elsewhere "unit phonemes" (tʃ dʒ), thus,
for example, "bench" and "hinge" may possess tʃ and dʒ respectively, but only, according to Bloch, as a consequence of
excrescence/intrusion due to early velum-raising (bɛnʃ ∼ bɛntʃ,
hɪnʒ ∼ hɪndʒ): "That [tʃ] and [dʒ] are unit phonemes and not
like [ts], [dz], clusters of two phonemes each, appears from
their patterning elsewhere (their distribution, their occurrence
before and after other consonants, etc); yet at the end of a
stressed syllable after a nasal, they behave exactly like ordinary
clusters of stop plus spirant" (p. 281). Bloch concludes that "[t]he
simplest way to describe the facts ... is to posit partial intersection: in all positions except the one here defined, the sounds in
question are phonemic units; in this one position they are
clusters of two phonemes each, [t]+[ʃ] and [d]+[ʒ], and alternate
in free variation with the corresponding simple spirants [ʃ] and
[ʒ] just as other clusters do" (p. 281). Again employing Bloch's
formulation of partial overlap, and considering only the voiceless values for now, in this case the values in partial overlap are
the "unit phoneme" t͡ʃ and a tʃ sequence. So, x is tʃ or ʃ, a is t+ʃ,
and b is t͡ʃ. We find a (t+ʃ) when x is immediately preceded by a
nasal (N__), and b (t͡ʃ) may be any other context in which x is
found (∼N__).

The flaw: once again, the conclusion that this is a case of partial
phonemic overlap is unmotivated. Bloch is claiming that the phonetic
sequences tʃ and dʒ are unit phonemes in all contexts except when a

nasal immediately precedes in a stressed syllable. In this and only this context, t͡ʃ and d͡ʒ are phonologically sequenced. But how does he know? Unlike the cases in which an interdental or an alveolar suffix may variably trigger alternation (for example, wɔɹm "warm" but wɔɹmθ ~ wɔɹmpθ "warmth", feɪn "fine" but feɪnz ~ feɪndz "fines"), English possesses no alternations involving the palato-alveolars. Consequently, there is no phonological evidence – either by alternation or by context – for the conclusion that we are dealing with phonemic overlap: in the (always static) context of a preceding nasal it cannot be determined whether phonetic ʃ or t͡ʃ is phonological ʃ or t͡ʃ, or whether phonetic ʒ or d͡ʒ is phonological ʒ or d͡ʒ: there are no alternations to make such a determination. A better way of stating this is that there is actually no need for such a determination. Rather, once again, we are dealing with a static contrast suspension: when a nasal immediately precedes, English suspends the ʃ–t͡ʃ and ʒ–d͡ʒ contrasts.

We are forced to conclude that none of the three cases considered by Bloch is a legitimate instance of partial phonemic overlap according to his own definition of the term; all are, rather, instances of contrast suspension. This is not to say that the phenomenon does not really exist, or that he has failed in isolating and defining it. Indeed, as shown by our Canadian English example, partial phonemic overlap, as Bloch defines it, is a very real phenomenon. But Bloch has not provided any genuine cases of the effect. More often than not, he has, alas, been seduced into faulty phonemicizations due to orthographic interference; a distressingly common mistake among linguists, even those of Bloch's fully justified high standing.

Bloch's definition of the effect is fine (recall: "[t]he intersection or overlapping of phonemes will be called partial if a given sound **x** occurring under one set of phonetic conditions is assigned to phoneme **a**, while the same **x** under a different set of conditions is assigned to phoneme **b**"), but we need *linguistic evidence* that values **a** and **b** are genuinely in opposition, such that, upon partial overlap, they may be unambiguously assigned to one value or the other. Bloch fails to provide this evidence.

GUREVICH (2004)

Let's now move on to consider several more cases of partial phonemic overlap – *genuine* cases now – not considered by Bloch. These were compiled by Gurevich in her important book from 2004, which focuses on lenition, and the absence of neutralization that results from most such weakening processes. Gurevich uses the term "phonetic neutralization" to characterize the sorts of partial overlap introduced by Bloch, since, indeed, in such cases the phonetic distinction within an opposition is neutralized when considered out of context, though the contrastive information itself is cued by other means. Gurevich documents and exemplifies these "other means" by which phonetically neutralized values eschew genuine (i.e. "phonological") neutralization. It should be noted that Gurevich ultimately embraces an especially narrow definition of "neutralization", subsequently also embraced by me in my 2006 book, and also the definition we are building towards in the present study: neutralization as derived homophony, that is, NEUTRALIZATION. Still, this narrowed definition need not concern us yet, as the elements of Gurevich's discussion we now consider may be applied to more standard approaches to neutralization.

In her corpus of 230 leniting processes, Gurevich documents 52 cases in which the phonetic distinction is neutralized for a particular opposition, with the contrast surviving by various other means. She typologizes Bloch's partial phonemic overlap phenomenon into several structurally unique though functionally equivalent types. They are unique in that each involves a different means of preserving the opposition that has been "phonetically neutralized", but they are functionally equivalent in that, indeed, for each sub-type, the relevant contrast is maintained.

(1) Contrast shifts: "[W]hen the phonetic distinction between the two contrastive sounds is neutralized, the contrast previously embodied by the neutralized opposition may shift elsewhere." One example would be our tapping-and-raising case already discussed. Gurevich (2004:52): "[I]n ... [Canadian] ... English ... intervocalic t and d are both realized as ɾ, obliterating the phonetic distinction between the two phonemes. However, the contrast previously embodied by the t/d opposition shifts to the length and height of the preceding vowel." Here, both values are cued by alternation: both alternate with ɾ, and the site of overlap is disambiguated by the difference in vowel quality. Indeed, as shown by Kelly and Local 1989:158–161, the site of disambiguating cues stretches much further than the immediately preceding vowel, manifesting itself across the entire lexical span.

A related example of a "contrast shift": in Cardiff English, Collins and Mees report that "/b d g dʒ/ are markedly devoiced in final position, and that the contrast with /p t k tʃ/ is mainly indicated by the length of the preceding vowel". Thus, assuming for the moment that final devoicing here is complete, the contrast nonetheless survives in the form of preceding vowel quality. In Cardiff English then, a = **b d g dʒ**, b = **p t k tʃ**, c = **p t k tʃ**, x = **V·__**, y = **V__**.

(2) Synchronic chain shifts: "[I]n some context a phoneme **a** shifts to **b**, which is also phonemic in the language, but the a/b opposition is maintained because in that same context, **b** is realized as another sound, **c**" (2004:52). Gurevich labels such "synchronic chain shifts" as cases of (partial) "phonemic overlap", as, indeed, they are examples *par excellence* of the phenomenon. In Northern Corsican, for example, Gurevich writes that "intervocalic **p t k** are voiced to **b d g**, and in the same [intervocalic] context, **b d g** are spirantized to **β ð ɣ**", for example, <u>pe</u>ðe – u+<u>be</u>ðe "foot"–"the foot", <u>bok:ɑ</u> – ɑ+<u>βok:ɑ</u> "mouth"–"the mouth" (where the underlined sounds are in alternation for each pair). Thus, although both values possess voiced stop alternants, neutralization is never encountered, because the voiced stops in alternation with the voiceless stops are *only* present intervocalically, and the voiced stops in alternation with the voiced spirants are *never* found intervocalically. In Northern Corsican, a = **p t k**, b = **β ð ɣ**, c = **b d g**, x = **V__V**, y = ~[**V__V**].

A second example: in Malayalam, voiceless stops are voiced after sonorants, and before vowels if a non-nasal precedes. Also, the voiced stops spirantize (/flap) in these same contexts. Thus, in exactly those contexts where the voiceless stops possess voiced alternants, the voiced stops possess spirantized (/flapped) alternants; a classic synchronic chain shift, in which no value is neutralized. In Malayalam, a = **p t ʈ k**, b = **β ð ɽ ɣ**, c = **b d ɖ g**, x = $C_{sonorant}$ __, C_{oral} __ V, y = ~[$C_{sonorant}$ __], ~[C_{oral} __ V].

(3) Distributional differences are found "if a phonetic distinction between two phonemes is obliterated but [these two phonemes] never surface in the same [prosodic] context ... For example, in Haia Amele ... **b** and **f** are contrastive (**fæ** 'doubt'; **bæ** 'today'), but both can be realized as **p** under certain conditions: **b** surfaces as **p** word-finally in polysyllabic words (**hiˈnup**, 'five days hence'), and **f** may surface as **p** elsewhere (**puˈpu** ~ **fuˈfu**, 'wind')." Thus, "it is always clear which phoneme is represented by **p**" (2004:51). In Haia Amele, a = **b**, b = **f**, c = **p**, x = σ ...__#, y = ~[σ...__#].

Another example documented by Gurevich: in Warndarang, word-initial stops **b** and **ɟ** correspond to glides **w** and **j** upon reduplication (with certain lexical exceptions), for example, **ɟaɽi-jaɽi** "to do continuously", **biji-wijima** "(reciprocal aux v.)".

Meanwhile, the glides **w** and **j** are in opposition with the stops intervocalically under all other circumstances. Thus, glides may appear intervocalically under two different circumstances: (1) as lexical (non-alternating) glides, and (2) as reduplication-conditioned alternants of the stops. Nonetheless, despite their "phonetic neutralization" in intervocalic position, no "phonological neutralization" is ever encountered: in non-reduplicating contexts, the glides are always, simply, glides. In reduplication contexts, the glides are transparently affiliated with the stops, with which they are in correspondence. Consequently, the neutralization is merely "phonetic", and never "phonological".

Observe that in Warndarang, it is the "correspondence" relationship that provides contextual morphological information about the nature of a given opposition. In Warndarang, glides may appear in identical phonological contexts (that is, intervocalically), yet still be in opposition, because some intervocalic glides are transparently in correspondence with stops, whereas others are transparently not.

Gurevich shows that, of the 52 cases in her corpus of the Bloch variety (his "partial phonemic overlap"; her "phonetic neutralization"), 15 avoid "phonological neutralization" due to contrast shifts, 19 due to synchronic chain shifting, and seven due to distributional differences. Her findings are quite remarkable, not only for demonstrating so unambiguously that leniting processes are overwhelmingly contrast-preserving (92 percent of all cases in her corpus are contrast-preserving, rather than contrast-neutralizing), but also because, in the process of showing this, she typologizes the various means that languages have at their disposal to avoid "phonological neutralization" while tolerating "phonetic neutralization".

CONCLUSION

Given the constraints imposed by a phonemic/segmental account of phonological structure, it is not fully clear how we might generalize across all cases of partial phonemic overlap in clear and concise structural terms. But for now, at least, we conclude with Bloch that partial phonemic overlap involves two contrastive values **a** and **b** for which one or both possess(es) a conditioned alternant **c** that eliminates the phonetic distinction between **a** and **b**, though **a** and **b** may still be phonologically differentiated here by virtue of **c**'s distinct contexts.

One thing is perfectly clear though: partial phonemic overlap – especially in light of Gurevich's success in both exemplifying *and* typologizing the phenomenon – is in no sense a variant of neutralization.

DISCUSSION QUESTIONS AND FURTHER READING

(1) Bloch's partial phonemic overlap is an example of what **Kiparsky (1973)** terms "phonological opacity", in which a pervasive phonological generalization is not always surface-present. Opacity has been synchronically characterized within rule-based phonology (such as Kiparsky's) and in constraint-based phonology, including the "constraint conjunction" approach of **Kirchner (1996)**, the "sympathy" approach of **McCarthy (1999)**, and the "targeted constraints" approach of **Wilson (2001)** and **McCarthy (2007)**. By contrast, both **Silverman (2002)** and **Gurevich (2004)** characterize patterns of partial phonemic overlap in diachronic terms, characterizing the effect as a passive consequence of functional pressures on language use. For these authors, phonological opacity is not a problem to be solved for language users; it is only a problem for linguists' diachronic analyses. Discuss both the synchronic and diachronic accounts of partial phonemic overlap, focusing especially on the insights that each approach makes regarding its linguistic basis.

(2) Recall that **Gurevich (2004)** finds that upwards of 92 percent of all the leniting processes she investigates actually preserve contrasts, rather than neutralizing them. She concludes that such lenitions "do not operate independently of functional considerations". Consider Gurevich's take on her findings, and compare it to those of her predecessors, specifically **Lavoie (2001)** and **Kirchner (1998, 2004)**. Also of relevance is a paper by **Kaplan (2011b)**.

6 Near-neutralization

Unless we were to admit the possibility of "spelling pronunciations" serving to undo a merger, then values that were phonetically different in the past, but are now identical, cannot become different again. Thus if historic **a** and historic **b** merge towards **b** such that, for instance, historic forms **ac** and **bc** both end up **bc**, the collapse of historic **a** and **b** cannot be undone ("unmerged") at a later point in time; **bc** will indeed be subject to further changes, but will never split such that the historic **a**–**b** contrast is re-introduced as **a**–**b**, or as any other phonetic values, say, **e**–**f**, along the same lexical lines as their historical antecedents. This fact of sound change goes by the name of Garde's Principle (after Garde 1961): "A merger realized in one language and unknown in another is always the result of an innovation in the language where it exists. Innovations can create mergers, but cannot reverse them. If two words have become identical through a phonetic change, they can never be differentiated by phonetic means" (translated from the French by Labov 1994:311).

In this chapter we consider some putative cases of so-called "unmergings" in light of documented cases of "near-merger", and "near (or incomplete) neutralization". Apparent counter-examples to Garde's Principle are, in fact, only that: apparent. The values that were assumed to be merged in the past, or neutralized in the present, can be shown to be (or argued to have been) merely nearly-merged or nearly-neutralized. Near-mergers and near-neutralizations thus cannot be classified as neutralization.

LABOV (1994)

Taking Garde's Principle into consideration, let's look at some sound changes discussed at length by Labov (1994) that, at first blush, seem to violate it. We will see, of course, that no violation of Garde's Principle is encountered. Rather, the incontrovertible truth of the Principle demands an alternative analysis, one, we will see, that is both plausible on its face, and confirmable to its depths.

The first case: in the eighteenth century, the English diphthong əɪ split into aɪ and ɔɪ. This split might not require much commentary except for the fact that the əɪ diphthong itself was a consequence of the Middle English merger of iː and ʊɪ, which was part of the Great English Vowel Shift: as iː began to diphthongize towards modern-day aɪ, it passed through an əɪ-like phase. Meanwhile as uː began to diphthongize towards au, it passed through an əu-like phase. During this period, the u in ʊɪ also began to lower in tandem with uː such that it, like iː, went through an əɪ-like phase on its way to modern-day ɔɪ. That is, historic iː and historic ʊɪ seem to have merged in the seventeenth century, only to later split into modern-day aɪ and ɔɪ. For example, Middle English liːn "line" and lʊɪn "loin" supposedly merged to ləɪn, and then split to modern-day laɪn and lɔɪn. Indeed, the merged values split along the exact same lexical lines on which they supposedly merged, in an apparent violation of Garde's Principle.

	iː	aɪ	əɪ		ɔɪ	ʊɪ
>16th c.:	line					loin
17th c.:			line	loin		
18th c.>:		line			loin	

If we take Garde's Principle seriously, we must conclude that iː and uː never did, in fact, merge to əɪ. Rather, as advanced by Labov, they engaged in a *near-merger*: they came perilously close to each other, so close that neither did the linguists of the era detect their difference (remember, there were no spectrographs back then), nor did speakers report that the two were actually different values. We might propose that the near-merger took the form iː > ə̣ɪ, ʊɪ > ə̱ɪ.

	iː	aɪ	ə̣ɪ	ə̱ɪ	ɔɪ	ʊɪ
>16th c.:	line					loin
17th c.:			line	loin		
18th c.>:		line			loin	

If the values were merely nearly-merged, Garde's Principle remains inviolate, as well it should.

Apart from the logical necessity of our conclusion that the two patterns exemplified by "line" and "loin" never actually merged in the past, but only nearly-merged, what empirical support might we appeal to? This is an especially pressing concern since we obviously have no extant samples of seventeenth-century speech. We turn to this issue now.

In its broadest application, the doctrine of Uniformitarianism states that the laws governing the patterning of natural phenomena are equally valid across all space and time. Consequently, as Labov writes, we might use the present to explain the past. If we find near-mergers in the present in exactly those cases that seem to have violated Garde's Principle in the past, then we may conclude that the Principle was never in fact violated: the near-merger found today is good evidence of a near-merger in the past, one that has survived to the present. Indeed, the "line"–"loin" near-merger that developed in the seventeenth century actually does survive today, for example, in Essex. In the village of Tillingham, Labov interviewed several speakers, eliciting the relevant vowel qualities in both spontaneous speech and recitation speech. He found (1) there were indeed minor acoustic differences between the supposedly merged values, more pronounced in spontaneous speech, less pronounced in recitation speech, and (2) despite these minor differences in vowel production, the Tillingham residents were unable to perceive them accurately, even when listening to their own speech; this is known as a "commutation test". Labov reasonably asserts that a "passing grade" on the commutation test requires a score approaching 100 percent, since contrastive values are expected to be readily distinguished in their positions of relevance. We return to these curious results in a few moments, but for now, Labov plausibly concludes that the near-merger in evidence today embodies the same near-merger that developed in the seventeenth century.

The second case: in Middle English "meet", "meat", and "mate" possessed distinct vowel qualities: eː, æː, aː. During the sixteenth century, the vowels æː ("meat") and aː ("mate") reportedly merged towards ɛː, but during the seventeenth century they unmerged, with (historic) æː ("meat") and eː ("meet") now merging towards iː (and historic aː ("mate") rising to eː).

	iː		eː	ɛː		æː	aː
>16th c.:			meet			meat	mate
16th c.:			meet	meat	mate		
17th c.>:	meet	meat	mate				

The assumption that æː and aː merged to ɛː in the sixteenth century is based on a number of lines of evidence, including bidirectional spelling errors found in contemporaneous texts, and reports by several of the era's grammarians.

Actually, certain sixteenth-century orthographic "ea" words alternated between ɛː and (short) ɛ when followed by two consonants ("break"–"breakfast", "clean"–"cleanliness", "mean"–"meant"), which might have left a route open for these particular words to unhinge from ɛː, and merge with iː. That is, since their phonological behavior was different from non-alternating ɛː-words, there might be a basis for their distinct diachronic trajectories. However, this source of the supposed unmerging would not account for the many other words that changed from ɛː to iː that did not engage in the ɛː–ɛ alternation, such as the first members of the pairs "beat–bate", "meat"–"mate", "feet"–"fate". It is thus apparent that the changes were not sensitive to the ɛː–ɛ alternation, but instead applied to all ɛː words historically deriving from æː (for example, "meat"), and excluded all ɛː words historically deriving from aː (for example, "mate"); an apparent violation of Garde's Principle.

We are, of course, dealing with another near-merger: æː and aː both drifted towards ɛː in the sixteenth century, coming extremely close to each other without actually merging. As in the "line"–"loin" case, we again have contemporary dialectal evidence in favor of this analysis, this time from Belfast. As in Tillingham, Belfast speakers were recorded employing both spontaneous speech and recitation speech. It was found that the "mate"–"meat" near-merger survives in the stigmatized vernacular, though is lost in the prestige dialect. It should thus not be surprising that spontaneous speech provided evidence of the near-merger, whereas recitation speech contexts – in which speakers more carefully and self-consciously monitor their behavior – did not. Moreover, speakers reported that the vowels in question were always the same, even when their attention was specifically drawn to the near-mergers that they produced in spontaneous speech. (Whether this conclusion on the part of Belfast speakers was itself influenced by social factors remains unexplored.) The nature of the Belfast "mate"–"meat" distinction is one of vowel height and off-gliding, the "mate" class now possessing the higher vowel, and a sporadic off-glide (iəː), though overlap of the two vowel qualities – even in spontaneous speech – is not insignificant.

Assuming for now that the modern Belfast reflexes are phonetically comparable to the sixteenth-century distinction – that is, "mate" with a slightly higher, off-glided value in comparison to "meat" – then the supposed unmerging never, in fact, took place in the seventeenth century, since the forms remained distinct in the sixteenth.

	iː		eː	ɛː	i̧ɔ̧ː	æː	aː
>16ᵗʰ c.:			meet			meat	mate
16ᵗʰ c.:			meet	meat	mate		
17ᵗʰ c.>:	meet	meat	mate				

Labov (1994:387): "The overlap [in the distribution of the two vowel qualities] has not prevented the distinction between the two classes from being maintained for almost three hundred years. The first report of the merger in Hiberno-English was as early as 1700, and by Garde's well-established principle of the irreversibility of mergers, the distinction found in today's Belfast vernacular could not have been maintained if complete merger had occurred then or at any time thereafter. It follows that speakers are capable of tracing the frequency of occurrence of the two classes ... and that this differential distribution is a part of their fundamental knowledge of the language ... ."

Were near-mergers merely an areal peculiarity of the British Isles, then other supposed cases of unmergings would remain problematic for Garde's Principle. Of course, no such areal peculiarity exists; the doctrine of Uniformitarianism requires us to delve deeper into other apparent counter-examples to the principle, regardless of their region or era of origin.

Some of Labov's most famous research investigates near-mergers in North American English. Let's consider a case from New York, that of "source" and "sauce". In so-called "r-less" dialects, the non-prevocalic ɹ found in other dialects typically corresponds to a schwa-like off-glide. Since these very same dialects possess ɔə in words like "sauce", the pronunciation of these two words – "source" and "sauce" – is nearly identical. Labov reports that in recitation contexts, the two vowels are rather distinct from one another, in apparent imitation of the prestige (non-r-dropping) dialect: "source" possesses a higher tongue position compared to "sauce". In spontaneous speech, however, the height difference all but disappears, and the vowels are only barely distinguished by a very slight backing and/or rising for "source", thus, sɔ̧əs ("source") – sɔəs ("sauce").

Another case: in Albuquerque, a high school student was found who nearly merged the vowels in "fool" and "full". Despite a slight though persistent difference in their phonetic properties, this student felt that all the relevant words possessed but a single vowel quality. He was recorded reciting a list of "fool"–"full", "pool"–"pull" words. When this recording was played to speakers who possessed a better separation of the vowel qualities, they correctly identified the words only 83 percent of the time.

A third case: in the 1990s, central Pennsylvania possessed the eastern-most isogloss of the a–ɔ merger, and thus, for example, "cot" and "caught" began to merge here. An older speaker in the town of Duncannon maintained a robust a–ɔ distinction in spontaneous speech, but in minimal pair recitation forms, the distinction was nearly merged. Other researchers report comparable patterns among other older speakers.

Other such cases are discussed by Labov – "fool"–"full" in Salt Lake City, "too"–"toe" in Norwich, etc. – that further document dialectal differences involving near-mergers.

Consider a three-by-three matrix in which local and standard dialects possess discrepancies among fully-merged, nearly-merged, and well-separated values.

		Standard Dialect		
		a. fully-merged	b. nearly-merged	c. well-separated
Local Dialect	1. fully-merged		1b.	1c.
	2. nearly-merged	2a. Tillingham		2c. NYC
	3. well-separated	3a.	3b.	

All the cases discussed by Labov involve local dialects that possess nearly-merged values (the 2-cells), while the standard dialect possesses either fully-merged values (for example, Tillingham, cell 2a), or well-separated values (for example, New York City, cell 2c). Following Garde's Principle, in cases where the local dialect possesses fully-merged values (the 1-cells) it is this dialect – not the standard dialect (the b-cells and c-cells) – that is innovative. In cases where the standard dialect possesses fully-merged values, it is this dialect (the a-cells) – not the local dialect (the 2-cells and 3-cells) – that is innovative. For cells 2c and 3b, either dialect class may be innovative.

Moreover, assuming for the moment that the local dialect is stigmatized (an assumption that is certainly not always correct, of course), then in the 2-cells, near-mergers are more likely to be found in spontaneous speech, and less likely to be found in recitation speech; in the b-cells, near-mergers more likely to be found in recitation speech, and less likely to be found in spontaneous speech.

Finally, regarding the empty cells, the fact that the **b**-cells remain unfilled is a mere accident of intellectual history: Labov and his colleagues emphasize research into current dialectal variation in their efforts to use the present to explain the past. Meanwhile, examples for the cells **3a** and **1c** are readily available, but are not of present concern, as they do not involve near-mergers.

One may wonder why systems tolerate near-mergers in the first place, especially if the system sometimes eventually wends its way towards the better separation of the values, as in our "line"–"loin" example. In fact, rare is the case in which a single corner of the sound pattern can be satisfactorily analyzed without understanding its place in the system as a whole. Consider the "line"–"loin" near-merger. Recall that the near-merger here was part of a much more extensive pattern of upheaval, the Great Vowel Shift. The cause(s) of the Great Vowel Shift are unknown, but nonetheless Labov shows that certain aspects of its patterning are seen over and over again in patterns of vowel change, suggesting that its origins are at least partly phonetic. Indeed, a "trigger" of such shifts is likely to reside in certain phonetic attributes of low vowels. Let's briefly consider why this might be so.

It is well established that low vowels tend to involve a degree of velum lowering. It is unlikely that velum lowering here evolved in service to *enhancing* the contrast between low and non-low vowels, because, in fact, the introduction of nasal resonant energy serves to lower the "center of gravity" of the first formant region for low vowels. This lowering of the velum thus serves to make low vowels sound more like mid vowels, because the higher the vowel, the lower the first formant. Consequently, it should be obvious that velum lowering here does not serve to *enhance* the acoustic distinction between low and non-low vowels. Rather, all else being equal, it serves to *diminish* this distinction. For this reason, the velum-lowering that accompanies low vowels is likely to be an automatic physiological development – with potentially function-negative consequences – and not a product of contrast enhancement as a product of passive evolutionary pressures.

What is the nature of this potentially function-negative development? Given that low vowels tend to rise due to their concomitant nasalization, they may begin to encroach on the acoustic space of their higher neighbors. The eventual result may be a merger of the mid and low vowels (an outcome that is sometimes found in nasal vowel sub-systems). Obviously, this could be a function-negative development. More likely though, the mid vowels too will begin to rise, thus encroaching on the acoustic space of the high vowels, and a full-fledged chain shift is set in motion. Now, the high vowels cannot be made any higher, of course. Rather, in English as we know, it was specifically the long high vowels that began to diphthongize. This is a natural development from an auditory perspective: the acoustic distinction between long and short vowels may indeed be enhanced by modulating its formant frequency characteristics. Diphthongization is thus a natural way to enhance a distinction that would otherwise depend primarily on duration differences. Indeed, the diphthongization of contrastively long vowels is a common diachronic development.

In this proposed scenario, the near-merger of "line" and "loin" is simply the by-product of a change having its origins in a wholly unrelated corner of the sound system, that is, the automatic velum-lowering accompanying low vowels.

NEAR-NEUTRALIZATION

The existence of near-mergers makes the existence of near-neutralizations (often termed incomplete neutralization) a virtual inevitability, and indeed, shortly after Labov's pioneering work, phoneticians and phonologists set about investigating the issue. Results were positive: certain alternations that were traditionally assumed to be completely neutralized sometimes turn out to be nearly neutralized, for example, in Polish (Slowiaczek and Dinnsen 1985), German (Port and O'Dell 1985, Port and Crawford 1989), Russian (Pye 1986), Catalan (Charles-Luce 1993), Dutch (Warner, Jongman, Sereno, and Kemps 2004), Andalusian Spanish (Bishop 2007), Cantonese (Yu 2007), etc. We'll consider two cases in depth: final devoicing in Dutch and in Catalan.

Warner, Jongman, Sereno, and Kemps (2004) discuss final devoicing of obstruents in Dutch. In their first of a series of experiments, they had subjects read a list containing stop-final words that contrasted for voicing, words that were assumed to be completely neutralized towards voicelessness in the elicited context (that is, word-finally). In comparison to lexically voiceless stops, they found devoiced stops were produced with a minor though statistically significant longer duration of their preceding vowels, thus indicating that the voicing contrast is nearly-neutralized.

The authors then administered the commutation test. Speakers who produced a more robust distinction performed a bit better than those who produced a lesser distinction, but still, as expected now, all subjects failed, with scores around 50–60 percent. When vowel duration differences were artificially increased, subjects performed much better, and when stop closure duration differences were artificially increased, also, subjects performed somewhat better. Moreover, subjects produced more robust distinctions when their attention was specifically drawn to orthographic or morpho-phonological distinctions among potentially neutralized forms.

Warner, Jongman, Sereno, and Kemps (2004:252) write: "This finding is rather disturbing in its implications for phonological theory because it runs contrary to the idea of categorical distinctions among [contrasting] segments." This statement may, in fact, be questioned. I consider two components of their statement in turn: (1) their assumption regarding what does and what does not fall within the rubric of "phonological theory", and (2) their assertion that the existence of near-neutralizations runs contrary to the idea of categorical distinctions among contrastive values.

First, one may question these authors' assertion that the existence of near-mergers and near-neutralizations is problematic ("disturbing") for phonological theory. Really, it is only problematic for phonological theories that are not capable of readily incorporating these findings; for a phonological theory that predicts the existence of near-mergers and near-neutralizations, and offers a compelling account of their patterning, such phenomena are not "disturbing" at all.

This brings us to these authors' assertion that the existence of near-mergers and near-neutralizations "runs contrary to the idea of categorical distinctions among segments". This assertion, too, may be questioned. Despite the gradient, variable, and continuous nature of speech production, phonological categories themselves remain clearly defined. The absence of discreteness at the level of speech production may indeed culminate in neutralizations and near-neutralizations, but the categories themselves remain discrete. In the case of complete neutralization, there is a lack of phonetic evidence for a listener to conclude which discrete category the speech token belongs to, but this fact has no bearing on the genuine discreteness of the categories themselves. In the case of near-neutralization, there exists a certain amount of variability, such that when we plot an array of tokens in the phonetic space, these tokens' distribution does indeed seem gradual, variable, and continuous. However, it is logically impossible for an individual speech token to ever embody such variability at the phonological level of analysis. Rather, this variability is observable only when we investigate the phonetic properties of pools of speech tokens: despite the phonetic continuousness observable within a pool of tokens, phonological discreteness is necessarily maintained for any single token.

Writing in 1975, André Martinet (1975:25) offers a prescient rejoinder to these authors' concerns:

> One wonders whether the habit of constantly operating with graphic notations does not make some linguist(s) deaf to the gradual shifts which any painstaking observation can reveal. If one has been taught, not only that phonological systems are made up of discrete units, but also that these units are basically the same in all languages, and that even if a discrete unit may well appear under the form of different allophones, these allophones can be listed and identified, so that they, in a sense, partake in the discreteness of the phonemes, one can hardly avoid concluding that no change can take place except by means of jumps from one unit or allophone to another. Only those who know that linguistic identity does not imply physical sameness, can accept the notion that discreteness does not rule out infinite variety and be thus prepared to perceive the gradualness of phonological shifts.

Martinet was writing about sound change, but the same argument may be applied to near-neutralization. Indeed, until this point, we have considered near-mergers and near-neutralizations in a near-vacuum, that is, without making specific reference to the functional consequences that such patterns may or may not have for the linguistic system as a whole, or for situation-specific semantics. More to the point, we have not yet investigated the possible relationship between near-neutralization (as opposed to complete neutralization) and derived homophony, that is, NEUTRALIZATION. If (1) we investigate minimal pairs that are involved in a neutralizing alternations, and if (2) we find that forms have a tendency to nearly neutralize (as opposed to completely neutralize) in contexts where derived homophony might induce semantic confusion, and if (3) we find that forms are more likely to completely neutralize in contexts that do not induce semantic confusion, then we might have uncovered a functional motivation for the diachronic persistence of such near-neutralizing patterns. We consider some evidence now.

Charles-Luce (1993) reports on a study of near-neutralization, finding that a Catalan voicing alternation is more likely to be nearly-neutralized (as opposed to completely neutralized) in contexts that would otherwise be semantically ambiguous. Her results are especially important for our purposes, because they show that the tendency towards neutralization is indeed affected by semantic factors: "[T]he perception and production of spoken words is affected differentially by the presence and absence of higher levels of linguistic information and ... the degree of precision of articulation is inversely proportional to the presence of semantic information" (p. 29).

Charles-Luce employed five minimal pairs in Catalan involving voicing in contexts of neutralization: **rik-** ("rich") – **rig-** ("I laugh, pres. ind."); **duk-** ("duke") – **dug-** ("I carry, pres. ind."); **fat-** ("fate") – **fad-** ("tasteless, masc."); **sɛk-** ("dry, masc.") – **sɛg-** ("I set down, pres. ind."); **sɛt-** ("seven") – **sɛd-** ("thirst"). The voiced forms are traditionally assumed to undergo complete devoicing – that is, complete neutralization – in the context of a following voiceless sound. In such cases, purported complete neutralization induces homophony. In turn, homophonous forms may induce semantic ambiguity under particular conditions.

Charles-Luce measured several different phonetic properties of the contrastive values, including the duration of the preceding vowel (which is typically longer in the context of a following voiced stop), closure voicing, and closure duration (which is typically longer during a voiceless stop). She reports that in semantically biased contexts, devoicing was usually complete. That is, complete neutralization was tolerated when it nonetheless resulted in a semantically unambiguous speech signal. However, in semantically unbiased contexts, devoicing was often incomplete. That is, complete neutralization was observed less often if it would have resulted in a semantically ambiguous speech signal; instead, near-neutralization was found, thus salvaging all the semantic information. Overall, the contrast was maintained in the form of vowel duration about 60 percent of the time in semantically ambiguous contexts, but only about 20 percent of the time in semantically unambiguous contexts.

Thus, concludes Charles-Luce (1993:39), "vowel duration distinguished underlying voicing in the neutral context and not in the biasing context ... suggest[ing] that when semantically biasing information is absent, underlying voicing is distinguished, regardless of the assimilatory environments. However, when semantically biasing information is present, vowel duration shows the predicted effects of regressive voice assimilation."

Charles-Luce's study focused on minimal pairs, the neutralization of which induces homophony. It is further predicted that neutralized heterophones are more likely to engage in complete neutralization, since doing so should not induce semantic ambiguity due to derived homophony.

As Charles-Luce (1993:41) concludes: "[T]here may be some on-line assessment by the speaker as to the degree of biasing information present [that] may be quite automatic and learned through experience . . . ."

Echoing Labov's commutation test results, Charles-Luce (1993:41) observes that "it is not uncommon for speakers to produce phonetic distinctions but for listeners to be unable to perceive the difference". This statement is completely accurate, but, alas, is readily subject to misinterpretation. On a fundamental level, it is, quite frankly, impossible for a speech community to possess systematic differences in production that are not perceived as such by the members of the community, because if such differences were not perceived, then these systematic differences in production would immediately and irrevocably be filtered out during the perception process; a preposterous scenario. Instead – and logically – any systematic differences in speech production are necessarily perceived by listeners. The evidence stems from the simple fact that when these listeners become speakers, they produce these patterns; as a matter of course, they would not produce them if they did not perceive them.

Still, the issue remains that speakers may fail the commutation test when listening to speech – even their own speech – that contains examples of nearly-merged or nearly-neutralized forms. How to reconcile this fact with its apparent logical impossibility? The answer, I believe, is rooted in Labov's (1994:387) observation that "speakers are capable of tracing the frequency of occurrence of the two classes . . . and that this differential distribution is a part of their fundamental knowledge of the language . . .". Language users are sensitive to patterns of speech variation, as evidenced by the fact that they largely recapitulate this variation in their own speech. That is, speech variation is conventionalized within a speech community. (This phenomenon, known as *probability matching*, is considered in depth by Labov in his 1994 book, in my 2006 book, and in Chapter 11 of the present volume.)

Hardly a conundrum, the results of the commutation test may actually open a remarkably clear window into speakers' knowledge of speech variation. Let's suppose values **a** and **b** are contrastive, but in the context of a following **c**, **a** nearly-neutralizes towards **b** 80% of the time, and genuinely neutralizes to **b** 20% of the time. During a (particularly grueling, though thankfully hypothetical) commutation test, listeners are exposed to a series of 1000 individual tokens, 500 of which possess **a**+**c** morphological structures (cell **1** in table below), and 500 of which possess **b**+**c** morphological structures (cell **2**); all

1000 tokens are instances of minimal pairs along the **a+c** – **b+c** dimension. For now, let's assume that the (non-alternating) **b+c** forms are all implemented **bc** (cell **5**), and are perceived correctly 100% of the time (cell **8**). So far, our subjects are doing perfect work. Now consider the (alternating) **a+c** tokens. These are implemented as nearly-neutralized (call them b_ac) 80% of the time (400 times; cell **3**), and completely neutralized (**bc**) 20% of the time (100 times; cell **4**). Let's assume that all 400 nearly-neutralized b_ac forms are accurately perceived by listeners (that is, as **a+c** words), and so our subjects are still performing perfectly (cell **6**). But now consider the 100 fully-neutralized **bc** words (deriving from **a+c**) (cell **7**). Assuming that these are always perceived as **b+c** words, this results in 100 mistakes (cell **10**). In sum, subjects correctly interpret 400 of the 500 **a+c** tokens (cell **12**) for a score of 80% (cell **14**), and also correctly interpret all of the **b+c** tokens (cell **13**) for a score of 100% (cell **15**). Under these circumstances, subjects receive a final grade of 90% on the commutation test (cell **16**). Since, recall, passing the test requires a score of 100% (indicating that we are dealing with a "genuine" contrast), then our subjects will inevitably fail the commutation test in such cases.

The preliminary proposal, then, is that listeners have little trouble interpreting *nearly* neutralized tokens, their failure on the commutation test instead being due to the ambiguity of *genuinely* neutralized tokens.

Speakers			Listeners				
Semantic Production	Phonetic Production	Phonetic Perception	Semantic Perception	Correct Answers	Score		
1. 500 a+c	3. 400 b_ac	6. 400 b_ac	9. 400 a+c	12. 400	14. 80%	16. 90%	
	4. 100 bc	7. 100 bc	10. 100 b+c				
2. 500 b+c	5. 500 bc	8. 500 bc	11. 500 b+c	13. 500	15. 100%		

In fact, however, in the scenario just considered, we were probably too optimistic about subjects' performance on the commutation test. Far more likely, among genuinely neutralized test stimuli, subjects' responses will more closely mirror the perceived distribution of words in their linguistic experience. That is, instead of always concluding that **bc** stimuli are actually **b+c** words (remember: during the commutation test the tokens are not embedded in a disambiguating semantic context), their responses may recapitulate the actual rates of perceived occurrence, in an example of probability matching. What does this predict? There is any number of ways we might proceed, so we'll just consider one possibility for now. Recall that **a** nearly-neutralizes towards **b** 80% of the time, and genuinely neutralizes to **b** 20% of the time. All else being equal (which it surely would *not* be in the real world) 500 tokens derive from **a**+**c** words (cell **1** in the table below), and 500 tokens derive from **b**+**c** words (cell **2**). Among the **a**+**c** tokens, recall that 400 are likely to be implemented as $b_a c$ (cell **3**), and 100 as **bc** (cell **4**). Meanwhile, all 500 **b**+**c** tokens are implemented **bc** (cell **5**). Now, if we assume that subjects' perception of ambiguous tokens matches their perceived distribution, then, of the 600 tokens perceived as **bc** (100 from **a**+**c**; cell **7**, and 500 from **b**+**c**; cell **8**), they will correctly interpret 40 of the 100 **bc** tokens derived from **a**+**c** (40%) as **a**+**c** (cell **10**), and incorrectly interpret 60 of these **bc** tokens (60%) as derived from **a**+**c** (cell **11**). Also, out of the 500 words deriving from **b**+**c**, they will incorrectly interpret 200 tokens (40%) **a**+**c** words (cell **12**), and correctly interpret 300 tokens (60%) as **b**+**c** words (cell **13**). In total then, subjects will correctly identify 440 of the **a**+**c** word (cell **14**), a total of 88% correct (cell **16**), and will correctly identify 300 of the **b**+**c** words (cell **15**), a total of 60% (cell **17**). In this scenario, subjects earn a final score of 74% (cell **18**) – utter failure!

Speakers			Listeners			
Semantic Production	Phonetic Production	Phonetic Perception	Semantic Perception	Correct Answers	Score	
1. 500 a+c	3. 400 $b_a c$	6. 400 $b_a c$	9. 400 a+c	14. 440	16. 88%	18. 74%
	4. 100 bc	7. 100 bc	10. 40 a+c			
			11. 60 b+c			
2. 500 b+c	5. 500 bc	8. 500 bc	12. 200 a+c	15. 300	17. 60%	
			13. 300 b+c			

Of course even this more plausible scenario is much-simplified, not taking into account any number of relevant factors, including the effects of lexical frequency, the small possibility of phonetic misperception, the role of dialect status influencing subjects' judgments, and surely many others. Nonetheless, the point is made: listeners' failure on the commutation test is not a conundrum at all, but is, rather, fully consistent with the nearly-neutralized status of the values under consideration.

As remarked by Labov, the conventionalization of nearly-merged values in a speech community may remain remarkably stable over the course of decades, even centuries, such as the pattern found in Belfast. Such long-term stability of these supposedly "unstable" nearly-merged values provides fantastically compelling evidence for both (1) the statistically nuanced nature of linguistic knowledge (2) the articulatorily nuanced nature of speech production.

In fact, it follows from Charles-Luce's work that speakers are engaging in complex calculations "on the fly", in that they employ speech variants that are appropriate to situation-specific semantics: they are more likely to avoid a completely neutralized variant (and instead employ a nearly-neutralized variant) in those specific instances when doing so would result in confusion-inducing homophony.

Still, it would probably be a mistake to suppose that speakers are engaging in any sort of on-line goal-directed strategy. Rather, this behavior on the part of speakers may be yet another example of probability matching. Consider a case of the sort Charles-Luce discusses: in their experience as listeners, speakers have typically encountered nearly homophonous variants (as opposed to fully homophonous variants) in contexts that would otherwise induce confusion. Such nearly-neutralized tokens are thus pooled with other tokens that they have encountered in comparable situations, that is, in situations where genuine homophony might confuse them. Now these listeners become speakers. As a consequence of their own listening experience, they select speech variants that they have already encountered. Thus, in contexts where a completely neutralized token might result in confusing homophony, they dip into their pool of tokens encountered in comparable listening situations. As a mere by-product of their randomly sampling the tokens in this pool, the probability is high that this token is nearly-neutralized, as opposed to completely neutralized.

In this scenario, speakers are not striving to make the speech signal clearer for the listener "on the fly". Rather, clear speech signals are a passive consequence of speakers matching their own speech patterns to those in their linguistic experience.

CONCLUSION

Near-mergers and near-neutralizations are facts of linguistic life, and all theories of linguistic structure and linguistic knowledge are compelled to address the remarkably nuanced nature of these phenomena. In this chapter I have discussed in only the most superficial fashion these endlessly rich data sets that are suffused with phonetic detail, detail oftentimes invisible to the naked ear. Thoroughgoing knowledge of this phonetic detail is absolutely essential if we are ever to understand the various pressures that are responsible for language structure and language change.

Having now considered two neutralization "false positives", in Section C we move on to consider explanatory approaches to neutralization.

DISCUSSION QUESTIONS AND FURTHER READING

(1) In light of the prevalence of near-neutralization (**Slowiaczek and Dinnsen 1985, Port and O'Dell 1985, Port and Crawford 1989, Pye 1986, Charles-Luce 1993, Warner, Jongman, Sereno, and Kemps 2004, Bishop 2007, Yu 2007**) consider again Warner, Jongman, Sereno, and Kemps' remark that any such pattern is "rather disturbing in its implications for phonological theory because it runs contrary to the idea of categorical distinctions among [contrasting] segments". Consider the nature of these "categorical distinctions" (contrastive values) in both phonetic terms (that is, the nature and extent of their phonetic distinct-ness) and functional terms (that is, their role of keeping elements phonetically distinct that differ in meaning). Now, unpack the quoted statement by considering arguments both for and against it. You might also look at papers by **Ernestus (2006, 2011), Scobbie (2007), Scobbie and Stuart-Smith (2008), Scobbie and Sebregts (2011),** and **Yu (2011)**, and also papers in **Faneslow Féry, Schlesewsky, and Vogel (2006)**.

(2) I just asserted that: "speakers are engaging in complex cal-culations 'on the fly', in that they employ speech variants that are appropriate to situation-specific semantics: they are more likely to avoid a completely neutralized variant (and instead employ a nearly-neutralized variant) in those specific instances when doing so would result in confusion-inducing homo-phony". Now, consider my assertion that "it would probably be a mistake to suppose that speakers are engaging in any sort of on-line goal-directed strategy. Rather, this behavior on the part of speakers may be yet another example of probability matching." Can this provocative proposal be defended? How might we experimentally investigate it?

7   Ease of production

Speaker-based approaches to neutralization that reference "ease of production" have often been mentioned in passing in the phonological literature, though have rarely been pursued with much rigor (one exception being Kirchner 1998, 2004), perhaps because even a rather superficial thinking-through of any potential arguments in their favor leads to patently false predictions.

Proponents of this general approach typically invoke intuitively appealing references to speaker "laziness", "energy conservation", "articulatory anticipation", or "articulatory undershoot" in their accounts of neutralization that derive from assimilation and/or gestural reduction. As we'll see, it's one thing to propose that speakers – and, by extension, phonological patterns – are, at some level, partially influenced by general movement constraints such that, over long periods of use, phonological systems may bear the mark of such limitations. It is quite another, however, to propose that speakers' physical prowess is taxed in ways that have an on-line influence on their speech patterns, such that these speakers habitually ease their articulatory burden, or anticipate a following speech gesture, or undershoot some proposed articulatory target. As I write in my 2006 book, in the context of the topic of neutralization deriving from anticipatory assimilation: "... [T]he sound substitutions that we observe can probably *never* be reduced to such one-dimensional, proximate influences on speech, articulatory or otherwise; we observe articulatory anticipation in the present state of the language, but this doesn't mean that the pattern has its origins in present-day articulatory forces" (2006a:66).

Let's start by briefly considering, "articulatory undershoot" and then go into some detail about "articulatory anticipation", focusing in particular on nasal assimilation, which is emerging as something of a leitmotif in the present volume.

ARTICULATORY UNDERSHOOT

The proposal that neutralization may derive from "articulatory under-shoot" is predicated on the notion that, due to the complex demands of speech production, speakers do not always have sufficient time or energy to implement all the gestures that they are "fed" from the phonology. That is, speakers are attempting – though, on occasion, crucially failing – to reach their "articulatory target". Under certain conditions, their inability to achieve their articulatory goals results in gestural reduction such that the articulatory distinction among con-trastive values is neutralized (for example, Liljencrants and Lindblom 1972, Flemming 2009).

We may consider English schwa as an example case. Recall from Chapter 3 that Barnes (2006) discusses the fact that some full vowels alternate with schwa when in stressless contexts: ɹəˈlæks "relax" – ˌɹiˌlækˈseɪʃn̩ "relaxation"; ˈʔærə̃m "atom" – ʔəˈtʰamɪk "atomic". A syn-chronic approach to this neutralizing alternation that invokes "articu-latory undershoot" would propose that reduction to schwa here is probably related to the shortening of the relevant vowels under stress-lessness: speakers are, by hypothesis, attempting to implement a full (non-neutralized) vowel, but the decreased duration of stressless con-texts inhibits their achieving this articulatory goal.

But note that, under this account, it remains to explain why (1) speakers should have articulatory targets that are nowhere in evidence in the speech they perceive, and (2) speakers fail in achieving their goals to virtually the same extent, each and every time, as their interlocutors. Thus, the "articulatory undershoot" approach to ges-tural reduction and neutralization suffers from a fatal malady: since speakers successfully reproduce the very speech that they hear – including elements that are reduced and/or neutralized – there is no evidence that their articulatory goals are not being met. Over time, a sound pattern may indeed evolve such that the magnitude of particu-lar speech gestures in particular contexts is lessened (this, recall, is the proposal of Barnes 2006), but the difference between the (historical) larger gesture and the (latter-day) reduced gesture is wholly immaterial to speakers, playing no role in the knowledge that language users bring to the task of speech production or phono-logical organization. Moreover, such articulatory reductions are more likely to have *semantic* origins rather than *phonetic* origins (Silverman 2006a, Gahl 2008). In our example case then, clearly, no such unmet articulatory goals exist in the minds of speakers. Whatever the genuine origins of the schwa alternant, it surely has nothing to do with any given speaker's knowledge of their language.

ARTICULATORY ANTICIPATION

As we know, one common source of neutralizing assimilation is found in nasal–stop sequences: nasals are very often assimilated to a following stop in terms of their place-of-articulation. For example, in Dutch monomorphemic contexts we find non-alternating **panter** "panther", **wimper** "eyelash", **aŋker** "anchor". Across morpheme and word boundaries, **n** assimilates: **ɪn+trɛk** "move in", **ɪm+pɑk** "wrap to", **ɪŋ+kɛik** "look into" (where the underlined values are in alternation). This is indeed a neutralizing alternation, since all three nasals are contrastive in morpheme-final position, for example: **hɑn** "Han (a name)", **hɑm** "ham", **hɑŋ** "bent".

As with "articulatory undershoot", some proponents of a specifically articulation-centered approach to such patterns of assimilation and neutralization might implicate speakers' articulatory goals, such that, instead of achieving the supposedly distinct oral configuration required of the relevant nasal consonant, these speakers anticipate the oral configuration of the following stop consonant during the nasal itself. The result is a simplified articulatory routine involving only a single oral gesture, an assimilated nasal–stop sequence of the sort we find over and over again in linguistic sound patterns.

The "gestural simplification" or "ease-of-articulation" approach to nasal assimilation makes two further predictions: (1) stops should as readily assimilate to following nasals as do nasals to stops (**ɑt+ɑ, ɑp+mɑ, ɑt+nɑ, ɑk+ŋɑ**); and (2) stops and nasals should as readily progressively assimilate as they do regressively assimilate (for example, **ɑ+nɑ, ɑp+mɑ, ɑt+nɑ, ɑk+ŋɑ** and **ɑ+tɑ, ɑm+pɑ, ɑn+tɑ, ɑŋ+kɑ**). Both predictions are incorrect.

Thus, two asymmetries need to be accounted for: (1) nasals often assimilate to following stops in terms of their place-of-articulation, but stops do not assimilate to following nasals in terms of their place-of-articulation; and (2) assimilation is typically regressive, not progressive. If assimilation (neutralizing or not) were a speaker-controlled measure implemented in order to relieve articulatory burden, we would not expect such asymmetries. Rather, we would expect all patterns, possibly with equal prevalence; it should suffice that two oral gestures turn into one gesture.

Let's then briefly consider why, in fact, we do observe the patterns we do, and why we don't observe the patterns we don't. We'll see that a more compelling explanation emerges upon investigating the acoustic properties of the relevant speech signals: more-salient acoustic cues are more effective in encoding contrastive information than are less-salient acoustic cues. We consider, in turn, cues to nasals in the relevant contexts, and cues to stops in the relevant contexts.

There are four major acoustic cues to the location of the oral occlusion among the nasals:

(1) Formant transitions out of the nasal consonant
(2) Formant transitions into the nasal consonant
(3) Location of the nasal anti-formant during the oral closure (*the farther back the oral occlusion, the higher in frequency the nasal anti-resonance*), and
(4) Duration of nasalization on the preceding vowel (*the farther back the oral occlusion, the greater the extent of preceding vowel nasalization*).

Now let's consider what happens to these cues when nasals are placed in various contexts. First, when a morpheme-initial nasal is immediately preceded by a heterorganic stop, but is immediately followed by a vowel, for example **ap+na**:

(1) Formant transitions out of the nasal consonant are present (...**na**)
(2) Formant transitions into the nasal consonant are only partially present, since a consonant immediately precedes the nasal (...**p+n**...)
(3) The nasal anti-formant is present (...**n**...), and
(4) There is no nasalization on the preceding vowel, since a non-nasal consonant immediately precedes the nasal (...**ap+n**...).

When a nasal immediately precedes a heterorganic stop, for example, **ãn+pa**:

(1) Formant transitions out of the nasal consonant are partially present, since a consonant immediately follows (...**n+p**...)
(2) Formant transitions into the nasal consonant are present (**ãn**...)
(3) The nasal anti-formant is present (...**n**...), and
(4) Nasalization on the preceding vowel is present (**ãn**...).

This, recall, is the context in which we typically observe neutralizing assimilation of the nasal: **ãn+a** and **ãn+ta**, but **ãm+pa** and **ãŋ+ka**. Also, recall, we don't find the stop assimilating to the nasal. Consequently:

(1) The formant transitions from the nasal into a following vowel seem to be very important in the determination of a nasal's

place-of-articulation. Without these formant transitions, the distinctive oral properties of the nasal may eventually be lost.

(2) Formant transitions from the vowel to the nasal are not especially important, since their presence here does not salvage the nasal's oral properties.

(3) The anti-formant is not extremely important for the determination of a nasal's place-of-articulation, since it is present whether the nasal assimilates or not.

(4) The duration of nasalization on the preceding vowel does not seem crucial to determining the place of oral closure, since its presence here does not salvage the nasal's oral properties.

Consider now the major cues to place-of-articulation in stop consonants (there are additional cues, including closure duration for example, but we'll stick to certain major cues for illustrative purposes):

(1) Formant transitions out of the stop
(2) Burst frequency
(3) Formant transitions into the stop.

When a morpheme initial stop is preceded by a morpheme-final nasal, for example, **ãn+pɑ**:

(1) Formant transitions out of the stop are present (...**pa**)
(2) The burst is present (...**pa**)
(3) Formant transitions into the stop are only partially present (**n+p**).

When a morpheme-final stop is followed by a morpheme-initial nasal, for example, **ap+na**:

(1) Formant transitions out of the stop are only partially present (**p+n**)
(2) The burst is attenuated or absent (**p+n**)
(3) Formant transitions into the stop are present (**ap**...).

Since stops do not assimilate to nasals regardless of their respective sequencing, we may tentatively conclude that:

(1) Formant transitions out of the stop robustly cue place-of-articulation, and/or
(2) The stop burst robustly cues place-of-articulation, and/or
(3) Formant transitions into the stop robustly cue place-of-articulation.

Thus, when a stop precedes a nasal, neither stop offset transitions nor burst frequency are fully present in the speech signal, but still, stops in such contexts do not forfeit their place-of-articulation to a following nasal, indicating that the remaining cues are sufficiently robust for listeners to recover their oral posture.

So, the asymmetry in the (assimilatory) behavior of pre-stop nasals and (non-assimilatory) behavior of pre-nasal stops reduces to the robustness of the first consonant's onset cues. Why should this be? The answer is likely to reside in the overlay of nasal resonance structure on the formant transitions into a nasal. It is well established that the velum lowers for nasal consonants before the oral occlusion is made; after all, were the velum to lower after the oral occlusion were made, a brief oral stop would be produced between the vowel and the nasal. Lowering the velum a little early thus produces a fully nasal stop. Upon the introduction of the nasal resonance structure during this stretch of the speech stream, the formants deriving from oral cavity configuration are partially obscured. It is, by hypothesis, the partial obscuring of oral resonance structure during the implementation of nasals that is the likely culprit in cases of nasal-to-stop assimilation. As the cues to the nasal's place-of-articulation are rendered less robust, they are less likely to be successfully communicated to listeners.

Still, we have yet to motivate the specifically *assimilative* nature of nasal alternation here (**mp nt ŋk**) rather than, say, the uniform presence of a single nasal sound regardless of context (for example, **np nt nk**). Both of these results are possible outcomes, so why is it only the assimilative pattern that we find? Must we ultimately embrace an "articulatory ease" account of this pattern, such that the span reduces to a single oral gesture? While there have been any number of attempts to explain the widely attested pattern of nasal assimilation (some of which are inventoried in Ohala 1990), I consider now the approach that (for my money, anyway) seems the most promising, first brought to my attention by Jack Bowers in 2010 (pc).

Nasals are sonorants, and more to the point are *resonants*; they possess a harmonic structure, and consequently allow information about their oral configurations to "bleed through" during the nasal murmur itself. Consequently, when a lowered velum is temporally coextensive with a dynamic oral closing gesture (from vowel to nasal to stop) a certain amount of acoustic information about oral posture – specifically, dynamic F1 transitions (due to the pharyngeal cavity's resonance frequencies) and especially, dynamic Z1 transitions (due to the oral cavity's anti-resonance frequencies) – is present on the nasal murmur itself. The result is that, in addition to conveying information about the oral quality of the *nasal's* oral posture, the nasal murmur begins with spectral cues that convey information about the preceding *vowel's* oral posture, and ends with spectral cues that convey information about the following *stop's* oral posture, and thus the acoustic signal comes to cue this *de facto* homorganicity to a following stop closure during the course of the nasal's production. Listeners hear the nasal undergoing a shift in its oral configuration, and faithfully reproduce this shift in their own speech. In due time, the nasal's oral posture may become more temporally coordinated with the velic lowering posture, and full-fledged assimilation results.

Moreover, the absence of assimilation in stop–nasal sequences is also readily accounted for under this proposal. Even if cues to oral posture "bleed through" during the nasal murmur here, it is the overriding perceptual robustness of the nasal's offset transitions – from the nasal to the following vowel – that is the likely acoustic source for listeners as they determine the nasal's oral posture. The result, of course, is the retention of heterorganicity in such sequences.

Note especially that this proposed scenario answers the question of homorganicity, and also disinvites an analysis that invokes "ease of articulation": it is not due to a lack of articulatory effort that oral formant transitions are present during the nasal murmur. Rather, such transitions are purely epiphenomenal: one oral posture cannot instantaneously change into another; instead a certain amount of time is required to achieve a postural reconfiguration. This is not "ease-of-articulation"; it is plain old pre-quantum physics.

Consider also the explanatory value of this proposal with respect to neutralization of word-final nasals. Recall Jun's (2010) observation that in some languages – for example, Ancient Greek, Spanish, and Japanese – whereas lexical pre-*consonantal* nasals assimilate to a following stop, word-*final* nasals do indeed collapse to a single oral configuration. Under the present analysis, this asymmetry may be accounted for with relative ease. Considered on a word-by-word basis, unlike word-internal nasal–stop clusters – whose motor routines are necessarily heavily entrenched due to their constant repetition – the coarticulatory properties of cross-word nasal stop clusters may be less entrenched, less routinized, than their word-medial counterparts. This is due to the fact that the post-nasal context here varies in unconstrained ways (depending only on the phonological shape of the following word-initial value). Consequently word-final nasals may not as readily possess fixed coarticulatory properties. The result is that word-final nasals may display less context-specific entrenchment than their word-medial counterparts, and thus are more likely to settle towards a value that is not fixed by the following phonetic context.

In these proposed scenarios, note especially two essential components: (1) neither "ease of articulation" nor "gestural anticipation" plays any role whatsoever; and (2) the explanation for the sound pattern resides in slow-acting diachronic pressures, not in the minds of individual speakers. Regarding this second component, the proposal is that speakers are not recapitulating the diachronic pressures that have given rise to the sound pattern they are exposed to; how the sound pattern evolved to its present state is immaterial to latter-day speakers.

CONCLUSION

To sum up, in accounting for patterns of neutralizing assimilation, "articulatory undershoot" and "ease of articulation" arguments are intuitively appealing, but, even upon a cursory investigation, such analyses are found wanting, as they make many incorrect predictions. Consequently, instead of considering *articulation* as an explanatory locus for phonological patterning (neutralizing or otherwise) in the next four chapters we focus our attention on *acoustics* as a source of explanation for sound patterning (again, neutralizing or otherwise).

DISCUSSION QUESTIONS AND FURTHER READING

(1) Probably the most rigorous implementation of the "ease of production" approach to speaker-based accounts of neutralization is that of **Kirchner (1998, 2004)**. Consider Kirchner's formal approach with the following questions in mind: (1) What is the empirical basis of Kirchner's proposals regarding the amount of energy involved in speech production? (2) What are the advantages and disadvantages of recapitulating real-world phonetic/diachronic pressures on sound patterning in their proposed mental representation? (3) Assuming for the moment that you are swayed by the arguments presented in this chapter, what role(s) remain for "ease of production" in phonology? You might also consider discussion by, for example, **Martinet (1955)**, **Diver (1979)**, and **Tobin (1997)**.

(2) Regarding nasal assimilation in particular, further consider the ease-of-production approach in light of the following investigative reports: **Fujimura (1962)**, **Ohala (1975)**, **Takeuchi, Kasuga, and Kido (1975)**, **Kurowski and Blumstein (1984, 1987)**, and **Recasens (1983)**.

8   Ease of perception

As discussed in Chapter 7, at first blush, it might seem perfectly reasonable to assume that linguistic structure is influenced at least in part by speakers looking to (presumably unconsciously) ease their own articulatory burden. Just as quickly, however, such a hypothesis encountered insurmountable difficulties, and we concluded that "ease-of-articulation" influences on linguistic sound structure are at the very least several times removed from the world of individual speakers.

There are, however, variations on the fatally flawed theme of speaker-controlled approaches to sound patterning in general – and neutralization in particular – that we turn to now. These approaches center on the hypothesis that speakers control their speech in order to ease the perceptual burden of their interlocutors. We consider, in turn, Lindblom's "H&H hypothesis", Jun's "production hypothesis", and Steriade's "P-map hypothesis". We conclude by discussing some outstanding issues that arise from these accounts.

LINDBLOM'S H&H HYPOTHESIS (1990)

Lindblom (1990) does not specifically address the issue of neutralization. Nonetheless, as we shall see, his "H&H" (hyper- and hypo-articulation) proposal readily lends itself to such an application. The underlying assumption of this speaker-oriented approach to speech organization is that language users have an awareness of listeners' ability to extract information from the speech signal. Consequently, speakers adjust their speech such that it varies along a hypo-articulation–hyper-articulation continuum. Hypo-articulation involves a "default to some low-cost form of behavior". If speech sounds are hypo-articulated up to or surpassing the point of their unique discriminability, neutralization may result. Hyper-articulation involves a higher-cost form of behavior in which speech gestures are greater in magnitude and/or duration, thus enhancing the ease with which listeners recover information, perhaps especially in contexts in which non-hyper-articulated speech sounds would run the risk of non-recoverability. In short: (1) speakers are constrained by certain production limitations that are both physiological and cognitive in origin; and (2) speakers are aware of the receptive constraints of listeners, which are social and communicative in origin. Thus, overall, his model is certainly speaker-oriented, but speakers nonetheless take listening constraints into consideration as they plan and implement their speech.

Lindblom considers studies of animal motor behavior that suggest organisms' actions are planned "on the fly" in ways that incorporate the goal or end-product of these very actions. The same idea, he claims, may be applied to speech. Lindblom's (1990:404) approach is thus teleological in orientation: "Speech motor control is future-oriented. It is purpose-driven and prospectively organized." Moreover, H&H speech computations are active *on-line* such that, for example, the final word in "The next word is nine" may be hyper-articulated (since it enjoys no contextual cues), whereas the last word in "A stitch in time saves nine" may be hypo-articulated (since it is quite predictable) (see also Charles-Luce 1993). In general, *hyperspeech* is observed when output (perceptually oriented) constraints dominate, and *hypospeech* is observed when input (production-based) constraints dominate (thus, as we see shortly, H&H readily lends itself to optimality-theoretic analyses). Speakers, he asserts, have a choice with respect to (1) whether or not they will engage in hypo- or hyper-articulated speech, and (2) what particular degree – or even what particular strategy – of H&H speech they might engage in.

His discussion of coarticulation – especially, observed patterns of *variable* coarticulation – moves him closer to the issues of most relevance to us, since coarticulation is often a diachronic precursor to assimilation; a very common source of neutralization. Since (1) speakers may or may not choose to hypo-articulate in appropriate phonetic and/or semantic contexts, and (2) they vary in the degree of coarticulation in such contexts, then we do not expect particular speech sounds to possess invariant properties. Rather, we expect a *range of variability*, such that more coarticulation may be observed when speakers choose to hypo-articulate; a correct prediction when we investigate the variable nature of speech production.

JUN'S PRODUCTION HYPOTHESIS (1995, 2004, 2010)

As already demonstrated in Chapter 3, Jun's work (1995, 2004, 2010) is rich in data and detail regarding patterns of C_1C_2 neutralization. Overall, Jun observes that more likely targets of assimilation are acoustically less salient than less likely ones. As many scholars before him do, Jun views place assimilation (and perhaps other aspects of phonological patterning as well) as a compromise between the two aforementioned conflicting pressures of "ease of articulation" and "ease of perception", though as we will see, he has quite novel ideas on the subject. Employing optimality theory, he proposes two sets of constraints that are based on these two demands. He characterizes patterns of neutralization by ranking his "ease of articulation" constraints higher ("markedness" constraints), while the preservation of contrasts is characterized by higher-ranked "ease of perception" constraints ("faithfulness" constraints). The interaction of these two constraint families models an array of neutralization patterns that, by and large, form an implicational hierarchy of consonant neutralization, as discussed in Chapter 3.

As we have already observed, Jun's cross-linguistic investigation into patterns of consonant assimilation yields very interesting results. Recall that he reports, first off – and as expected – that in C_1C_2 sequences, C_2 is usually the trigger of place assimilation, whereas C_1 is usually the target. That is, consonant place assimilation is usually regressive, from onset to coda. Regarding potential targets' manner of articulation: (1) if oral sonorants and fricatives assimilate, then stops and nasals assimilate as well; and (2) if stops assimilate, then nasals do as well. Regarding potential targets' place-of-articulation: (1) if non-coronals are targets of place assimilation, so are coronals; and (2) usually, if velars are targets of place assimilation, so are labials. In general then, nasals and coronals are most susceptible to regressive place assimilation.

Regarding triggers' manner of articulation: (1) if oral sonorants trigger place assimilation, so do nasals and fricatives; and (2) if nasals or fricatives trigger place assimilation, so do stops. Regarding triggers' place of assimilation: if coronals trigger place assimilation, so do velars. In general then, stops and non-coronals are the most common triggers of regressive place assimilation.

Jun proposes a cue-based explanation for these observed implicational hierarchies. For example, regarding the resistance of fricatives and oral sonorants to regressive place assimilation: (1) fricatives have more robust place cues than stops during their constriction phase, in the form of their noise spectra; and (2) oral sonorants have more robust cues than nasals in the form of clear onset formant transitions. Meanwhile, pre-consonantal stops are more readily subject to regressive place assimilation than are oral sonorants and fricatives, due to their absence of release cues (primarily bursts and formant transitions) and their absence of place-of-articulation cues during the constriction itself. Also, as already discussed, pre-consonantal nasals are even more readily subject to regressive place assimilation due, by hypothesis, to the superimposition of nasal resonance structure onto their onset formant transitions.

Regarding the place-of-articulation of regressively assimilated consonants, Jun again discusses the relevance of acoustic cueing: when preceded by a vowel and followed by a consonant, velars are claimed to possess more robust cues than labials, which in turn have stronger cues than coronals. Jun follows Byrd (1994) in proposing that coronal gestures are rapid, and thus have rapid transition cues which are expected to be less robust in comparison to the slower motion of tongue dorsum and lip gestures. But consider another possibility, rooted in the fact that the tongue tip is not significantly involved in the formation of vowel sounds. In the context of a vowel which precedes a **t**, the tongue tip itself can almost achieve the correct posture for the ensuing stop well before it actually makes contact behind the upper teeth, without having a significant effect on vowel quality. Consequently, the formant transitions from the vowel into this oral closure are rather diminished in terms of both their duration and their magnitude, resulting in a rather meager conveyance of information regarding the actual coronal gesture, thus rendering such coronals rather susceptible to place assimilation. (This might also account for the intimate relationship enjoyed by **t** and **ʔ**, the latter completely lacking formant transitions.)

While Jun is clearly sensitive to the specific role of acoustic cueing, he has not completely abandoned discussion of prosodic positions, as he talks quite freely in terms of "onsets" and "codas". Still, it should not be concluded that Jun, like, for example, Itô (1986, 1989) or Beckman (1997, 2004), is assuming that cues are "licensed" in some prosodic positions, and "unlicensed" in others. Rather, his discussion makes clear his assumption that the acoustic context itself, and not the proposed prosodic slot that a segment might occupy, is the ultimate determinant of the patterns of neutralization being investigated. In this way, he prefigures Steriade's related work on this topic (to be discussed presently).

Above and beyond his discussion of "raw" acoustic influences on patterns of place assimilation, Jun also considers the role that speakers' knowledge of acoustic cueing plays in patterns of neutralization, and relatedly, whether neutralization is "speaker controlled" or not. The notion of "speaker control" requires some explication, because, at the most basic level, all speech is (of course) speaker controlled, in that it is accomplished due to the intent of speakers themselves. Rather, the issue of speaker control in the sense intended by Jun focuses on the role that *speakers' linguistic intentions* (unconscious or otherwise) – as opposed to raw physical constraints due to vocal tract physiology, the laws of physics, etc. – may or may not play as speakers formulate their mental grammar and engage in speech acts. The idea to be explored for Jun's speaker-based account, then, is whether patterns of neutralization are best accounted for in terms of strictly passive, physical constraints, or whether speakers exert some independent control over their speech, apart from any raw physiological floor or ceiling effects. And if speakers *do* exert such control, what is its nature? Is it to ease their own articulatory burden, to ease the perceptual burden for listeners, some combination of these, and/or something else?

Jun's answer to these questions resides in his "production hypothesis": speakers exert more energy in their production of sounds that possess more salient acoustic cues, and exert less energy in their production of sounds that possess less salient cues. As a consequence of the greater energy expended on salient cues, these are less likely to be lost, and thus contribute to the maintenance of contrasts. Conversely, as a consequence of the lesser amount of energy expended on less salient cues, these are more likely to be lost, thus rendering their associated contrastive values more susceptible to neutralization. Metaphorically speaking, money goes to money: the rich get richer and the poor get poorer.

Consider four aspects of the production hypothesis. (1) Most obviously it is a hypothesis about the *production of speech*, and only indirectly relates to *perception*. (2) It assumes a specifically *teleological* role for speakers: rather than assuming a passive role for speakers, whose speech – irrespective of any intent or effort on their part – merely produces a variety of acoustic cues (some of which are more salient, and some of which are less salient), the production hypothesis proposes that speakers are organizing their speech such that they exert more effort on "strong" cues, and less effort on "weak" ones. (3) Although the production hypothesis places specific emphasis on acoustic cues, it directly focuses on *speakers' knowledge* of those cues, and only indirectly on listeners' ability or inability to discern them. (4) Most interestingly, unlike Lindblom, Jun is not suggesting that speakers may engage in compensatory measures to make poorer cues more salient. On the contrary, according to Jun, speakers may allow poor cues to get left by the wayside.

Let's now summarize the similarities and differences between Lindblom's H&H hypothesis, and Jun's production hypothesis. Regarding their similarities: (1) both are speaker-oriented; (2) both assume goal-directed behavior on the part of speakers; (3) both assume speakers exploit their knowledge of phonetics; and (4) both assume there is a conflict between the pressures that might enhance the salience of cues and those that might diminish the salience of cues.

Regarding the main difference between the two, whereas Lindblom's approach assumes that speakers are taking listeners' needs into consideration as they speak, listeners play a far less direct role in Jun's approach. More specifically, Lindblom assumes that the conflict to be resolved resides in whether to hyper-articulate on behalf of listeners, or hypo-articulate when listeners' perception is not in jeopardy; in Lindblom's approach, poor cues may be hyper-articulated. For Jun, the conflict resides in the inherent salience of the acoustic cues themselves. When these cues are robust, speakers expend more effort to produce them, and when cues are less robust, speakers expend less effort to produce them; in Jun's approach, poor cues may be hypo-articulated.

STERIADE'S P-MAP HYPOTHESIS (2008)

In her investigation of alternating values, Steriade (2008) is concerned with two sorts of phonological relations, and their interaction: (1) those between one contrastive value and another; and (2) those between *proposed* underlying values and *observed* surface values. She observes that contrasts are better cued in certain positions, more poorly cued in others, a proposal that falls within her "licensing by cue" hypothesis (Steriade 1999, 2001). When contrastive information is poorly cued, neutralization is the common result. Moreover – and this is Steriade's main point – the output of alternations tends to be phonetically similar to – and confusable with – the input, in comparison to other output candidates. Schematically, assume alphabetic proximity is the sole determinant of confusability. Thus, if **a**, **b**, **c**, and **d** are contrastive values, and if **b** is never found before **d**, then input string **b+d** will correspond to output string **cd**. Importantly, **a** and **c** are equally confusable with **b**, but **ad** and **bd** are less confusable with each other than are **cd** and **bd**. Consequently, for input **b+d**, the best output candidate is indeed **cd**.

On the face of it, Steriade's proposal seems to be a phonetically based restatement of Halle's (1962) "evaluation metric", which proposes that a grammar is more highly valued to the extent that it involves fewer terms, and thus, under many circumstances, minimal augmentation may be preferred: "Given two alternative descriptions of a particular body of data, the description containing fewer ... symbols will be regarded as simpler and will, therefore, be preferred over the other" (p. 55); optimality theory's "faithfulness" criteria play a comparable role in that theory. However, for Steriade, similarity or dissimilarity is not determined by a raw tally of distinctive feature changes, as Halle and many subsequent theorists might propose. Rather, Steriade makes direct reference to psycholinguistic studies that focus on confusability (a quantifiable value) and/or some as-yet-unknown method of calculating similarity, in order to arrive at output candidates that are minimally distinct from their inputs.

Steriade's proposal stems from the observation that alternations that are (by hypothesis) induced by phonotactic constraints are only a subset of the logically possible repair strategies. For example, devoicing a stop before a voiceless obstruent – a very common alternation – is but one of innumerable possible ways to make a morphologically ordered voiced stop–voiceless obstruent sequence conform to a phonotactic constraint that prohibits such sequences. Thus, while acoustically similar contrastive values are more likely to neutralize, Steriade is more concerned with the acoustic similarity of proposed underlying values and their observed surface forms: input–output acoustic dissimilarity is minimal.

Steriade considers the absolute and relative perceptibility of acoustic cues, and proposes that language users establish optimality-theoretic constraint rankings that determine the distribution of allophones. For example, the fact that obstruent voicing is better perceived before vowels than before consonants is part of speakers' grammatical knowledge, and is thus characterized in terms of constraint ranking. Her "P-map" hypothesis proposes that language users exploit their phonetic knowledge to determine which allophone (in a theoretically infinite set) is optimal, in the sense that it deviates least from the input. It is this determination that, in turn, determines the ranking of constraints: the more similar a candidate is to the input, the more likely it will emerge as the output. The constraint ranking thus exploits speakers' resultant knowledge of these P-map calculi. Speakers within a speech community share a common knowledge of similarity/ confusability judgments, and are assumed by Steriade to be actively engaged in exploiting and refining this knowledge.

Despite the prominent role that listeners' perception plays in this account of alternation, it is clear that Steriade (like Lindblom and Jun) nonetheless implicates *speakers'* cognitive apparatus as the locus of these phenomena, and implicates it in a specifically teleological manner: "Any modification must be tolerably similar to the original; and must involve an improvement, in articulation, perception or paradigm structure, over the original ... [T]he critical assumption then is that speakers exert some control over the incipient sound change: that they do so, in part, by computing the distance in perceptual space between a lexical norm and potential modifications of it" (2001:232).

Let's look at a few more cases to see how Steriade's ideas work. Consider word-final devoicing. Both Steriade's intuitions as a language user, as well as the results of several studies on rhyming, lead her to conclude that word-final voiceless stops (say, **t#**) – as opposed to word-final sonorants (**n#**), or zero (**Ø#**), or word-final epenthesized vowels (**tə#**) – are most similar to word-final voiced stops (**d#**). Due to their maximal similarity, the P-map projects correspondence constraints that rank voiceless stops highest, and so a language in which voiced stops are disallowed in final position may possess devoiced stops here, as opposed to neutralizing towards a sonorant, or deleting the voiced stop, or triggering epenthesis.

Consider another case. In a language where obstruent clusters agree in voicing, **kud+ta** may, in theory, be realized **kutta, kudda, kunta, kulta, kudra, ku_ta, kud_a, kudəta, kudat, gutta**, etc. In fact, we might only find the form that displays regressive voicing assimilation, **kutta**. Proponents of the P-map hypothesis would thus seek independent evidence that, among all possible pair-wise comparisons, **kudta** and **kutta** are maximally confusable.

Steriade further observes that if a phonotactic violation can be repaired by modifying either place-of-articulation or stricture, it is typically the case that place-of-articulation is changed, while stricture remains unchanged, again, because stricture differences are typically less confusable than place-of-articulation differences. For example, heterorganic clusters like **tp and tk** were disallowed in Ancient Greek and Classical Latin. When the morphology would create such sequences, we find gemination, and not, say, spirantization. Thus, Latin **at+keleraːre** "to accelerate" is realized **akkeleraːre**, not **askeleraːre**. If speakers were to simply count distinctive features, and use these totals for their determination of phonotactic repairs, such facts cannot be accounted for, since changing a stop into a spirant is no more "costly" than changing a coronal into a velar, using the standard evaluation metric. Instead, it seems that certain features are intrinsically more likely to undergo modification in some contexts than are other features. For Steriade, the relevant intrinsic quality is the salience of the contrastive acoustic cue in the particular context: the less salient the cue, the more likely it will change.

Another case: consider a language in which nasal–stop clusters are always homorganic. In the sequence **an+pa**, the nasal has been experimentally shown to be highly confusable with **m**, and thus **anpa** may be heard as **ampa**; we don't expect progressive assimilation here, because speakers know that **anpa** and **anta** are saliently distinct from each other, more distinct from each other than are **anpa** and **ampa**. Speakers exploit such knowledge, as evidenced by their employing **ampa**, a surface form that is minimally acoustically distinct from input **anpa**.

Steriade observes that this particular scenario begs the question (one we have already considered in Chapter 7) why nasals specifically *assimilate* before consonants. After all, for any given morphologically ordered nasal–stop sequence (say, **n+p**, or **ŋ+t**), it is surely not the case that a specifically assimilated nasal (**mp**, or **nt**) always constitutes the smallest perceptual deviation from the input, in comparison to other non-assimilated sequences (**ŋp**, or **mt**). Since assimilated alternants are, in fact, commonplace here, Steriade – again, like Lindblom, and unlike the proposals laid out in Chapter 7 – imparts a further role for the speaker: in addition to calculating the perceived similarity between inputs and outputs, speakers also engage in "improvement[s] in articulation" or "*tolerated* articulatory simplification[s]" (italics in original). In this way, Steriade offers an explanation for the specifically *assimilatory* nature of many neutralizing alternations: "ease of articulation" thus, after all, plays a fundamental role in her analysis of neutralizing assimilation.

Most cases we have discussed up to now involve regressive assimilation in CC contexts, such that the first consonant undergoes the neutralizing alternation. However, one subclass of neutralization – that involving retroflexes – operates progressively: apical (alveolar–retroflex) contrasts are typically realized post-vocalically (**V__**), but are neutralized post-consonantally (**C__**) and word-initially (**#__**). Steriade's task, then, is to show that the retroflex–alveolar acoustic distinction – unlike other place contrasts – is better cued in the context of a preceding vowel (**V__**), rather than in the context of a following vowel (**__V**), and indeed, she marshals phonetic experimental evidence in support of her hypothesis. A significant lowering of the upper formants is observed on vowels that precede retroflex consonants. This formant lowering seems to be the acoustic analog of tongue retroflexion, which begins before the consonantal constriction is achieved, that is, on the preceding vowel. Moreover, the tongue apex seems be in a state of forward motion during the implementation of a retroflex such that, by the time of its release, the apex is sufficiently forward in the mouth to be rather indistinguishable from an alveolar release.

Thus, retroflexes – unlike other consonants – are more acoustically distinct from alveolars during their approach phase in comparison to their release phase. This phonetic fact, coupled with the phonological pattern of retroflex progressive assimilation, is consistent with Steriade's proposal that contrasts are less likely to be maintained in contexts of relatively reduced perceptibility. As retroflexes are difficult to distinguish from their alveolar counterparts at their respective releases, then languages are less likely to possess this contrast in post-consonantal contexts, and are more likely to possess it in post-vocalic contexts.

Most interestingly, retroflex nasals pattern exceptionally in some cases (for example, in Sanskrit and Malayalam), in that they may neutralize in the context of a following consonant (__C). Steriade attributes this to the attenuation of the higher formants in nasals: "[S]ince [the attenuation of upper formants] is a diagnostic value for the alveolar/retroflex distinction this means that in an apical+apical cluster where C_1 is a nasal and C_2 is a stop, there may be no constant perceptual advantage of C_1 over C_2, as there is in heterorganic apical clusters" (p. 11).

The importance of Steriade's results involving retroflexes cannot be overstated. Until this point in her discussion, all facts could be handled equally well by a "prosodic licensing" account of assimilation, since onsets trigger assimilation, and codas undergo assimilation. To be sure, any analysis that offers an externally consistent explanation (as Steriade's does) should be given more weight than one reliant solely on theory-internal constructs, but still, taken on solely their own terms, both hypotheses are equally adept at characterizing the observed patterns. However, the unique patterning of retroflexes lends strong support to Steriade's approach, as this patterning cannot be compellingly handled in the "prosodic licensing" account without special pleading: it is not the case that we can generalize over prosodic positions in our characterization of assimilatory phenomena. Rather, what Steriade demonstrates is that the apparent success of "prosodic licensing" is merely a consequence of the strong tendency for contrastive cues to be better-perceived in prevocalic contexts as opposed to pre-consonantal ones. It is thus the exception of retroflexes that reveals the illusory success of the prosodic account.

Steriade goes on to consider additional cases that would prove difficult to reconcile under a "prosodic licensing" account, but for our purposes, the point is made.

To summarize the main points, Steriade observes that inputs and outputs tend to be very similar. She employs a phonetically informed variant of the standard evaluation metric in her proposal that speakers exploit their phonetic knowledge of similarity/confusability (the P-map) when determining which output form to employ.

DISCUSSION

Lindblom, Jun, and Steriade all implicate a critical role for the speaker in their analyses. But whereas previous proposals on the role of speakers typically emphasize "ease of articulation" as the primary factor in neutralization, what makes the analyses covered in this chapter especially noteworthy is their emphasis on speakers' knowledge of phonetic cueing: speakers are assumed to be aware of the perceptual consequences of their speech, and may thus adjust this speech accordingly. While Lindblom seems primarily interested in accounting for on-line speaking activity, both Jun and Steriade propose that this awareness on the part of speakers has deeper effects on phonological patterning.

A persistent problem for all such analyses, however, is a dearth of evidence. For example, Lindblom refers to experiments in which subjects attempt to overcome physical obstructions that interfere with normal speech. When natural speech patterns are physically interfered with, speakers engage in compensatory articulatory measures in apparent attempts to achieve a normal acoustic output. Based on these results, he proposes that all speakers, in all natural settings, employ comparable strategies. But the only thing such studies indicate is that speakers are aware of what their speech sounds like, such that when it doesn't sound normal, they attempt to improve it. So far so good. But when it *does* sound normal, no such pressure towards improvement need exist, and so it may be premature to extrapolate from such experimental conditions by proposing that these goals are present in everyday speaking situations. Indeed, as Lindblom (1990:419) himself writes: "It might be suggested that the fact that subjects do well on experimental tasks involving compensatory articulation ... is interesting but irrelevant to phonetic theory since [such studies] create unnatural, non-speech conditions." While he feels such concerns are unwarranted, it is not so obvious they should be dismissed out of hand.

Even deeper concerns may be raised about Jun's and Steriade's proposals, exactly because they propose a *systemic* effect of speaker's goals, that is, that speakers' knowledge of phonetic cueing plays an organizing role in their phonologies. But surely, how the sound pattern of their language achieved its present state is completely independent of the speakers who come to possess it, since its organization is a consequence of linguistic evolution, not a consequence of individual speakers' knowledge of its structure. Under normal circumstances, speakers are merely recapitulating the speech patterns that they have always heard. Steriade herself raises just this concern: "[I]f [phonotactic constraints are] not viewed as a problem to be solved, or as a standard of well-formedness that is independent of the lexicon's contents, but rather as a static generalization over the words that happen to be attested in one's language, then no … problem arises: learners, on this view, do not seek to find solutions … but to learn whatever patterns happen to be instantiated by their lexicon." Alas, this possibility remains unexplored in any detail by Steriade.

Another source of concern stems from Steriade's proposal that speakers' grammatical knowledge is in part a consequence of their comparing outputs (actual speech patterns that are, by hypothesis, subject to phonotactic constraints) to inputs (hypothesized underlying representations that are not subject to phonotactic constraints, called the "inferred input" in Jun 2002). Indeed, phonotactic "violations" are, by definition, not actually encountered in the speech stream. Rather, at most, the "disallowed" patterns might be inferred by their absence. Consequently, speakers' basis for comparison when establishing their P-maps would involve *actual speech* compared to *imagined speech*: "Speakers can compute relatively consistent similarity values for sound differences and … this computation of similarity takes into account cue distribution." "Perceived similarity" between input and output is thus a misnomer, because inputs are not perceived by language users – they are (by hypothesis) abstract mental constructs that may or may not have "faithful" phonetic analogs. For example, in a language in which all obstruents are voiceless in final position such that alternations are present involving final devoicing, speakers possess no linguistic experience on which they might draw to conclude that a voiceless stop is most similar to a voiced stop in this context, for the obvious reason that, exactly due to the sound pattern of their language, they have never actually *heard* voiced stops in this context. It seems then, that the P-map hypothesis involves speakers picking and choosing their speech patterns based on a calculated similarity between actual percepts and "imaginary percepts", and thus veers towards logical incoherence.

Steriade is of course correct in her observation that alternants tend to be similar to each other, but this fact does not require us to posit a speaker-based grammatical locus of this tendency. Rather, the explanation may more plausibly reside in the evolutionary pressures that exist on the sound pattern, pressures that have almost nothing to do with individual speakers or their knowledge of language.

Similar questions arise with Jun's production hypothesis. More robust cues are clearly better than poorer cues, but this physical fact need not be recapitulated in speakers' grammatical knowledge such that these speakers exert more effort when producing robust cues, less effort for weaker cues. Surely, the very fact that strong cues are strong is sufficient for them to "do their job" of saliently cueing linguistically relevant information. By the same token, as a natural consequence of the weakness of certain cues might they be susceptible to loss, thus resulting in the neutralization of certain values in certain contexts. Again, individual speakers have almost nothing to do with these patterns, since the patterns existed long before any individual language user came on to the linguistic scene.

An issue concerning all of Lindblom's, Jun's, and Steriade's approaches centers on the role of articulatory ease. Each of these scholars makes critical use of this questionable factor in patterns of neutralization. As discussed in Chapter 7, it is not at all clear that "ease of articulation" arguments play any role whatsoever in individual speakers' grammatical knowledge. Rather, at most, this factor might constitute a slow-going diachronic pressure on linguistic sound systems, a pressure of *semantic*, not *phonetic* origin.

Finally, neither Jun's nor Steriade's proposals consider the genuine functional consequences of neutralization, that is, whether or not the development of a neutralizing alternation interferes with the flow of information between speaker and listener. It may be the case that neutralization is more likely to be tolerated if it does not reduce information flow, and is less likely to be tolerated if it does. For example, although we have herein focused on patterns of neutralization, Steriade assumes the same analysis for non-neutralizing alternations. According to Steriade, schwa is a common word-medial epenthetic vowel because it is highly confusable with its absence. Thus, for Steriade, whether an alternation is neutralizing or contrast-preserving does not seem to be a factor in whether an alternation might be induced or not. It does not matter that, say, /tab/ surfaces as neutralized [tap] instead of contrast-preserving [tabə]. Instead, solely because **tab** is more confusable with **tap** than **tabə** is, the P-map constraints rank [tap] above [tabə].

CONCLUSION

Despite all of these shortcomings, it must be emphasized that the issues brought to the fore in Lindblom's, Jun's, and Steriade's research constitute bold steps forward in phonological theorizing on the subject of phonological patterning in general, and neutralization in particular. In the next chapter, we make extensive use of these findings, considering how acoustic cueing, rather than playing a direct role in *speakers'* linguistic knowledge behavior, instead points to *listeners* as a source of neutralizing alternations.

DISCUSSION QUESTIONS AND FURTHER READING

(1) "Ease of production" and "ease of perception" are typically grouped together as intertwined (if opposing) pressures acting on phonological systems and phonological change. However, these two supposed agents are far from parallel in terms of the locus of their relevance: "ease of production" is solely relevant to the speaker (not the listener), whereas "ease of perception" crucially relies on a role for both the speaker *and* the listener. That is, perception is inherently dependent on an interlocutionary event, whereas production is not. Consider this important difference between these two proposed usage-based pressures on phonology in general, and on neutralization in particular, especially in light of the fact that usage-based factors necessarily reference both speakers and listeners. Might one or the other of these pressures be jettisoned as an explanatory factor in phonology, or do both (or, perhaps, neither) serve important roles in this regard? (You might change your mind by the end of Part 1.)

(2) Remember my claim that all of Lindblom's H&H hypothesis, Jun's production hypothesis, and Steriade's P-map hypothesis suffer from a dearth of evidence in their favor. Further recall that Lindblom (1990:419) writes "It might be suggested that the fact that subjects do well on experimental tasks involving compensatory articulation ... is interesting but irrelevant to phonetic theory since [such studies] create unnatural, non-speech conditions", though he apparently feels such concerns are unwarranted. Also, In his unpublished manuscript of 2002, Jun implicitly acknowledges a lack of evidence for an "inferred

input" as the basis of comparison for phonetically attested forms, and consequently addresses this concern. Finally, recall that Steriade writes: "if [phonotactic constraints are] not viewed as a problem to be solved, or as a standard of well-formedness that is independent of the lexicon's contents, but rather as a static generalization over the words that happen to be attested in one's language, then no ... problem arises: learners, on this view, do not seek to find solutions ... but to learn whatever patterns happen to be instantiated by their lexicon." With respect to the speaker-controlled listener-oriented approaches to neutralization considered in this chapter, how serious do you regard these concerns? Are they readily dismissible? Do they require a more a thorough investigation to determine their seriousness? Are they insurmountable problems? Some further discussion of Steriade's theorizing on the topic of cue expression may be found in papers by **Gerfen (2001)**, **Hansson (2003)**, **Yu (2004)**, **Kochetov (2006)**, and an unpublished manuscript by **Boersma (2008)**.

9   Phonetic misperception

A major thread woven into in the sturdy fabric of Ohala's research program (for example, 1981, 1989, 1990, 1992, 1993a, 1993b) is a prominent role for *listeners* as progenitors of sound change. Now, while traditionally, the term "sound change" does not encompass patterns of neutralization (rather, it refers to diachronic modifications such that the overall functional organization of the system remains unchanged), and while Ohala himself often discusses sound change in this traditional sense, nonetheless, his scholarship has far-reaching consequences that may quite readily encompass such patterns. Indeed, his research occasionally forays into the relevant domain of assimilation, a common source of neutralization. Consequently, in this chapter, we consider Ohala's ideas in some detail as they specifically relate to our present concerns, that is, how listeners' "phonetic misperceptions" may bear on patterns of neutralization. I begin with some of the basics of Ohala's extremely important and influential program, then move on to consider some outstanding remaining issues.

So, a little background first. As also considered (and summarily rejected) in Chapter 7, Ohala observes that traditional approaches usually trace the locus of sound change to *speakers*, not listeners, typically invoking "ease of articulation" argumentation. Ohala challenges this tradition by proposing that listeners take an active (if, of course, unconscious) role in sound change, in the form of formulating hypotheses about the *articulatory intentions* of the speakers they hear. The source of this role for listeners, Ohala argues, is an occasional *inherent ambiguity* in the speech signal: given the imperfect match-up between articulatory and acoustic states – most crucially for Ohala, the many-to-one relationship between articulation and acoustics – listeners may have multiple ways of interpreting the acoustic signal as articulated by speakers. On occasion, such ambiguous speech signals may be interpreted by listeners in a way that does not exactly match speakers' articulatory intentions. If such mismatches iterate and propagate, a sound change may be set in motion.

According to Ohala, four major scenarios may play themselves out over time as a consequence of this interplay between the acoustic signals speakers produce and the interpretations of these signals by listeners: (1) *correction* of acoustically unclear signals, resulting in diachronic stability, (that is, no sound change); (2) *confusion* of acoustically similar sounds (also, presumably, no sound change); (3) *hypo-correction*; and (4) *hyper-correction*. It is these last two scenarios that Ohala explores in depth.

Consider *hypo*-correction. Hypo-correction involves listeners interpreting a context-dependent phonetic property as context-independent. Thus, for example, voiced stops typically induce pitch lowering as they are released into vowels; voiceless stops do not induce such pitch lowering at their release. So, is vocalic pitch lowering an "automatic" and "unintended" consequence of stop voicing, or is it an intended property of the vocalism itself? For Ohala, this is not only a question for linguists; it is also a question for listeners, and has significant implications for the future state of the system. If listeners interpret these vocalic pitch perturbations as due to the intentions of speakers, rather than as an ancillary artifact of the voicing state during the stop itself, then these supposedly *context-dependent unintended phonetic* pitch *distinctions* may be reinterpreted as *context-independent intended phonological* tone *distinctions*, and a sound change may be set in motion, one that eventually shifts the contrast from one of stop voicing to one of vocalic tone. Such patterns of sound change are well attested crosslinguistically, for example, in Indic and Sinitic.

Another example of hypo-correction: in back vowel–dental consonant sequences, coarticulation may induce an "automatic" rise in the second formant of the vowel. Again, this may result in an acoustic signal that is ambiguous from the point of view of listeners: is the higher F2 here a consequence of coarticulation with the consonant, or rather, is it an inherent property of the vocalism? If speakers "intend" the former, but listeners "interpret" the latter, then, again, an *unintended phonetic property* is being reinterpreted as an *intended phonological one*, and the context-dependent vowel fronting may be reinterpreted as context-independent, and, again, a sound change is set in motion. Such a change may result in contrast suspension and/or neutralization if the language already possessed **yt** and/or **y+t** configurations.

Regarding *hyper*-correction, listeners may "over-correct" a component of the speech signal, misinterpreting a context-independent property as a context-dependent one. For example, in Latin **kʷiŋkʷeː > kiŋkʷeː**, assuming an intermediate stage during which a degree of labiality persists from the first labial element through the first vowel and spans across to the release of the second velar ($k^wiŋk^we:$), a listener may mistakenly conclude that the labiality on the first vowel is simply an automatic "spillover" from the second velar release interval, so they "undo" it, "mis-"attributing it to solely the second **k**. The result of such a hyper-corrective sound change is labial dissimilation. As Ohala astutely notes, such patterns are typically observed among features that are not limited to short duration (stricture features), but instead are present across spans (labiality, tongue body features, tongue root features, laryngeal features, etc.).

Another example of dissimilation due to hyper-correction: consider a front round vowel in the context of a following dental stop (**yt**). This is the same phonetic context we considered above, one that might feed a process of hypo-correction; recall, listeners might interpret a context-dependent vowel fronting as context-independent. But now we can imagine that the vowel-fronting is context-*in*dependent, and listeners treat it as context-dependent. Ohala proposes that this "mis"-attribution on the part of listeners might feed a process of dissimilation, such that these listeners "undo" the fronting, diachronically culminating in a dissimilated back vowel–dental sequence (**ut**). Such a change results in contrast suspension and/or neutralization if the language already possesses **ut** and/or **u+t** configurations, as well it might.

In keeping with the strict empirical basis of his framework, Ohala harnesses the laboratory as an essential component of his research program. One example (of countless many): Ohala, Kawasaki, Riordan, and Caisse (no date) tested listeners' knowledge of vowel fronting in the aforementioned dental context. Eight gradient vocalic distinctions acoustically equidistant between both **i** and **u**, and between **ɛ** and **ɔ**, were synthesized, and placed in both **f_p** and **s_t** contexts. Subjects listening to these synthesized forms were more likely to interpret the more-back vowels as front in the labial context, and more likely to interpret the more-front vowels as back in the dental context: "What this means is that listeners will accept as an /u/ or an /ɔ/ a more fronted vowel if they can 'blame' the phonetic context for this fronting" (Ohala 1981:181). Unpacking this a bit, listeners seem to "tolerate" a degree of acoustic departure from the supposedly "intended" vowel, but only if this departure is interpretable as an unintended coarticulatory consequence of its context. Thus, a somewhat front vowel in a dental context may be synchronically "reconstructed" as an underlying back vowel; a somewhat back vowel in a labial context may be synchronically "reconstructed" as an underlying front vowel.

Consider now an example of assimilation, rather than coarticulation, discussed several times already in the present volume. While nasality itself tends to be fairly stable diachronically due to its distinct-ive acoustic properties (potentially confusable only with laterality, and, rarely, aspiration and obstruent pre-voicing), the oral states that accompany velic venting, by contrast are fairly indistinct in acoustic terms, and consequently tend to be diachronically changeable, particu-larly in the sense that these have a significant tendency to assimilate to a following consonantal closure. This is standard nasal assimilation. Ohala (1990) provides straightforward examples from Romance (Late Latin *primu tempus* > French *printemps*; Late Latin *amitas* > Old French *ante*) and Shona (**N+tuta** > **nt^{h}uta** > **nfiuta**; **N+bato** > **mbato**), though such patterns may be found virtually everywhere.

Ohala suggests that derived homorganicity in nasal–stop sequences may be rooted in the auditory ambiguity of the nasal class as a whole. Specifically, given that the oral configurations of nasal consonants are not perspicuously distinct from one another in acoustic terms – especially in the context of a following oral stop, where nasals lack their all-important release cues – they may be "articulatorily reinter-preted". This "reinterpretation" may be such that all the nasals' contrast-ive oral configurations (canonically, **m n ŋ**) collapse towards the oral value of a following consonant (**mp nt ŋk**). Ohala (1990:261): " . . . [W]hen joined to a following stop it is not surprising that the listener has relatively less trouble hearing the nasal consonant as such but takes the place cue from the more salient stop release."

Note that such patterns are neutralizing only if the language in question possesses a *series* of nasals such that the phonetic distinction among the relevant contrastive values is neutralized or suspended (in the relevant context). Thus, for example, it might be argued that, say, Finnish or Japanese – which do not contrast different nasals in morpheme-final position – do not neutralize under nasal assimilation. Still, nasal assimilation has a strong tendency to be neutralizing, as we have already considered, especially in the context of Jun's work.

The other example of assimilatory neutralization discussed in Ohala (1990) involves (oral) stop–stop sequences. As often noted, C_1 has a tendency to assimilate to C_2 with respect to its place-of-articulation. As we have already discussed the listener-based motivation for such patterns, we forgo its repetition here.

DISCUSSION

Let's start our discussion by continuing with Ohala's proposals regarding the source of nasal assimilation, and then move on to discuss certain other issues that arise from his approach.

With respect to nasal assimilation, Ohala's proposals actually beg the question of why such nasals should be reinterpreted in a specifically *homorganic* way. Specifically, why should listeners assign an oral configuration to the nasal by "reading off" the cues present at the following consonantal release? Granted, nasality is perceptually perspicuous, and nasals' oral properties are perceptually imperspicuous, but still, as we discussed in Chapters 7 and 8, why not simply collapse the distinct oral postures to a single place-of-articulation in this context, for example, perhaps ŋp ŋt ŋk? Ohala is tellingly silent on the question, his silence reinforcing the fact that the question remains, and calls out for a satisfying answer. I hope to have provided a compelling answer in Chapter 7. Recall: nasals allow information about their oral configurations to "bleed through" during the nasal murmur itself. Consequently, listeners hear the nasal undergoing a shift in its oral configuration, and faithfully reproduce this shift in their own speech. In due time, the nasal's oral posture may become temporally coordinated with the velic lowering posture, and full-fledged assimilation results.

Let's now consider some additional questions that arise as we investigate the details of Ohala's approach. Despite Ohala's often emphasizing the many-to-one relationship between articulation and acoustics, he ultimately argues for a rather different locus of sound change: the supposed ambiguity of which Ohala speaks is *not* rooted in this *empirically verifiable* articulatory–acoustic mismatch, but rather, lies squarely within a *conjectural* mismatch between *speaker intent* and *listeners' conclusions about speaker intent*. The acoustic signal itself is rarely ambiguous. Ohala himself implicitly assumes as much, as his examples consistently rely on the role of listeners formulating hypotheses about speakers' *mental states*, not about these speakers' *physical states* (recall, hypo- and hyper-correction crucially rely on such hypotheses). Thus, for Ohala, the supposed ambiguity centers on listeners' uncertainty about *speaker intent* and does not center on listeners' uncertainty about *speaker behavior*. Especially given Ohala's praiseworthy emphasis on empiricism, it is unfortunate that the crux of his analysis is rooted in the decidedly unempirical domain of language users' "mental states", and further, implicates listeners as engaging in the very sorts of "guessing games" about speaker intent as does Ohala himself.

Moreover, Ohala's approach ultimately makes crucial reference to the traditional segment, in the sense that listeners are formulating hypotheses about the *intended segmental affiliation* of particular acoustic cues. By extension (and as Ohala readily acknowledges), he is making use of the structural and generative theoretical construct "underlying form". Ohala's basic proposal is that listeners may take an active role in "undoing", "factoring out", or "correcting" supposed "distortions" in the speech signal. Such distortions, note, may be characterized as such only if we assume the existence of an idealized "undistorted" (underlying, phonemic) state. Such an assumption is part and parcel of structuralist, and especially generativist theories about phonological structure.

In this context, let's briefly reconsider Ohala's proposals regarding Latin labial dissimilation. Recall that, under his analysis, listeners hear a span of labiality – stretching from one velar release to another – and "mis"-attribute its segmental affiliation to the latter velar only, instead of two instances, one on each velar. In time, it is the labialization on the first velar that is treated as a redundant cue to the contrast, thus precipitating its withering away. Here we see the role of segmentation and phonemes in Ohala's approach, for his assumption is that speakers are formulating hypotheses about the underlying segmental affiliation of labiality.

Alternative hypotheses are readily available, however. Listeners may indeed hear a span of labiality from the first velar–vocoid sequence through the second velar–vocoid sequence ($k^w i \eta k^w e$ː), but the cues to this labial posture are *less* saliently encoded on the first of these sequences, *more* saliently encoded on the second. This is due to the presence of pervasive labiality during the early portion of the span, acoustically encoded as a rather meager F2 transition during the glide–vowel span ($k^w i \eta k^w e$ː). By contrast, the second glide–vowel sequence is characterized by a robust F2 transition, due to the change in lip posture from rounded to unrounded ($k^w i \eta k^w e$ː). The result is a span of labiality with its cues most prominent during the second glide–vowel sequence. Due to the cue robustness of these particular transitions, listeners may attend to – and come to rely most heavily upon – this particular acoustic component of the span. In time, the cues that precede this latter velar–vocoid sequence may become less important, thus precipitating their diachronic demise. Here, then, is a phonetically and functionally driven account of the dissimilatory change: no segments, no phonemes, no underlying representations, and no "guessing games" about speakers' mental states by either the linguist or the listener.

(Still, a crucial component is lacking in this scenario, and that is the role of minimal pairs: if historic $k^w i \eta k^w e$ː minimally contrasted with $ki \eta k^w e$ː, the change may be less likely to proceed. We consider such issues in detail in Chapters 10 through 13.)

Another example comes from American English, including my native dialect of English ("Nanuet English", spoken thirty kilometers northwest of Manhattan Island). Here, we observe rhotic dissimilation that is present (1) in lexically static contexts (that is, in certain contexts where certain dialects may possess two rhotics, we typically possess one; the latter), and also, increasingly, (2) in morphologically derived contexts (that is, in a form of dynamic dissimilation). For example, we have (static) **kʷɔɹʔ** ("quart") – **kʷɔɾɹ** ("quarter"; rhymes with **wɔɾɹ** "water"); **kʰɔɹn** ("corn") – **kʰɔnɹ** ("corner"), but we also have cases of (dynamic) variable alternation, as in **mɔɹn** ("mourn") – **mɔnɹ** ~ **mɔɹnɹ** ("mourner"), and **b̥ɔɹd̥** ("board") – **b̥ɔɹɹ** ~ **b̥ɔɹɾɹ** ("boarder") (compare to monomorphemic **b̥ɔɾɹ** "border", which rarely varies with **b̥ɔɹɾɹ**). This pattern of dissimilation is also readily understandable in a cue-based approached to dissimilation. First, it should be pointed out that the American English rhotic involves both pharyngeal constriction and lip protrusion, postures that are especially likely to be implemented as spans, such that the (historic) non-adjacent rhotics may indeed come to unify as a span. This evolved span of rhoticity (from the historic first rhotic to the second) possesses its most salient cues after the interrupting oral constriction, since here the span possesses clear formant transitions from the intervening consonant into the syllabic rhotic. Due to its salience, listeners may passively attend to – and come to rely most heavily upon – this particular acoustic component of the span. In time, the cues to rhoticity that precede the oral occlusion may become less important, thus, again, precipitating their diachronic demise. In an excellent paper, Hall (2009) goes into impressive detail on the pattern of rhotic dissimilation in American English, eventually embracing Ohala's account. While further recognizing the salience of certain cues over others, she remains silent regarding the relevance of segmental affiliation. The comparable analysis presented here overtly rejects segments, phonemes, underlying representations, and listener "guessing games" about speaker intentions.

Moving on now, recall also Ohala's (1981:181) conclusions concerning the findings of Ohala, Kawasaki, Riordan, and Caisse: "What this means is that listeners will accept as an /u/ or an /ɔ/ a more fronted vowel if they can 'blame' the phonetic context for this fronting." There is a fairly straightforward alternative interpretation of these findings – one based on listeners' overall linguistic experience with speech tokens – that need not make reference to phonemes, and surely need not make reference to speaker intent. It is plausibly the case that listeners are simply matching the experimental stimuli against sound patterns with which they have extensive experience. After all, vowels *are* somewhat fronted when flanked by dentals, and, consequently, if such vowels are "unnaturally" backed (in the sense of being statistically rare), speakers are, quite naturally, prone to interpret such vowels as something other than what experience has lead them to expect. Comparably, vowels may be less fronted when flanked by labials, and, if such vowels become "unnaturally" fronted, speakers again naturally interpret them as something different; a back vowel. Under this interpretation, there is no need to posit segments or underlying representations. Rather, there is, quite simply, an *experiential* explanation for the obtained results. Ultimately, this sort of experiment might thus tell us something about how listeners deal with language-*like* acoustic signals, but does not provide evidence for any supposed mental state that might be triggered by genuine linguistic stimuli.

CONCLUSION

Do these outstanding problems force a full reconsideration of the Ohalaian enterprise? Absolutely not. The flaws in its few components that require minor tweaking are far outweighed by the virtues of its many components that go significantly farther than virtually all preceding approaches to explanation in phonology. Ohala's theories on the social and psychological mechanisms of sound change properly recognize that linguistic sound structure is unambiguously influenced by the social setting in which language is used. His proposal that sound change begins in the low-level variation common to all speech, and may take root due to the role of listeners, was often bandied about by earlier scholars, but Ohala was the first to actually show how and why this is such a compelling explanation for many sorts of sound changes. His proposals on phonetic explanations for phonological sound patterns have proven a huge boon to philologists and historical linguists, who may now test their linguistic reconstructions and proposed sound changes against their articulatory and acoustic plausibility. His pioneering use of the laboratory as a "time machine" – that is, showing how real-world slow-acting sound changes can be sped up under the proper laboratory conditions – continues to provide remarkably fertile ground for researchers in phonetics, phonology, and historical linguistics. I could go on, but I believe my point is made.

DISCUSSION QUESTIONS AND FURTHER READING

(1) In this chapter I have only briefly investigated the assertion that Ohala's ideas on sound change are based less on listeners' misinterpretation of speakers' phonetic *productions*, and more

on listeners' misinterpretation of speakers' phonetic *intentions*. Read up on **Ohala**'s ideas in his **1981**, **1990**, **1992**, **1993a**, and **1993b** papers. How compelling do you find my criticism, and what sorts of experimental methods might be employed to tease apart the predictions of Ohala's assertions versus the predictions of my rejoinder?

(2) Consider Ohala's proposals on the preconditions and causes of sound change (correction, confusion, hypo-correction, hyper-correction) and compare them to subsequent theorizing by **Blevins (2004)** on this same topic, her "Change", "Chance", and "Choice".

10 Semantic misperception: early proposals

Having now considered Ohala's listener-based approach to neutralization – one rooted in the proposal that listeners may sporadically misinterpret speakers' *phonetic* intentions – in this chapter we move on to consider an alternative listener-based approach to the issue, one rooted in the proposal that listeners may sporadically misinterpret speakers' *semantic* intentions. On the face of it, this may seem a bizarre claim indeed, so the goal here is to build arguments in its favor, considering Martinet's (1952) proposals on sound change and functional load, as well as King's (1967) rejoinder.

MARTINET (1952)

Martinet (1952) starts from the validated assertion that speech is inherently variable in terms of its articulatory and acoustic properties. This variability is not only due to context-sensitive factors (that is, due to what he calls "allophonic deviations"), but also in a context-free sense. He argues that this low-level phonetic variation, generally speaking, is passively delimited such that a comfortable perceptual buffer zone is maintained between one value and its immediate systemic neighbors. However, Martinet notes that, under certain circumstances, this buffer zone may be fatally breached such that one value may (diachronically) merge or (synchronically) neutralize with another. Thus, while each value (in each context) has a "center of [acoustic and articulatory] gravity", there is likely to be sufficient low-level variation such that tokens of one value, **a**, might occasionally stray into the territory of a neighboring value, **b**. Under some conditions, such strays are tolerated, since the movement of **a** towards **b** is accompanied by a movement of **b** towards a new value, **c**. This constitutes a chain shift. But on other occasions, merger or neutralization of **a** and **b** does indeed take place. The question that Martinet contends with is this: What pressures exist on the phonological system to limit the likelihood of one value merging or neutralizing with another value?

First off, a major factor that influences the outcome of a potential neutralization, according to Martinet (1952:5), is "the basic necessity of securing mutual understanding through the preservation of useful phonemic oppositions" (we're talking about [synchronic] neutralizations, since that is our focus here, although all arguments are equally valid for [diachronic] mergers; many of Martinet's examples involve such mergers). Now, while all phonemic oppositions are inherently "useful", some, according to Martinet are more useful than others. Thus, if **a** occasionally drifts towards **b**, and listeners are confused by the result, this movement is unlikely to be imitated. However, if the occasional drift of **a** towards **b** does not induce listener confusion, then there are fewer functional pressures militating against such a movement. An opposition is thus likely to be more "useful" if it is responsible for keeping many words distinct from one another. That is, an opposition that is responsible for many *minimal pairs* is more useful than an opposition that is responsible for few minimal pairs. All else being equal, an opposition with a higher *functional load*, *yield*, or *burden* is thus less likely to neutralize; an opposition with a low functional load is more likely to neutralize.

Martinet (1952:8) writes: "In its simplest somewhat unsophisticated acceptation, [functional yield, burden, or load] refers to the number of lexical pairs which would be complete homonyms if it were not for that one word of the pair presents one member **a** of the opposition where the other shows the other member **b**: the pair *pack – back* is part of a functional yield of the **p-b** opposition in English, and so are *repel – rebel* (v.), *cap – cab*, and hosts of others."

Curiously, Martinet asserts that, while bilateral oppositions like English **s–ʃ** and **s–z** qualify as minimally contrastive, multilateral oppositions like English **s–ʒ** and **ʃ–z** do not, in an apparent echo of Trubetzkoy's problematic assertion that only bilateral oppositions might neutralize. Indeed, considering any single phonemic opposition may be insufficient to gauge the likelihood of merger. Rather, the extent to which this opposition is *correlated* should be considered as well. Trubetzkoy's notion of correlated opposition takes into account all the oppositions in a system that crucially hinge on one feature. For example, although the functional load of the English **θ–ð** bilateral opposition is exceedingly meager, it is merely one member of a correlated opposition involving voicing. Since sound changes tend to affect correlated values (that is, natural classes) rather than single members of a *correlated opposition*, then – because the functional load of the voicing opposition in English is rather high – merger of the **θ–ð** opposition might be curtailed. In short, the less correlated the opposition, the more likely that neutralization might take place; the more correlated the opposition, the less likely that neutralization might take place.

Moreover, Martinet's preliminary definition of the term "functional load" does not consider the number of minimal pairs belonging to different syntactic categories. Thus, as he notes, if there are many minimal pairs, but the respective members of these pairs belong to different syntactic categories, communicative success should not be jeopardized upon merger; the functional load of this opposition may be low, and so tendencies towards neutralization might not be curtailed. So, his *back–pack* and *repel–rebel* (v.) examples constitute relevant minimal pairs, but *thigh–thy* and *mouth* (n.) – *mouth* (v.) do not.

Also according to Martinet, it is important to consider the lexical (and probably token) frequency of each member. If the lexical/token frequency of one or both members of the relevant minimal pairs is low, then the functional load of this opposition may be low as well, and so neutralization might not be curtailed. If lexical/token frequency of one or both members of the relevant minimal pairs is high, then the functional load of this opposition may be high as well, and so neutralization might be curtailed. For example, the French $\tilde{\epsilon}$–$\tilde{œ}$ opposition may be lost not only because the values are phonetically similar, but because (1) the opposition is responsible for few minimal pairs, and (2) the lexical frequency of $\tilde{œ}$ is meager.

Finally, additional morphological markers may serve to disambiguate homophonic sets. For example, Martinet writes that, among Parisian speakers, the earlier **i–y–u–e** distinction is virtually lost, since these values were primarily responsible for gender distinctions, a function that has been taken up by the determiner and pronoun systems. Consequently, there are few functional pressures to maintain these distinctions. Though some mergers and neutralizations do indeed create annoying ambiguities (for example, French *l'amie–l'ami, mon amie–mon ami*) Martinet suggests that one or two useful minimal pairs may be insufficient to block an impending loss of contrast.

To summarize, according to Martinet, the tendency towards neutralization is favored to the extent that:

(1) The values in opposition are phonetically similar
(2) The number of minimal morpheme pairs that the opposition is responsible for is low
(3) The number of minimal pairs within a correlated opposition is low (or the opposition is uncorrelated)
(4) The minimal pairs belong to different syntactic categories

(5) The lexical/token frequency of one or both members of the minimal pairs is low

(6) The presence of additional morphological markers serves a disambiguating function

Ultimately however, neutralization is not likely to take place simply because some of the relevant morphemes have a low token frequency, or because some of the relevant minimal pairs happen to belong to different syntactic categories, etc. Rather, these totals should be cumulatively low across the totality of the lexicon in use. After all, if sounds are to neutralize, then, according to Martinet's criteria, the output of the process – across the lexicon in use – should not yield a significant increase in the amount of communicative confusion.

Having compiled these criteria as factors affecting functional load, Martinet (1952:9) is nonetheless quick to qualify his assertions: "[I]t is clear that the functional yield of an opposition can only be evaluated with any degree of accuracy if we deal with linguistic stages for which fairly exhaustive word lists are available. This circumstance makes it practically impossible to check the validity of the functional assumption in the case of prehistoric sound shifts." For example, even though we possess exhaustive knowledge of Latin vocabulary, we have precious little knowledge of actual Latin *usage*. Moreover, phonological patterning may interact in non-trivial ways with morphological patterning: "word composition and morphological reshuffling frequently afford easy solutions to the problems which may arise when a functionally important opposition is being threatened by the drifting together of two phonemes: as soon as the margin of security is invaded and danger of misunderstanding rises, speakers will be induced to give preference to such alternative words, phrases, or forms as will remove all ambiguity" (p. 10).

KING (1967)

In his 1967 rejoinder to Martinet, King acknowledges these problems in quantifying functional load: it is extremely difficult – or, at the time of King's writing, perhaps downright impossible – to gauge the degree of functional load in accordance with Martinet's criteria both before and after a merger has taken place, that is, at two different stages of a language's development. In his attempt to do just this, however, King embraces neither Martinet's first approximation of the term's working definition (the number of minimal pairs involving phonetically similar values), nor Martinet's qualifiers (the role of correlated oppositions, the role of syntactic category, the role of frequency, the role of morphology). Instead, he proposes his own criteria for the determination of functional load, crucially excluding the overriding importance of minimal pairs.

King's (1967:836) definition of the term "functional load" possesses two components: (1) "the global text frequencies of the two phonemes involved", and (2) "the degree to which [the two phonemes] contrast in all possible environments, where environment means, roughly speaking, one phoneme to the left and right".

Regarding his first criterion, note that the raw frequencies of a given set of phonemes do not provide any direct information about the role that this opposition plays in keeping morphemes phonologically distinct from one another. For example, if we tally the raw frequency of similar values, say, **x** and **y**, then words **axb** versus **ayb** are clearly relevant to the functional load of the **x**–**y** opposition; these are minimal pairs. However words **abx** versus **yab** would also be relevant to the **x**–**y** opposition, despite the fact they are not minimal pairs. Consequently, this first criterion fails to capture the genuinely relevant property that a proper characterization of functional load requires, that is, that the opposition create minimal pairs.

Regarding his second criterion, King would propose that instances of our example phonemes **x** and **y** should be counted towards the functional load of the **x**–**y** opposition when immediately flanked by identical values, say, **a** and **b**. Consequently, words **axb** versus **ayb** are, once again, clearly relevant to the functional load of the **x**–**y** opposition, as these are minimal pairs. However, words **axbc** versus **aybd** would also be relevant to the **x**–**y** opposition, despite the fact that they are not minimal pairs. Consequently, this second criterion also fails to capture the genuinely relevant property that a proper characterization of functional load requires.

Instead of considering the role that minimal pairs play in the tendency towards merger, King considers the following three hypotheses regarding the likelihood of merger (emphasis added):

(1) The weak point hypothesis: "If all else is equal, sound change is more likely to start within oppositions bearing low functional loads than within oppositions bearing high functional loads; or, in the case of a single phoneme, *a phoneme of low frequency of occurrence is more likely to be affected by sound change than is a high-frequency phoneme*" (pp. 834f.).

(2) The least resistance hypothesis: "If all else is equal, and if (for whatever reason) there is a tendency for a phoneme **x** to merge

with either of the two phonemes **y** or **z**, then that merger will occur for which the functional load of the merged opposition is smaller: i.e. **x** > **y** if L(**x**, **y**) is smaller than L(**x**, **z**), and **x** > **z** if L(**x**, **z**) is smaller than L(**x**, **y**), where L(**x**, **y**) designates the functional load of the opposition **x** ≠ **y**, and > designates merger" (p. 835).

(3) The frequency hypothesis: "*If an opposition* **x** ≠ **y** *is destroyed by merger, then that phoneme will disappear in the merger for which the relative frequency of occurrence is smaller: i.e.* **x** > **y** *if the relative frequency of* **x** *is smaller than that of* **y**, *and* **y** > **x** *if the relative frequency of* **y** *is smaller than that of* **x**" (p. 835).

The first component of his weak point hypothesis, as well as his least resistance hypothesis, purport to specifically target oppositions with low functional loads. However, as just discussed, King's criteria for the determination of functional load do not accord with Martinet's, as they do not directly isolate the number of relevant minimal pairs that would be rendered homophonous upon merger. Further, note the italicized portions of his three criteria. King is especially concerned with the phonetic quality of the merged value: does, say, **x** become **y**, or does **y** become **x**? But surely, in terms of the functional consequences of a merged opposition, directionality does not matter. Whether **x** merges towards **y**, or **y** merges towards **x**, the functional result is the same: a certain number of morphemes that were previously distinguished solely by the **x**–**y** opposition will be rendered non-distinct from each other. Furthermore, King does not consider whether the relevant forms are in the same or different syntactic categories; nor does he consider whether the token frequencies of the relevant forms are high or low; nor does he consider whether additional morphological markers do or do not serve a disambiguating function.

King's investigation of the role of "functional load" in Icelandic, Old Saxon, German, and Yiddish vowel changes yields largely negative results, that is, "functional load" (according to his criteria) does not seem to be a genuine pressure acting on patterns of sound change.

Regarding Icelandic, according to Benediktsson (1959), a series of mergers and changes has taken place in the following chronological order: õ>ø, ø:>ẽ (mergers), au>ø^i, e:>e^i, e:>a^i, o:>o^u, a:>a^u (changes), y>i, y:>i:, ey>ei (mergers). Let's consider the mergers in turn. King finds that the prevalence of the õ–ø opposition was quite low. Given his *frequency hypothesis*, however, it would be expected that the merger would be ø>õ, rather than õ>ø, since õ is roughly six times more frequent than ø. Still it should be recalled that Martinet's hypotheses make no predictions regarding the directionality of merger, as the functional consequences are equivalent regardless. Regarding the ø:>ẽ merger, the *least resistance hypothesis* fails, as the ø:–ẽ opposition reportedly possessed a higher functional load than ø: possessed with other values (though all the relevant oppositions yield extremely low values here). This merger passes the weak point test however, since ø: was less frequent that ẽ. Regarding y>i, y:>i:, ey>ei, the results are mixed as well: the *least resistance hypothesis* is not supported, but the *weak point hypothesis* is.

Let's also consider the Yiddish evidence. King readily acknowledges that usage data from Proto-Yiddish are lacking, and thus he uses data from Middle High German instead (while further acknowledging that there is little evidence suggesting a direct lineal relationship between Classical Middle High German and Yiddish). According to Herzog (1965), Proto-Yiddish possessed high vowel oppositions i–i:–u–u:. In Southern Yiddish, the back vowels merged towards the front vowels, yielding i–i:. Absent any reliable numerical results, King (1967:847) concludes that this merger "affected a highly useful opposition in the functional sense". In Northeastern Yiddish, the long vowels merged with the short vowels, yielding i–u. This length distinction "did not carry a high functional load in Middle High German" (p. 847), and thus King tentatively concludes that the merger "affected oppositions whose functional loads were probably less high [than the merged front–back opposition in Southern Yiddish]" (p. 835). Finally, in North Central Poland and Northern Ukraine, all four vowels merged to i: "[T]he functional load of the oppositions destroyed must have been considerably larger than the provisional functional load ... lost in the merger of Southern Yiddish" (p. 835).

Despite the obvious tentativeness of the majority of his conclusions, King asserts that Martinet's proposals (as King interprets them) are supported about 50 percent of the time. In other words, the functional load hypothesis is fully non-predictive. Still, King (1967:848) readily acknowledges that "Language has ... manifold devices for carrying on its business of communication [and] distinctiveness lost at the phonological level might be assumed without interruption of communication by higher-level markers in morphology and syntax", but this caveat remains unexplored.

King (1967:850) ultimately concludes that "[t]he theory of therapeutic sound change as developed especially in Prague School linguistics is predicated on (1) the assumption that the speaker, or at any rate some higher linguistic consciousness, is aware of certain informational indices in his language – relative frequencies of phonemes, functional loads of oppositions, etc. – and (2) that the speaker (or his higher consciousness, whatever it is) possesses the ability to act on this knowledge to avert possible linguistic changes. I know of no empirical findings which support this assumption. I think, therefore, that concrete evidence of the soundness of such an assumption should precede further speculations on the nature of therapeutic sound change" (indices added).

Hockett (1967:320), having viewed the galleys of King's report just as his own paper on the topic was going to press, has this to add: "[King's] is a sketchy report of an empirical study leading [him] to conclude that 'functional load, if it is a factor at all in sound change, is one of the least important of those we know anything about ... ' This puts the matter awkwardly, since as a matter of fact we know nothing about any other factor in sound change either. King used a mere 20,000 running phonemes of text for each stage of each language, which is not nearly enough ... Of course, it may be that functional load has no significant bearing on sound change, but King has by no means proved his thesis."

Hockett's criticisms aside, it should be emphasized that, whereas Martinet's is merely a skeletal proposal (and Hockett's is a rather impenetrable fleshing out of the notion), King's is the first genuinely numerical investigation into the functional load hypothesis. That his results were negative may be as much a consequence of the technological limitations of his era as anything else. Indeed, with today's computer-tallied corpora, quantitative explorations of the functional load hypothesis may be undertaken with relative ease. Moreover, research subsequent to King's has shown that (1) speakers are in fact keenly aware of so-called "phoneme distributions" and variability in their speech, and (2) there is no reason to assume that teleology, speaker intention, or any other form of goal-directed behavior plays a role in functionally motivated phonological change.

CONCLUSION

Due in great part to the technological limitations of the day, both Martinet's original proposals and King's preliminary quantitative disconfirmations regarding the functional load hypothesis must be treated as tentative in nature. Nowadays though, with the advent of modern computer technology, more thoroughgoing statistical investigations may be pursued with relative ease. In the next chapter then, we consider more recent theoretical proposals regarding the role of semantic misperception and homophony – those of Labov and the school of sociophonetic research he has pioneered – that harness modern computer-based documentary and experimental techniques. This is followed, in Chapter 12, by a case study – neutralization and anti-homophony in Korean – that constitutes the first of what may (and, indeed, should) be many quantitative corpus-based investigations into the issue of functional load and sound change.

DISCUSSION QUESTIONS AND FURTHER READING

(1) As noted, probably due to technological limitations, the twentieth-century literature on functional load is rather meager; the idea is there, but its investigation remains elusive (**Martinet 1952, King 1967, 1969, Hockett 1955, 1967**). Times have changed though, and modern technology now provides us the means to investigate the issue in a far more thoroughgoing and sophisticated manner (**Surendran and Niyogi 2003, 2006, Kaplan 2011a**, and, to a far less sophisticated degree, **Silverman 2010**). Reading these studies might inspire you to undertake your own investigations into the issue of functional load, merger, and neutralization.

(2) Unrelated to the issue of neutralization, an additional component to the **Martinet's (1952)** study addresses the observed "symmetry" of phonological systems, for example, the symmetrical dispersion of vowel systems in the acoustic space. Martinet seems to attribute this aspect of phonological systems to a cognitive pressure, itch, or bent, towards symmetry and dispersion. Consider Martinet's analysis, and compare to those found in **Liljencrantz and Lindblom (1972), Flemming (1995), de Boer (2001)**, and **Silverman (2006a)**.

11 Semantic misperception: recent proposals

For the bulk of his 1994 book, Labov employs a rather particular working definition of the term "functionalism". For Labov, the "functionalist hypothesis" is primarily *syntagmatic* in orientation, where "syntagmatic", for Labov, refers to "the stream of speech ... where the speaker has the opportunity to adjust the choice of variants at one point to compensate for the presence or loss of information at other points" (p. 570). In other words, in this narrow sense, "functionalism" refers to a synchronic "on-line" or "on the fly" monitoring of the semantic content of the speech signal such that this code is constantly being updated to ensure a lack of semantic ambiguity for the listener. As documented in Chapter 19 of his book, Labov's findings regarding functional pressures on language use (in this sense) are largely negative. Instead, "speakers are more influenced by the tendency toward structural parallelism" (p. 570). For example, in any given utterance, if one agreement marker is present in a construction, all tend to be present, but if one is dropped, all tend to be dropped; clearly not a "functional" result, since in the former case, the structure may possess unnecessary redundancy, and in the latter case, the structure is devoid of agreement markers.

However, by expanding the scope of "functionalism" to incorporate the *paradigmatic* structural properties of language – where, for Labov, "paradigmatic" properties include the slow, diachronic, and decidedly passive accumulation of structural changes to the system as a whole, such that the speech code naturally settles towards a semantically unambiguous state – he changes his tune considerably regarding the efficacy of functionalism. Here, in his Chapter 20, he indeed finds striking positive evidence for functional influences on the structure of the linguistic system, among them, a gravitational tug towards lexical semantic clarity as embodied in a passive pressure towards homophone avoidance.

In this chapter, we summarize Labov's findings pertaining to this matter, and move on to outline his proposed mechanism of sound change. We'll see that his approach is a direct descendant of Martinet's functional account, though applied with a great deal more rigor. Further, whereas Ohala's listener-based locus of sound change focuses on the supposed misinterpretation of speakers' *phonetic intentions*, Labov's proposals – also listener-based – focus on the misinterpretation of speakers' *semantic intentions*, and are, as a matter of principle, silent with respect to listeners' supposed hypotheses concerning speakers' phonetic intentions. Finally, we place Labov's proposals in the context of the matter at hand – neutralization, especially neutralization as derived homophony, that is, NEUTRALIZATION – arguing that imparting a prominent role for the functional consequences of *semantic misperception* in the speech stream (as Labov does) is consonant with the proposal that there are passive diachronic pressures towards homophone avoidance.

SEMANTIC MISPERCEPTION

Consider first a case of a shift in usage: in French, the plural marker -s has been lost except when a vowel follows, and thus, for example, the plural article (earlier, **las** in all contexts) runs the risk of being homophonous with the singular, **la**, thus deriving NEUTRALIZATION. However, the plural is now (usually) signaled by a change in vowel quality: **las** ≫ **le**. Labov: "[This] show[s] how long-range changes in the French phonological, morphological, and syntactic systems compensated for sound changes, in ways that suggest a causal link" (p. 570).

Another example: in Boston Puerto Rican Spanish (Hochberg 1986a, 1986b) the plural marker -s is variably absent, but its absence is less often encountered when the result would create semantic ambiguity, and more often encountered in inherent plurals, thus **mutʃa(s) planta(s)** ("many plants") is found, with *variable* presence of the plural marker (note the inherently plural nature of the quantifier), but **las plantas** ("the plants") is found with *consistent* presence of the plural marker (note the consequent ambiguity upon -s-dropping: **la planta** "the plant").

A third example: Flores, Myhill, and Tarallo (1983) consider Spanish data like the following: **el ombre** ("the man"), **lo(s) ombre(s)** ("the men"), **la mujer** ("the woman"), **la(s) mujere(s)** ("the women"). The masculine plural determiner has two marks **-os**, while the female has only one **-s**. The masculine **-s** deletes significantly more often than the feminine. As Labov (1994:572) writes, " ... [I]t appears that the vowel difference in the masculine article will carry some of the plural information." (Still, plurality in the feminine is also cued upon -s-dropping, since the noun retains an extra vowel, **-e**.)

A fourth and final example: in Spanish, pronoun drop is variably applied: (**jo**) ɛstuðio ("I study"), (**nosotros**) estuðiamos ("we study"), (**tu**) ɛstuðias̲ ("you (sg.) study)", (ɛl/eja/ustɛd) ɛstuðia ("he/she/you study"), (ejos/ejas/ustɛðɛs) estuðian ("they study"). Note in particular the distinction between 2nd sg. and 3rd sg. verb agreement; 2nd person is marked by **-s**, whereas 3rd sg. lacks this **-s** (Hochberg 1986a, 1986b). One might predict that the **-s** in the 2nd sg. (underlined) should delete the least often, since it is the sole marker of the 2nd–3rd distinction. As it turns out, the 2nd sg. **-s** drops more often than the overall average. Interestingly though, pronoun use increases in the context of this **-s**-drop, thus semantically "undoing" the NEUTRALIZATION. Tellingly, among educated Madrid speakers, in which **-s** is not undergoing attrition, pronoun use is significantly lower. Pronoun use increases upon switch-reference, however (when a new subject is introduced) (Cameron 1992), and thus the pronoun provides contrastive information that reinforces switch reference.

Recall that Labov's findings suggest the absence of a role for functionalism in the syntagmatic (synchronic, "on-line") sense. Yet clearly, the system seems to take a shape that maintains meaning, strongly suggesting that there is *some* functional pressure, acting *somewhere*, on the system as a whole. But where? "If speakers do not consciously or unconsciously adjust their sentences to maximize the transmission of meaning, then we need to find some other mechanism that accounts for the systemic adjustments that maintain informational content" (1994:585).

Labov's proposed mechanism is *probability matching*: animals (including humans) have the capacity to replicate observed frequencies of events in terms of their behavioral responses. For example, in one very straightforward lab experiment demonstrating this phenomenon, rats placed in a T-Maze are rewarded with food 75% of the time at one end, 25% of the time at the other. When provided with feedback, the rats' foraging behavior quickly comes to match the probability of reward – they run to the one end 75% of the time, to the other end 25% of the time, despite the fact that they would maximize their food intake by running exclusively to the "75%" end.

Comparable statistical calculations underlie aspects of human linguistic behavior: the nature and extent of variation in speech is indeed largely matched as listeners become speakers. That is, the statistical distribution of perceived speech tokens within the phonetic space is calculated by listeners, and, rather amazingly, is largely matched as these listeners become speakers. Such stable variation may persist for generations and generations, in fact. (We have already seen an example of this in our discussion of Belfast English.) Consequently, "much synchronic variation is a residue of historical processes, rather than the immediate product of linguistic or physiological factors" (Labov 1994:583). For example, differences in the variability of English "-ɪŋ" – such that -ɪn is favored for progressives and participles, but not for non-verbal categories like adjectives, gerunds, and nouns – may be a consequence of history, as the participle suffix derives from historic -inde/-ende, and the verbal noun suffix derives from -ɪŋ (Houston 1985). Such findings, then, are indeed consistent with a proposal presented in Chapter 1, that is, that certain so-called "low-level" or "phonetic" effects may in fact be the result of deep, systemic pressures many times removed from the physical systems that proximally underlie speech. For full explication of the mechanism of probability matching, I direct the reader to Labov's original discussion in his Chapter 20; a somewhat simplified and schematized presentation is available in my 2006 book. I provide a still-further simplified discussion now.

As stated, the basic idea behind probability matching is that language users are especially adept at matching in their own productions the variation they perceive, such that this variation is conventionalized in the speech community. But of course, if probability matching always takes place without error, such that variation is always perfectly matched generation after generation, sound change would never have the opportunity to proceed. Consequently, what must be emphasized in this scenario is the role of *ambiguous* speech signals. This ambiguity is not based on listeners' confusion about speakers' phonetic intentions, as considered by Ohala. Rather, the ambiguity is *semantic* in nature. As Labov writes (1994:586), "It is not the desire to be understood, but rather the consequence of misunderstanding that influences language change. This mechanism implies a mismatch between producer and interpreter: the type of built-in instability that we would expect to find behind long-term shifts in language behavior."

To see how this works, it might be best to consider an example, as adapted from Labov: if the word "drop" is, on rare occasion, produced with a fully fronted vowel (**dræp**) – a "wild stray" – it may very well be regarded as a speech error, and induce confusion for listeners: **dræp** might not be understood, and thus the token may simply be thrown out. Since this fronted token is not added to the pool of "drop" tokens, it serves to inhibit any forward shift of the vowel. However, if the word "drop" is produced with a certain amount of uncharacteristic *minor* vowel-fronting (**drap̈**) – a "mild stray" – it might yet be understood correctly, since it sounds similar to most tokens of "drop", and further, is unlikely to be confused with another word (there is no English word "drap"). No matter how small such an effect, repetition may come to shift the pool of tokens in terms of its phonetic properties, exactly because the variable pronunciations are unlikely to induce semantic confusion on the part of listeners. Consequently, such interlocutions may, over time, lead to an overall fronting of the low back vowel in this context. In this example, vowel fronting is possible exactly because semantic ambiguity is absent, and thus there are few passive pressures inhibiting the sound change.

By contrast, if a token of the word "block" is produced as either a mild stray **blɒk** or a wild stray **blæk**, there is a greater likelihood of misunderstanding, since "black" is a word as well. Here, the role of these misunderstandings is, again, to *inhibit* sound change, since such tokens will not be pooled with the listener's store of exemplars for the word "block". The contrastive vowel qualities in these contexts – as a passive consequence of language use – may thus maintain a comfortable perceptual buffer zone.

In both Labov's detailed presentation, as well as the schematic and stripped-down discussion in Chapters 5 and 6 of my 2006 book, such "mismatches between producers and interpreters" are considered in detail. Very briefly, if there is a natural listener-based tendency for a particular shift in a phonetic value in some context or other (say, final devoicing, or nasal assimilation), this shift may be inhibited if the lexical space towards which this value might naturally gravitate is already occupied such that the one word would end up sounding identical to another word. This, indeed, is an inhibition of NEUTRALIZA-TION. It is the semantic confusion that NEUTRALIZATION might induce which may inhibit the shift: those tokens of words that are not confusable with other words are more likely to be successfully recovered by listeners, hence are more likely to be produced as these listeners become speakers (due to probability matching), and hence are more likely to become conventionalized as the speech norm. Note: no listener "guessing games" about speaker intentions, no on-line monitoring of the semantic clarity of the signal, and no role for teleological pressures on language structure. The result? Due to passive diachronic pressures on language use, the system naturally settles towards a semantically unambiguous state, including low levels of homophony; low levels of NEUTRALIZATION.

So let's apply Labov's proposals, again, in a schematic fashion. In particular, let's return to Babelese from Chapter 1. Perhaps you recall that there are three distinct contexts in Babelese where nasal–stop sequences are encountered: (1) morpheme-internally, where the nasal is always assimilated to the following stop in a *static* (non-alternating) fashion (**mp nt ŋk**); (2) across word-internal morpheme boundaries, where, also, the nasal is always assimilated to the following stop, though in a dynamic fashion such that alternations may be induced (**m+p, n+t, ŋ+k**); and (3) across word boundaries, where nasals may remain unassimilated. Recall also that dynamic nasal assimilation in particular induces an increase in phonological RHYME, in the sense that the inventory of sounds undergoes an active reduction in such contexts. Moreover, recall that nasal assimilation is a phonetically natural process, since, when nasals are immediately followed by stops, their oral configurations may "bleed through" the nasal murmur, thus cueing an assimilated oral state.

The issue now becomes this: Due to dynamic nasal assimilation, is the consequent increase in phonological RHYME accompanied by a decrease in phonological REASON, in the sense that assimilation here produces a marked increase in the number of homophones, that is, NEUTRALIZATION? Or instead, is this increase in phonological RHYME accompanied by a negligible decrease in phonological REASON such that, overall, meaning distinctions are maintained? Labov's "paradigmatic functionalist hypothesis" would likely predict the latter possibility. Here's why: let's imagine a stage in the history of Babelese in which there is marked variability in the pervasiveness of cross-morpheme nasal assimilation, such that some tokens of some words tend towards assimilation, while others do not. What trajectory of change might the system engage in at this point? All else being equal, there are (at minimum) three possibilities: (1) it might remain largely stable, (2) it might move towards a state in which cross-morpheme nasal assimilation comes to pervade the system, or (3) it might move towards a state in which cross-morpheme nasal assimilation is fully absent, thus retaining heterorganicity across morpheme boundaries.

All else is never equal, of course. Phonological patterns are passively shaped by the linguistic uses towards which these patterns are put. In the case at hand, if language use proceeds unencumbered upon nasal assimilation – in the sense of maintaining semantic fluency in the speech code – then there are few functional pressures militating against it, and nasal assimilation may proceed. However, if language use is indeed encumbered upon nasal assimilation in the sense of adversely affecting semantic fluency in the speech code, the language will passively evolve – through its daily use and disuse – some or other structural property that salvages the overall use towards which the system is put. One solution here would be to passively inhibit the natural tendency towards nasal assimilation.

Indeed, we already built up this argument back in Chapter 1. Recall from Chapter 1, with respect to Babelese: "Nasal alternations in the context N+C result in a smaller number of contrastive values here, but this reduction in *phonetic* distinctness (this increase in RHYME) does not necessarily entail a reduction in *semantic* distinctness (a decrease in REASON), simply because, in most cases, there will be other contrastive values that function to keep morphemes phonetically distinct from each other. For example, we may observe taŋkan# – taŋkam̱+p – taŋkaṉ+t – taŋkaŋ+k versus tiŋkaŋ# – tiŋkam̱+p – tiŋkaṉ+t – tiŋkaŋ+k. For the two words taŋkan# versus tiŋkaŋ#, despite the dynamically imposed phonetic identity (or, more precisely, near-identity) of the nasal–stop sequences in particular morphologically complex contexts, the morphemes maintain phonetic distinctness due to V_1 differences, a versus i. Rather, only in those comparatively rare instances when morphemes are otherwise identical are increases in phonological RHYME accompanied by a decrease in phonological REASON: taŋkan# – taŋkam̱+p – taŋkaṉ+t – taŋkaŋ+k versus taŋkaŋ# – taŋkam̱+p – taŋkaṉ+t – taŋkaŋ+k. Stated more succinctly, most alternations do not involve minimal pairs such that particular alternations derive homophones. Consequently, most such alternations are heterophone-maintaining and thus not function-negative; crucial phonetic differences are maintained despite increases in phonological RHYME."

The proposal, then, is that nasal assimilations in Babelese (and elsewhere), and neutralizing alternations in general, are more likely to proceed if they do not significantly increase the amount of homophony, for it is exactly homophonic forms that might induce semantic confusion for listeners, and, due to the intricate workings of probability matching, it is exactly such forms that are likely to be passively filtered out of the system, resulting in lexical structures that are well distributed in the phonetic space.

Let's briefly consider a real-world example. In Hindi (recently discussed in Silverman 2011), schwa alternates with zero in would-be VCəCV contexts, with certain important exceptions to be discussed momentarily. Thus, for example, təʈəp ("restlessness") – təʈpa ("cause to be restless"), wapəs ("return") – wapsi ("on return"). Now, our working hypothesis is this: the schwa–zero alternation (which, by the way, is quite a natural phonetic development, given schwa's tendency to acoustically "camouflage" itself to its acoustic surroundings) entered the language because its presence did not induce a significant number of homophones.

But note that schwa is susceptible to confusion with its absence in many acoustic contexts, not just VC(ə)CV, for example, when it finds itself flanked by more than one consonant on either side (VCCəCV and VCəCCV). Nonetheless, schwa usually does not delete here. Why? Well, were schwa to delete in a VCCəCV or VCəCCV context, the medial consonant may suffer a significant cue loss, as it would lack both approach cues and release cues. Thus, were VCCəCV or VCəCCV to become VCCCV, the sequence might be confused with VCCV. That is, the loss of schwa in these contexts may lead to a percept involving only two – not three – consonants. At this point, the chances of inducing homophony – hence neutralization – increase considerably.

Most interestingly, there are patterned exceptions to the absence of schwa deletion in VCCəCV and VCəCCV contexts: **kadəmbəri** ~ **kadəmbri** ("a novel", name for a girl), **ustəra** ~ **ustra** ("razor"), **puɳɖərik** ~ **puɳɖrik** ("white lotus"). Schwa deletion is variably encountered in these forms, and thus Hindi indeed possesses three sequential consonants that are a consequence of schwa loss. However, these derived tri-consonantal sequences are usually of the form nasal – homorganic stop – sonorant. The development of schwa deletion in such forms is thus not completely unexpected: the phonetic properties of these particular tri-consonantal sequences are readily recoverable from the speech signal, since the medial consonant here does not possess place features that are distinct from the preceding nasal, and thus it does not contribute place cues of its own. Consequently, not only are such sequences more likely to be found elsewhere, but also – and perhaps even as a partial consequence of their presence elsewhere – such sequences may more readily enter the language through developments such as schwa deletion.

DISCUSSION

As emphasized, Labov clearly entertains very different hypotheses from Ohala's regarding listeners' role in certain aspects of sound change. Recall that, in general terms, Ohala proposes that listeners are intent on interpreting the *phonetic* intentions of speakers, and that certain types of sound change are a consequence of listeners' sporadic "incorrect" conclusions about these intentions. Labov, by contrast, observes that listeners are, rather, exceptionally talented at interpreting the phonetic signal produced by speakers, as evidenced by the fact that they are able to match in their own speech the very variation they perceive. Instead, certain sorts of sound change may be a consequence of listeners' sporadic misinterpretation of the *semantic* content that rides on the phonetic signal.

With this in mind, consider the findings of Öhman (1966) and Manuel (1990, 1999). These authors investigate patterns of coarticulation, with Öhman investigating cross-linguistic patterns of vowel-to-vowel coarticulation through intervening consonants (V̱C̱V̱), and Manuel investigating cross-linguistic patterns of vowel coarticulation due to consonantal context (C̱V̱C̱). Both find that different languages possess different patterns of coarticulation in these contexts, and further, that at least a certain amount of the observed language-to-language difference in coarticulation may be attributable to the language-particular system of contrastive values.

Öhman acoustically investigates V̱C̱V̱ coarticulation in Swedish, English, and Russian, emphasizing that Russian, unlike Swedish and English, has a series of palatalized consonants. This is a relevant fact in the context of the following observation: "[I]n Swedish and English, the stop consonants seem to coarticulate relatively freely with the vowels ... there are languages, such as Russian, in which the instructions for the stop consonants are made ... as in English or Swedish but with the additional feature that the vowel channel must simultaneously receive exactly one of two fixed commands [palatalization or velarization]" (1966:166).

The data discussed by Manuel (1990, 1999) and Manuel and Krakow (1984) are also consistent with the idea that coarticulation is influenced at least in part by the distribution of contrastive values in the phonetic space, and that it may be curtailed to the extent that it (at least sometimes) does not jeopardize these contrastive values. Manuel and Krakow find that there is a greater amount of vowel coarticulation in languages with smaller vowel systems, and a lesser amount of such coarticulation in languages with larger vowel systems. Thus, Shona and Swahili, with five-vowel systems, may display more vowel coarticulation than in a language like English: on the one hand, because the vowel inventories of Shona and Swahili are small, they can presumably tolerate larger ranges of production without running the risk of encroaching on each other's distinctive spaces. On the other hand, the vowels in English are more crowded in the articulatory/acoustic space, thus the range of production for each vowel should be rather small, so as to maintain distinctions among them.

These studies, along with quite a few others that investigate system-influenced patterns of conventionalized (co-)articulatory routines (among them Clumeck 1976, Beddor, Krakow, and Goldstein 1986, Recasens 1983, Recasens, Pallarès, and Fontdevila 1998, Beddor and Krakow 1999, and Beddor, Harnsberger and Lindemann 2002) are consistent with Labov's proposal that (1) variation in speech is conventionalized within speech communities, and that (2) coarticulation is limited in just those contexts where lexical contrasts would otherwise be jeopardized. It may thus indeed be the case that speech variation is conventionalized on a language-to-language basis in ways that bear the clear mark of lexical semantic pressure, and again, such findings are consistent with the proposal that certain so-called "low-level" or "phonetic" effects may in fact be the result of deep, systemic pressures many times removed from the physical systems that proximally underlie speech.

Consider also the results presented in Gahl (2008). Starting from the well-documented finding that frequency-of-word-usage inversely correlates with word duration, Gahl finds that "homophones" (either lexical or derived) are produced with different durations, depending largely on their frequency-of-use (the scare quotes around "homophones" are intended to raise the question whether we should indeed regard these as legitimate exemplars of the phenomenon). Thus, for example, "thyme" is longer than "time". Gahl convincingly argues that such frequency effects are inconsistent with standard generative proposals regarding lexical structure (for example, Newmeyer 2006), and are also inconsistent with proposals implicating the frequency of mere motor routines themselves (for example, Bybee 2001). Even taking into consideration the interesting finding that (Gahl 2008:487) "words shorten if they occur multiple times within a discourse" (for example, Fowler 1988), her findings indicate that "the effect of overall usage frequency on word duration is separate and distinguishable from the effect of repetition within a discourse; even the first time a word occurs in a conversation, its duration in part reflects its frequency" (Gahl 2008:487). Indeed, as I assert in my 2006 book, "*exactly because* certain words are frequently encountered in the speech stream, they are more *predictably* present. Because of their constant repetition and their consequent predictability, those particular spontaneous variants that are slightly simplified [or, *pace* Gahl's findings, slightly shortened] may yet effectively convey the intended meaning to listeners" (2006a:198).

In the next two chapters we continue our discussion of phonological RHYME and NEUTRALIZATION, first with an in-depth study of neutralization in Korean, and then moving on to consider the grammatical domains over which NEUTRALIZATION might hold sway.

DISCUSSION QUESTIONS AND FURTHER READING

(1) Read **Gallistel (1990)** (and references therein) on probability matching in many species of lower animals, among them, university students. Do you think it a legitimate hypothesis that such findings are relevant to linguistic behavior, and, by extension, linguistic structure, in particular, linguistic change? Consider other proposals for sound change, including those of **Chomsky and Halle (1968)**, **King (1969)**, **Kiparsky (1978)**, **van der Hulst (1980)** and **Bermúdez-Otero (2006)**. You might also investigate the volume edited by **Stockwell and Macauley (1972)**.

(2) Some generative theorists (the so-called "generative phoneticians") have proposed that there is a distinction between a phonetic component and a phonological component in the mental grammar, for example, **Keating (1985)**, **Zsiga (1997)**, and **Cohn (1993)**. This distinction hinges in part on a supposed difference in status between gradient and categorical implementation of contrastive values. Consider the findings of **Öhman (1966)** and **Manuel (1990, 1999)**, or for that matter, consider the existence of near-mergers and near-neutralizations. In light of these findings, how well do the assertions of the generative phoneticians hold up?

12   Case study

We have reached the point in our discussion of neutralization –
or, more to the point, NEUTRALIZATION; neutralization as derived
homophony – to test our predictions against a body of data. Recall
that NEUTRALIZATION involves limitations on the distribution of
phonetic information, limitations that possess genuinely function-
negative consequences. Assuming that language structure and language change are influenced by functional considerations, there
may exist passive diachronic pressures against the proliferation of
homophone-deriving alternations. Thus, recall from Chapter 1 my
overarching proposal: *alternations are more likely to be present in a language if they do not significantly increase the level of homophony; derived
homophony is not excessive.*

A particularly rigorous testing ground for these predictions would
involve a pattern or patterns of sound change that *do* significantly
increase the amount of (traditionally defined) neutralization. The
proposal would be that, in such cases, despite an overall decrease in
word-internal *phonetic* distinctions, evidence for *semantic* distinctions
emerges largely intact, as derived homophony remains negligible. In
this chapter then, we report on a single case study: neutralization in
Korean (Silverman 2010, Kaplan 2011a). Indeed, it emerges that despite
this language's huge amount of traditionally defined neutralizing
alternation, the amount of derived homophony resulting from such
alternations – that is, the amount of NEUTRALIZATION – is surprisingly
meager.

Indeed, Korean provides us with a textbook case of traditional
neutralization. For example, while the language possesses a three-
way laryngeal distinction among its prevocalic obstruents, (plain/
voiced, aspirated, tensed), all these distinctions are neutralized
towards their plain, unreleased (that is, aplosive) counterparts when
lexically non-prevocalic.

NEUTRALIZATION AND ANTI-HOMOPHONY IN KOREAN

Let's first recall Martinet's (1952) proposals regarding derived homophony. The tendency towards merger of an opposition is favored to the extent that:

(1) The values in opposition are phonetically similar
(2) The number of minimal morpheme pairs that the opposition is responsible for is low
(3) The number of minimal pairs within a correlated opposition is low (or the opposition is uncorrelated)
(4) The minimal pairs belong to different syntactic categories
(5) The lexical/token frequency of one or both members of the minimal pairs is low
(6) The presence of additional morphological markers serves a disambiguating function

Readers are encouraged to keep this list in mind as they read on.

Now, consider seven neutralizing patterns in Korean (as earlier presented in Martin 1992), to be defined and discussed momentarily:

(1) Aplosivization
(2) Nasal lateralization
(3) Liquid nasalization
(4) Nasal assimilation
(5) Coronal assibilation
(6) Cluster reinforcement
(7) Certain instances of variable assimilation

In the corpus study I undertook, I only investigated nouns (not verbs), since these nouns do indeed engage in neutralization at a rampant level of prevalence, whereas verbs (due to Korean's rich system of verbal suffixation) do not.

Overall (though not including potential variable cases for now), there are 42 homophonic sets out of 35,907 nouns, involving 86 words. In running Korean speech, out of 1,234,323 noun tokens encountered, chances are that about 7,671 will be homophonous. This, indeed, is a very low level of homophony.

Herein we focus especially on the case of aplosivization, and continue with a brief discussion of the additional patterns of neutralization. We follow this with a brief discussion of Kaplan's (2011a) far more sophisticated quantitative investigation of the pattern.

APLOSIVIZATION

As we know, laryngeal neutralization is quite prevalent among lexically non-prevocalic stops (∼[CV]), and virtually unattested among prevocalic ones (CV). This position of neutralization typically involves *the loss of stop release*, or *aplosivization*. While the phonetic origins of this asymmetry lay in aerodynamics acoustics, and audition, we forgo these details for now. The upshot, though, is that if a stop is not released into a more open gesture such as a vowel, it may lose the phonetic cues associated with this interval of the speech stream, among them, cues to the state of the larynx.

In Korean, two values (b pʰ) neutralize to the labial aplosive p̚, for example, pab̠-e ("rice, loc.") – pap̚ ("rice"), ipʰ-e ("leaf, loc.") – ip̚ ("leaf"). Seven values (d tʰ dʒ tʃʰ s h s') neutralize to the coronal aplosive t̚, for example, os̠-e ("clothes, loc.") – ot̚ ("clothes"), patʰ-e ("field, loc.") – pat̚ ("field"), nadʒ-e ("day, loc.") – nat̚ ("day, loc."), pitʃʰ-e ("light, loc.") – pit̚ ("light"). Three values (g kʰ k') neutralize to the dorsal aplosive k̚, for example, kug̠-e ("soup, loc.") – kuk̚ ("soup"), puəkʰ-e ("kitchen, loc.") – puək̚ ("kitchen"), pak'-e ("outside, loc.") – pak̚ ("outside"). Altogether, twelve values neutralize to three, which constitutes a remarkably high 75 percent reduction in the number of contrastive values here.

Among the 35,907 different nouns in the corpus I employed, 10,412 nouns possess aplosive alternants, which constitutes 29% of all nouns. Despite these large figures, the number of homophonic sets within the noun inventory turned out to be remarkably low: only 14 sets of nouns (30 nouns in all; less than 0.01%) may be rendered homophonous as a consequence of neutralizing aplosivization. Moreover, while the mean token count among nouns is 35, 8 of the 14 noun sets possess at least one member with a token count below ten. In all, out of 1,234,323 noun tokens the total number of homophones due to aplosivization is 3,894. For example, tʃip̚ may mean "house" (tʃib...) or "straw" (tʃipʰ...); tʃʌt̚ may mean "breast/milk" (tʃʌdʒ...) or "salted fish" (tʃʌs...); mat̚ may mean "taste" (mas...) or "nearby place" (matʰ...); pak̚ may mean "gourd" (pag...) or "exterior" (pak'...).

The results are very clear: (1) Korean aplosivization induces the neutralization of a remarkably high number of oppositions; (2) Korean aplosivization induces the NEUTRALIZATION of a remarkably low number of nouns.

So, how did it happen that so much neutralization developed in Korean with so few counter-functional consequences? Even casual readers of the current volume know where the proposed answer resides. These divergent results are, in fact, *intimately related*: the neutralization of so many values may be tolerated in Korean *exactly because* it has a negligible effect on the amount of derived homophony. Recall from Chapter 1: "The overarching proposal ... is that phonological RHYME may increase until encountering a counter-pressure that inhibits undue decreases in phonological REASON. More specifically, the inventory of motor routines that a language deploys is likely to be influenced by lexical semantic factors: coarticulation and assimilatory alternations may conceivably evolve rather freely, provided the transmission of *meaning* between speaker and listener is not adversely affected." How this came to pass in Korean requires an investigation of its history, especially in the context of its extensive contact with Middle Chinese. I turn to this issue now.

In its distant past – beginning at least 1,300 hundred years ago – Korean witnessed a massive influx of Chinese words, with the greatest amount of borrowing taking place about 1,000 to 600 years ago. This borrowing served to supplant a significant portion of its native vocabulary, particularly its noun inventory. During the era of borrowing, Chinese possessed a very limited set of consonants in root-final position: $p^\urcorner$, $t^\urcorner$, $k^\urcorner$, **m**, **n**, **ŋ**. The Korean of this era had these endings, but also possessed more complex root-final structures (termed "over-stuffed" by Martin 1992), among them **p^h, pt, pt^h, ps, pst, psk, pts, ts^h, t^h, sp, st, sn, sk, k^h, ks, lk, lp, lp^h, lm, nts, n^h**. Contemporary Korean root-final tensed values seem to be the subsequent reflexes of at least some of these previously complex root-final clusters. Moreover, by 400 years ago, non-prevocalic **s** (which was now an alternant of **ts, ts^h**, and **s**) had succumbed to aplosivization, neutralizing to $t^\urcorner$.

Significantly, the simplification of root-final obstruent values continues even into the present day. Whereas past neutralizing values have primarily been among *non*-prevocalic alternants, in present-day Korean there are additional neutralizations among lexical *pre*vocalic root-final values. Briefly, among roots that heretofore have contrasted **d t^h s dʒ tʃ^h** prevocalically, the distinction among these prevocalic root-final values appears to be breaking down. Simplifying somewhat, among the coronals, **s** is the favored variant; among the labials (**b, p^h**), **b** is the favored variant; among the dorsals (**g, k^h, k'**), **g** is the favored variant. Moreover, those coronal-final roots varying towards **s** tend to be low-frequency items. The upshot is that root-final obstruents are becoming increasingly subject to neutralization, both non-prevocalically *and* prevocalically.

In short, the inventory of root-final values in Korean seems to be in a rather constant – if slow-going – state of attrition. Aplosivization induces a significant decrease in the number of distinctions in non-prevocalic position, and variation towards frequent values is inducing such a decrease even prevocalically.

Now consider compounding. Korean has probably always possessed at least some compounding, but during the era of massive borrowing from Chinese (recall about 1,000–600 years ago), compounding in the noun vocabulary became one of the primary characteristics of the Korean lexicon. Sohn (1999) discusses three layers of Sino-Korean compound words. For our purposes, the first and third layers are the most important. The first layer consists of nouns borrowed directly from Chinese, consisting primarily of academic and scientific terms due to contact with the Chinese intelligentsia, for example tʃa-jʌn ("nature"), tʃil-mun ("question"), hakˀ-kʼjo ("school"), sɛŋ-mjʌŋ ("life"). The third layer consists of Sino-Korean compound nouns that were not directly borrowed from Chinese, but instead were coined in Korea. This third layer is a later development, perhaps best viewed as a result of "trickling down": as Sino-Korean vocabulary began to pervade the language of the elite, its patterns of word formation came to influence lower social strata, for example, tʃʌn-dapˀ ("rice field-dry field"; "paddies and dry fields"), tʃʰoŋ-kakˀ ("all-horn"; "bachelor"), il-gi ("day-energy"; "weather"), ʃig-u ("eating-mouth"; "family, members of a family").

Especially relevant for present purposes, the huge influx of Sino-Korean nouns was largely coincident with the onset of root-final consonant attrition. Although *coincident*, this development was, by hypothesis, not *coincidental*, for, as noted, the Chinese of the lending era possessed only pˀ, tˀ, kˀ, m, n, ŋ in root-final position. Consequently, the Sino-Korean vocabulary lacked the "overstuffed" root-endings found in Native Korean, and, especially relevant, also lacked the root-final *plosivization* distinctions, including laryngeal and fricative values. What seems to have happened is that this property came to influence Korean phonotactics at large: the slow-going attrition of the Korean system of root-final values was likely set in motion by the influx of Sino-Korean forms.

So, if the influx of Chinese compounds into Korean set in motion an attrition of root-final values, how did Korean avoid developing excessive homophony? The answer, of course, is inherent in the question itself: the attrition of root-final values was offset by the compounding nature of the Sino-Korean vocabulary. Two heads are better than one: compounding greatly increased the opportunity for nouns to contrast with each other. Any limitations on the number of contrasts imposed by the smaller inventory of root-final structures is offset by these roots' combining and recombining into new and varied compounds, which had always lacked these plosive distinctions in root-final position.

Non-prevocalic aplosivization is a natural phonetic development, since, as stated, without a vowel following, contrastive states of the glottis tend to be less saliently encoded in the speech signal. However, simply because a sound change is natural does not entail that it will be actuated every chance it gets. As noted by Martinet, functional factors may indeed play an intervening role. In the case of Korean at least, it is likely that aplosive stops became so pervasive only because communication was not adversely affected by the resultant neutralization: the number of values undergoing aplosivization increased exactly because of the compounding that was introduced by the Sino-Korean vocabulary, which offset any counter-functional developments.

Indeed, it is almost unimaginable that Korean would have tolerated the attrition of its root-final obstruent system had it resulted in extensive homophony/ambiguity of word meaning. Thus, Sino-Korean compounding may be seen as playing a dual role: first, it offset the potential homophony that aplosivization might have otherwise induced in the noun system, and second, due to this, it may have sped the attrition of root-final values, as there were now fewer functional pressures that would inhibit this development.

OTHER ALTERNATIONS

As already mentioned, components of the neutralizing aplosivization pattern seem to have been in place fairly early on in Korean, but it was likely due to Korean's extensive contact with Chinese that the pattern began to rapidly expand, coming to incorporate affricate- and fricative-final roots. This attrition seems to have indirectly led to the neutralization of certain non-prevocalic root-final values, though always with negligible counter-functional consequences.

In fact, the pattern of root-final neutralization did not stop there. In the centuries following the era of great borrowing, a number of additional neutralizing alternations entered the language, affecting both root-final and immediately following root-initial values (in the aforementioned compounds). So let's consider the more recent routes to neutralization and potential homophony in Korean, listed earlier: (2) nasal lateralization, (3) liquid nasalization, (4) nasal assimilation, (5) coronal assibilation, (6) cluster reinforcement, and (7) variable assimilation. None of these alternations induces a significant amount of homophony.

Table 12.1 provides intervocalic consonant values in Korean. The first column lists morpheme-final consonants; the first row lists following morpheme-initial consonants, and the table interior indicates the phonetic values of these morphologically ordered sequences (from Silverman 2010, adapted in turn from Martin 1992; see Kaplan 2011a for a better version of this chart).

Table 12.1 *Korean intervocalic consonant values*

+C→ C↓	b	pʰ	p'	d	tʰ	t'	s	s'	dʒ	tʃʰ	tʃ'	g	kʰ	k'	m	n	ɾ	h	∅
b	p'	pʰ	p'	pt'	ptʰ	pt'	ps'	ps'	ptʃ'	ptʃʰ	ptʃ'	k'	kʰ	k'	mː	mn	mn	pʰ	b
pʰ	p'	pʰ	p'	pt'	ptʰ	pt'	ps'	ps'	ptʃ'	ptʃʰ	ptʃ'	k'	kʰ	k'	mː	mn	mn	pʰ	pʰ
d	p'	pʰ	p'	t'	tʰ	t'	s'	s'	tʃ'	tʃʰ	tʃ'	k'	kʰ	k'	mː	lː	lː	tʰ	d
tʰ	p'	pʰ	p'	t'	tʰ	t'	s'	s'	tʃ'	tʃʰ	tʃ'	k'	kʰ	k'	mː	nː	nː	tʰ	tʰ
s	p'	pʰ	p'	t'	tʰ	t'	s'	s'	tʃ'	tʃʰ	tʃ'	k'	kʰ	k'	mː	nː	nː	s'	s
s'	p'	pʰ	p'	t'	tʰ	t'	s'	s'	tʃ'	tʃʰ	tʃ'	k'	kʰ	k'	mː	nː	nː	s'	ʃ'
dʒ	p'	pʰ	p'	t'	tʰ	t'	s'	s'	tʃ'	tʃʰ	tʃ'	k'	kʰ	k'	mː	nː	nː	tʃʰ	dʒ
tʃʰ	p'	pʰ	p'	t'	tʰ	t'	s'	s'	tʃ'	tʃʰ	tʃ'	k'	kʰ	k'	mː	nː	nː	tʰ	tʃʰ
g	kp'	kpʰ	kp'	kt'	ktʰ	kt'	ks'	ks'	ktʃ'	ktʃʰ	ktʃ'	k'	kʰ	k'	ŋm	ŋn	ŋn	kʰ	g
kʰ	kpʰ	kpʰ	kpʰ	kt'	ktʰ	kt'	ks'	ks'	ktʃ'	ktʃʰ	ktʃ'	k'	kʰ	k'	ŋm	ŋn	ŋn	kʰ	kʰ
k'	kp'	kpʰ	kp'	kt'	ktʰ	kt'	ks'	ks'	ktʃ'	ktʃʰ	ktʃ'	k'	kʰ	k'	ŋm	ŋn	ŋn	kʰ	k'
m	mb	mpʰ	mb	md	mtʰ	mt'	ms'	ms'	mtʃ'	mtʃʰ	mtʃ'	ŋk'	ŋkʰ	ŋk'	mː	mn	mn	mh	m
n	mb	mpʰ	mp'	nd	ntʰ	nt'	ns'	ns'	ntʃ'	ntʃʰ	ntʃ'	ŋk'	ŋkʰ	ŋk'	mː	nː	nː	nh	n
ŋ	ŋb	ŋpʰ	ŋp'	ŋg	ŋtʰ	ŋt'	ŋs'	ŋs'	ŋtʃ'	ŋtʃʰ	ŋtʃ'	ŋk'	ŋkʰ	ŋk'	ŋm	ŋn	ŋl	ŋh	ŋ
l	lb	lpʰ	lp'	ld	ltʰ	lt'	ls'	ls'	ltʃ'	ltʃʰ	ltʃ'	lg	lkʰ	lk'	lm	lː	lː	lh	l
∅	b	pʰ	p'	d	tʰ	t'	s'	s'	dʒ	tʃʰ	tʃ'	g	kʰ	k'	m	n	ɾ	∅	∅

Discounting root-final clusters for now, there are 304 possible morphologically ordered sequences here. Variable values are bold-boxed and shaded. Including these among the neutralized values for now, the 304 morphologically ordered sequences reduce to only 77 phonetic values. So let's consider in turn our list of additional neutralizing alternations.

(2) *Nasal lateralization.* Coronal nasals and laterals bear certain perceptual similarities since their formant transitions are rather comparable, and they both possess formants and anti-formants. In Korean, their perceptual confusability may have influenced the evolution of a neutralizing alternation: a sequence of a lateral or tap and a coronal nasal in either order is realized as a long lateral: n+ɾ, l+ɾ, l+n → lː, a process that entered the language about 400 years ago.

Out of 1,001 nouns in the corpus possessing lː, there are only ten homophonic sets. Eight of these sets possess at least one member with a token count under ten.

(3) *Liquid nasalization.* Another neutralizing alternation in Korean involves the nasalization of non-coronal obstruent–liquid (tap) sequences: p+ɾ → mn, p+ɾ → ŋn. As there is no phonetic motivation for the pattern, this alternation has the "feel" of being analogically derived from nasal assimilation (to be discussed presently). In all, there are only four homophonic sets of nouns, a total of 520 tokens out of 1,234,323 are homophonous, which verges on 0 percent of the total.

(4) *Nasal assimilation.* Korean has a process of nasal assimilation such that any obstruent that comes to precede a nasal becomes nasal itself. Due to this alternation, there are ten homophonic sets out of 2,293 neutralized nouns in the list of 35,907 nouns, 732 out of 1,234,323 tokens.

(5) *Coronal assibilation.* Coronal obstruents assibilate before s and s', resulting in (neutralized) s'. Out of the 35,907 nouns in the corpus, 131 words possess the relevant value. There is a total of one homophonic set as a result of this alternation, 14 tokens in all.

(6) *Cluster reinforcement.* When a non-aspirated obstruent comes to follow another obstruent, the second value tenses. This also is a neutralizing alternation. Still, though there are 4,048 nouns in the corpus that possess word-medial tensed obstruents, there is no derived homophony as a consequence of cluster reinforcement.

(7) *Variable assimilation.* In colloquial Korean speech, coronals (excluding the lateral) variably assimilate to a following consonant, and labials variably assimilate to a following dorsal. This assimilation process, unlike the others discussed herein, has the potential to induce a non-negligible amount of homophony. But this is a *variable* pattern of neutralization: sometimes neutralization occurs (more often in casual speech), and sometimes it doesn't (more often in formal speech). Jun (1995), for example, reports gestural reduction of labials (in **p+k** sequences) to occur about 35 percent of the time in casual speech, and about 15 percent of the time in formal speech. However, Jun finds that this variable pattern does not vary between discrete values **k:** versus **pk**. Rather the variation is gradient, such that tokens may, in theory, fall anywhere on the phonetic continuum between these two endpoints. This sort of variation sets up a situation in which near-neutralizations are practically inevitable. Indeed, among variable processes such as Korean coronal assimilation, it is quite possible that potentially homophonic forms in particular are more likely to maintain their distinctive status than are neutralized heterophones, at least in semantically ambiguous contexts. This, recall, is consistent with the findings of Charles-Luce (1993). The relevant investigation, alas, has yet to be undertaken.

In sum, in running Korean speech, out of 1,234,323 noun tokens encountered, chances are that about 8,384 will be homophonous. This is a very low level of homophony.

In her follow-up to my 2010 paper, Kaplan (2011a) undertakes a far more sophisticated quantitative investigation of homophony in Korean. Kaplan investigates eight (as opposed to my seven) neutralizing patterns. For each pattern, she investigated whether neutralization created fewer homophones than expected, by creating 1,000 "hypothetical" neutralizations that don't actually occur in Korean but are structurally similar to the actual patterns. In most cases, the actual pattern created fewer homophones than the hypothetical ones, and thus her results actually substantiate mine.

Goal-directed behavior, speaker intention, and teleology play no role here, nor anywhere else in phonology, for that matter. The present-day patterns of neutralization are simply the passive consequence of selectional pressures acting on the variation inherent in speech and language. Homophony was minimal at the outset, and, despite an ever-increasing amount of neutralization, has remained minimal to the present day.

CONCLUSION

Even when there is a natural phonetic tendency towards a particular phonetic state, say non-prevocalic aplosivization among obstruents, a given language will most likely *not* evolve towards that state if excessive homophony were to result, for the very speech tokens that are produced with homophone-inducing aplosives are also the very speech tokens that would likely confuse listeners. And so, as an automatic, natural, passive consequence, such tokens would not be reproduced as these listeners become speakers. Rather, in such a language, there is likely to be an unguided, natural, passive maintenance of contrast – either through the maintenance of plosivization or by some other means – for it is exactly those speech tokens that are communicated successfully to listeners that are more likely to take hold, and become conventionalized as the speech norm. Quite simply, successful speech variants, like successful mutations, are naturally selected.

And although triggered by our proposed anti-homophonic pressure, the modified motor routines that result may eventually routinize, and so a sound change that has semantic origins may eventually come to pervade the system.

By contrast, for a language like Korean, in which – due to the huge influence of Chinese – root-final distinctions are not especially dependent on plosivization, we see massive neutralization in root-final values both non-prevocalically, and even, increasingly, prevocalically. Since communication remains unencumbered, natural tendencies towards such simplifications encounter little resistance: phonological RHYME may increase until it encounters a passive counter-pressure ensuring phonological REASON. Recall: "It is not the desire to be understood, but rather the consequence of misunderstanding that influences language change" (Labov 1994:586).

Other patterns of alternation (nasal lateralization, liquid nasalization, nasal assimilation, coronal assibilation, and cluster reinforcement) – all of which seem to have entered Korean subsequent to the expansion of aplosivization – may also have been tolerated, and, indeed, sped along, exactly because the compounding introduced by Chinese offset any counter-functional consequences. Thus, all of these slow-acting developments on the sound pattern of Korean may be seen as responses – however indirect – to the contact Korean enjoyed all those centuries ago with its influential neighbor.

Like the flapping of a butterfly's wings in that very same land, the consequences of which have been jocularly implicated in the formation of tornadoes in the American heartland, the Chinese lexicon of a millennium ago may be seen as possessing a reach that continues to press – however passively – on the minds of Korean speakers, even to this very day.

DISCUSSION QUESTIONS AND FURTHER READING

(1) Opinions differ regarding the existence of an anti-homophonic pressure on phonological patterning. Among those favoring a role for this pressure are **Gilliéron (1910)**, **Bloomfield (1933)**, **Martinet (1952)**, **Hoenigswald (1960)**, **Hockett (1955, 1967)**, **Ichimura (2006)**, **Gahl (2008)**, **Blevins and Wedel (2009)**, **Mondon (2009)**, **Silverman (2010)**, and **Kaplan (2011a)**. Among the dissenters are **King (1967, 1969)**, and **Surendran and Niyogi (2003, 2006)**. Taking these differing approaches into consideration, what is your opinion on the matter? What sorts of studies should be undertaken (diachronic, corpus, experimental) that might shed further light on the issue?

(2) At the end of Chapter 8 I asked whether one or both of "ease of production" and/or "ease of perception" might be jettisoned as (an) explanatory factor(s) in the shaping and changing of phonological systems, especially with respect to patterns of neutralization. In light of subsequent discussion about NEUTRALIZATION in particular, has your opinion changed at all on this issue?

13 Domains of application

In Chapter 11 we considered in some detail the mechanism by which anti-homophony might act as a passive pressure on language change, discussing Labov's (1994) *semantic misperception* proposals (also, by the way, considered in Silverman 2000, 2004, 2006a, 2006b, Blevins and Wedel 2009, and Mondon 2009). Recall: NEUTRALIZATION may result in a semantically ambiguous speech signal. Those tokens of words that are not confusable with other words are more likely to be successfully recovered by listeners, hence are more likely to be produced as these listeners become speakers, and consequently are more likely to become the conventionalized speech norm. Recall further that, in such a scenario, there are no listener "guessing games" about speakers' phonetic intentions, no on-line monitoring of the semantic clarity of the signal, no role for teleological pressures on language structure, no need for features, segments, syllables, or underlying representations. Instead, due to passive diachronic pressures on language *use*, the system naturally settles towards a semantically unambiguous state, one involving low levels of homophony; low levels of NEUTRALIZATION.

In Chapter 12 we investigated alternation in Korean as a testing ground for the role of NEUTRALIZATION in language evolution. We found that, despite the fact that Korean possesses a huge amount of (traditional) neutralizing alternation, the amount of NEUTRALIZATION is remarkably low. The overarching proposal, then, was that increases in phonological RHYME may be tolerated to the extent that undue decreases in phonological REASON are avoided.

In Korean, the grammatical domain in which this proposed anti-homophonic pressure exerts its force is the phonology itself: the proposal was that *across-the-board* phonological alternations are more likely to enter the language when they do not result in significant increases in NEUTRALIZATION; alternations that *would* result in significant NEUTRALIZATION are more likely to be globally absent. But this isn't the only domain in which an anti-homophonic pressure might manifest itself. Consider, then, some of the domains that might bear the mark of a passive pressure towards homophone avoidance, each of which is discussed and exemplified in this, our penultimate chapter on phonological RHYME.

(1) Anti-homophony in the *lexical* domain: an otherwise pervasive phonological or morphological process is blocked in those cases where it would derive homophony between or among particular lexemes. We'll briefly consider a well-known example from French.

(2) Anti-homophony in the *morphological* domain: root homophony is indeed tolerated, but any counter-functional consequences are offset by a concomitant morphological response. The classic example here is coda attrition vis-à-vis compounding in Chinese.

(3) Anti-homophony in the *phonological* domain: neutralizing alternations are fully blocked from entering a language if they would induce significant increases in derived homophony. This is, by and large, the Korean case, of course.

(4) Anti-homophony in the *phonotactic* domain: neutralizing alternations that otherwise apply pervasively are blocked from applying in particular phonotactic contexts, because their application here would result in significant increases in derived homophony. This is the case of Hindi schwa retention as discussed in Chapter 11.

(5) Anti-homophony in the *paradigmatic* domain: neutralizing alternations that otherwise apply pervasively are blocked in those morphological paradigms where semantic ambiguity would otherwise result. Trigrad Bulgarian and Banoni will provide our examples here.

(6) Anti-homophony in the *pragmatic* domain: neutralizing alternations that otherwise apply pervasively are blocked "on line", due to situation-specific semantic or pragmatic factors. Charles-Luce's results from Catalan will be reiterated here.

Although I am shamelessly repeating myself, please do keep in mind that when I use the term "blocked", or any other comparable term, this usage should not be interpreted in any agentive, prophylactic, or teleological sense. Rather, it is due to strictly passive, evolutive, and self-organizing pressures that play themselves out over generations of language *use*, that NEUTRALIZATION tends towards curtailment. With this in mind, let's consider in a bit more detail these six domains of anti-homophony.

ANTI-HOMOPHONY IN THE LEXICAL *DOMAIN*

Reports of lexical anti-homophony are anecdotal by their nature, so let's consider just a few cases for now.

A marginal example is discussed by Ichimura (2006), who elaborates on a suggestion by Aronoff (1976) that a form like "stealer" ("one who steals") may be absent from the lexicon of English due to the presence of "thief". That is, a pervasive word-formation process is blocked in those cases where a synonym is already present in the lexicon. Ichimura asserts that a comparable lexicon-based pressure may serve to block the creation of homophones. For example, Clark and Clark (1979) observe that the denominals in "to *summer/autumn/winter* in France" are fine, but those in "to *fall/spring* in France" are not, presumably because "fall" and "spring" already exist as verbs. As I said, this is a marginal case, since, due to their zero-morphology, the derived homophones are actually lexical homophones as well. A more clear-cut example: Bloomfield reports that, in certain Southern French dialects, final **l** has merged with final **t**. For example, where Standard French has **bɛl** "pretty", this dialect has **bɛt**. Because of the sound change, the Standard Southern French word for "cock" ("chicken") (**gal**) is pronounced **gat**. However, these southern speakers don't use the word **gat** anymore. Instead, they use a variety of other local terms, including *vicaire*, and the word for "chick" (**pul** in Standard Southern French, but **put** here). Bloomfield presents the explanation suggested by **Gilliéron** (1910) for the lexical shift: if **gal** had been maintained, it would have been pronounced **gat**, which is also the word for "cat", both in the standard dialect, and in the rural dialect. Bloomfield (1933:398) writes that "This homonymy must have caused trouble in practical life; therefore **gat** was avoided and replaced by makeshift words." (While discussing this case in class one day, a student of mine wondered aloud how they say "Beauty and the Beast" in this region.)

As I said, cases of anti-homophony in the lexical domain are anecdotal by their nature. This is not to suggest that the phenomenon is not prevalent, though still, its rigorous documentation may prove elusive.

ANTI-HOMOPHONY IN THE MORPHOLOGICAL *DOMAIN*

According to most written evidence, Middle Chinese, unlike its modern counterparts, was predominantly a so-called monosyllabic language, one in which, recall, only consonants that possessed oral occlusions (pʰ tʰ kʰ m n ŋ) appeared in root-final position. Some contemporary dialects like Cantonese retain these six consonants, but others, such as Mandarin, have drastically reduced this set to only two members (n ŋ). The general tendency towards loss of final consonantal elements is well documented both in Chinese and else-where, and lends itself to well-understood phonetic pressures that may (or, of course, may not) come to hold sway. For Mandarin, this drastic loss of phonetic content resulted in a significant amount of root homophony: Cantonese has about 1,800 syllable shapes, but Mandarin has only about 1,300, with largely equivalent semantic reference. Still, while Mandarin was now bereft of options to scrounge for phono-logical solutions to its problem of root identity, lo and behold, its morphology came to the rescue: concomitant with the attrition of its root-final consonants, Mandarin – unlike Cantonese – co-evolved a huge inventory of two-root compounds, which means that its words are now usually two syllables in length, and so have ample opportunity to maintain distinctness amongst themselves.

ANTI-HOMOPHONY IN THE PHONOLOGICAL DOMAIN

As stated, this is our Korean case. Here, quite a few neutralizing alterna-tions were allowed a "free pass", because (by my hypothesis) there existed no anti-homophonic counter-pressure inhibiting their entrance into the system. Although the reasoning is rather indirect, alternations that *would* have function-negative consequences – in the form of produc-ing significant amounts of NEUTRALIZATION – may have been passively filtered out before ever having had a chance to get off the ground. The result in Korean, of course, is massive neutralization with minimal NEUTRALIZATION; a staving-off of counter-functional developments.

Actually, the Korean case is (inevitably, of course) more complicated. Recall that the neutralizing alternations in Korean seem to really have gone full throttle as Chinese-influenced phonotactics and root-compounding entered the language. Thus, whereas Mandarin conso-nant attrition and root compounding seemed to be co-evolutionary developments that fed off each other, culminating in genuine *lexical* homophony among roots, in Korean, a comparable compounding development was *not* accompanied by a proliferation of lexical homo-phones. Rather, compounding in Korean co-evolved with alternations that are neutralizing, though, crucially, rarely derive NEUTRALIZATION.

ANTI-HOMOPHONY IN THE PHONOTACTIC DOMAIN

Recall that Hindi has a pervasive schwa–zero alternation, though with patterned exceptions. Specifically, while schwa alternates with zero in would-be **VCəCV** contexts, it does not alternate in certain **VCCəCV** and **VCəCCV**; contexts, that is, when the alternation would result in three sequenced consonants, the middle of which would be perilously susceptible to misperception. That is, the loss of schwa in these contexts may lead to a percept involving only two – not three – consonants. At this point, the chances of inducing homophony increase dramatically.

Moreover, under even more particular phonotactic conditions – typically, when the schwa–zero alternation would result in a nasal-homorganic stop–sonorant sequence – the alternation is indeed observed, since the phonetic properties of these particular tri-consonantal sequences are readily recoverable from the speech signal, and hence run little risk of deriving homophonic forms.

This neutralizing alternation in Hindi is tolerated under certain phonotactic conditions, but not tolerated under others. Specifically, in phonotactic contexts where the alternation does not result in a significant increase in neutralization, it may freely apply. But in phonotactic contexts where the alternation would likely induce a significant amount of neutralization, it does not apply. Now, of course, we have not yet numerically investigated the amount of derived homophony in either context (the actual case, and the would-be case), and so, for now, our proposal that neutralizing alternation in Hindi is sensitive to the amount of resultant homophony is simply our working hypothesis.

ANTI-HOMOPHONY IN THE PARADIGMATIC *DOMAIN*

As discussed by Crosswhite (1997) and Mondon (2009), Trigrad Bulgarian has a vowel alternation whereby **o** lowers to **a** under stresslessness, for example, ˈr**o̱g** "horn", ˈr**o̱g**-ave "horns", r**a̱g**-aˈve-te "the horns". Since, of course, the language possesses non-alternating **a** as well, this is a neutralizing alternation.

Inflectional suffixes engage in a phonetically comparable form of allomorphy, though with a telling class of exceptions. So, for example, we observe ˈkl**ɔ̱b**-a "ball of thread" and ˈr**e̱br**-a "rib" (with the lowered allomorph), but, in a large group of neuter nouns, we observe ˈz**ɔ̱rn**-o "grain, seed", ˈpetal-o̱ "horseshoe" (*without* the lowered allomorph). Both Crosswhite and Mondon propose the following: were **a** to be employed here, the singular forms would be rendered homophonous with their plural counterparts, since the nominative plural marker is *always* **a** in neuter nouns. As Mondon (2009:6) writes, "to prevent singular–plural homophony, vowel reduction does not apply to these forms", thus, ˈzɔrn-o (sg.) – ˈzɔrn-a (pl.), ˈpetal-o (sg.) – ˈpetal-a (pl.).

Crosswhite proposes an optimality-theoretic anti-homophonic constraint to characterize the pattern, while Mondon's approach is much closer in spirit to the proposals advanced herein: also inspired by Labov's pioneering theorizing in this area, Mondon proposes that slow-going usage-based pressures resulted in the system's passive evolution towards a state in which inflectional semantic clarity is maintained.

Now consider another example. As discussed by both Mondon (2009) and Blevins and Wedel (2009), the Austronesian language of Banoni has a lexical vowel length distinction that has evolved due in part to the diachronic loss of singleton consonants between identical vowels. The loss of these consonants has resulted in certain words being minimally distinguished by the consequent vowel length contrast, for example, **vom** "turtle" versus **voːm** "new". Interestingly despite the language's earlier evolution *towards* a vowel length distinction, more recently, it has been undergoing a change *away* from the contrast: the vowel length contrast seems to be collapsing, though, as in Trigrad Bulgarian, with some telling exceptions. In Banoni, possessed nouns are marked *solely* by vowel length, and are resisting the length merger. Thus **tama** "father" – **tamaː** "my father", **kasi** "brother" – **kasiː** "my brother". As earlier reported by Lincoln (1976:58), "Banoni speakers tend to shorten long vowels, except when necessary for disambiguation."

The patterns in Trigrad Bulgarian and Banoni are examples of anti-homophony in the *paradigmatic* domain: certain grammatical paradigms are apparently susceptible to a passive, usage-based anti-homophonic pressure, such that inflectional semantic content is communicated intact to listeners, even at the expense of phonological or phonotactic regularity.

ANTI-HOMOPHONY IN THE PRAGMATIC DOMAIN

Recall from Chapter 6 the results of Charles-Luce (1993:29), who found that, in Catalan, "[T]he perception and production of spoken words is affected differentially by the presence and absence of higher levels of linguistic information and … the degree of precision of articulation is inversely proportional to the presence of semantic information." Further recall her finding that a Catalan voicing alternation is more likely to be nearly-neutralized (as opposed to completely neutralized) in contexts that would otherwise be semantically ambiguous, concluding that "[T]here may be some on-line assessment by the speaker as to the degree of biasing information present [that] may be quite automatic and learned through experience ... " (p. 41). Further recall that, despite appearances to the contrary, there is really no need to assume a goal-directed pressure acting on language users in these semantically ambiguous contexts. Rather, this behavior on the part of speakers may be yet another example of probability matching: in contexts where a completely neutralized token might result in confusing homophony, speakers dip into their pool of tokens encountered in comparable listening situations. As a mere by-product of their randomly sampling the tokens in this pool, the probability is high that this token is merely nearly-neutralized, as opposed to completely neutralized.

DISCUSSION

At this point, the stubborn and skeptical reader (and I hope that includes you) might ask the following: If language is structured so as to avoid semantic ambiguity (in the form of anti-homophony, among other pressures), then why should systems *ever* put themselves at risk, only to "seek out" a response that countervails the ensuing threat?

As superficially vexing as this question may seem, it stems from a misunderstanding of the proposals I have been making. First and foremost, language is *not* inexorably destined towards any particular end-state, functionally efficacious or otherwise. Rather, just as in the evolution of ecosystems (of which a phonological system may certainly be seen as a metaphorical example), there is a plethora of pressures, some working in harmony, others in a state of antagonism, that are all subject to any number of contingent factors. Yes, there may be a slow-going diachronic tendency towards a lack of acoustic clarity among neighboring speech motor routines, resulting in coarticulation that, left unchecked, might further evolve towards a genuinely assimilatory state, oftentimes resulting in neutralization. But along with such slow-going *phonetic* pressures on language structure, there are also slow-going *semantic* pressures: any passive pressure towards an increase in phonological RHYME will ultimately encounter a counter-pressure that inhibits undue decreases in phonological REASON. These pressures are "end-state-blind": one pressure will not be inhibited because it "knows" that it might someday culminate in a counter-functional linguistic state. Rather, quite simply, it is solely a function of language *use* – an inevitable outcome of ever-present pressures on the interlocutionary act – that languages settle towards a semantically unambiguous state.

Another question that might arise: If anti-homophony really *is* a driving (though passive) pressure on language structure and language change, then why don't we see evidence of its power all over the place?

Well, I believe we *do* see evidence for an anti-homophonic pressure on linguistic structure, "all over the place", even. Quite simply, if coarticulatory and assimilatory tendencies were left wholly unchecked, languages would indeed evolve towards a state in which distinctions among the motor routines put in service to speech would diminish towards the vanishing point. The fact that speech motor routines typically maintain their distinctive status is likely due to two pressures.

First, inertia. Language would not be worth the air that carries it were it not successful in its communicative function. This requires that languages be sufficiently stable in their structural properties so that, quite simply, speaker and listener know what they are saying to each other. A major mechanism by which linguistic stability is largely maintained has already been discussed: probability matching. Interlocutors are exceptionally adept at *matching* their speech patterns to each other. By and large, they accurately perceive and accurately produce the very variation that is inherent to speech production, this variation thus being uniquely conventionalized in any given speech community.

Still, there is an inherent counter-pressure to this overwhelmingly powerful inertial force. Just as in genuine natural selection, it is the very variation inherent to the system that provides the fodder for change: speech variation is indeed copied very accurately and hence conventionalized in the speech community, but crucially, copying isn't *perfect*. This is the source of our semantic counter-pressure. Speech tokens that induce semantic confusion – as when one word ends up sounding too similar to another word – are less likely to become the conventionalized norm. Successful speech propagates; unsuccessful speech does not. Confusing speech tokens may be misunderstood, and thus not pooled with the exemplars of the intended word, and so the system maintains its state of semantic clarity. Anti-homophony is thus not an *active* pressure for which there is an abundance of overt evidence. Rather, it is a *passive* result of the pressures that inherently act upon the interlocutionary process. And though, pointing to an *absence* as evidence is much less compelling than pointing a *presence*, still, the very fact that language is not chock full of homophones provides evidence – however indirect – that anti-homophony is indeed a genuine pressure acting on language structure and language change.

DISCUSSION QUESTIONS AND FURTHER READING

(1) Consider the differing accounts of anti-homophony in Trigrad Bulgarian proposed by **Crosswhite (1997)** and **Mondon (2009)**. In your opinion, which provides the more explanatorily compelling account of the phonological patterns under investigation? Additional insights may be gained by reading the proposals of **Itô and Mester (2004)**, **Kenstowicz (2005)**, and **Gessner and Hansson (2004)**.

(2) I have proposed that that the *semantic misperception* approach to NEUTRALIZATION involves "no need for features, segments, syllables, or underlying representations". Regarding the necessity or superfluousness of (distinctive) features, consider the fine and relevant papers in the **Clements and Ridouane (2011)** volume. These are by (a) **Cohn (2011)**, (b) **Serniclaes (2011)**, and finally (c) **Lindblom, Diehl, Park, and Salvi (2011)**. Regarding segmentation, consider **Twaddell (1935)**, **Jones (1950)**, **Linell (1982)**, **Faber (1992)**, **Derwing (1992)**, **Read, Zhang, Nie, and Ding (1997)**, **Ladefoged (2005)**, **Port and Leary (2005)**, **Port (2006)**, **Silverman (2006a)**, and **Lodge (2009)**. Regarding syllables, consider again the work of **Vennemann (1988)**, **Kahn (1976)**, **Bell and Hooper (1978)**, **Ito (1989)**, **Blevins (1995)**, **Goldsmith (2011)**, **Szigetvari (2011)**, and papers in the **Féry and Van de Vijver (2003)** volume on syllables in optimality theory. Compare these to **Steriade (2008)**, which assumes the irrelevance of syllables. Consider also the relevance of "lexically prevocalic" and "lexically non-prevocalic" contexts.

14 "Distinctions are drawn that matter"

In Chapter 12 we explored in detail a single case study, testing the overarching proposal advanced herein: a language is more likely to tolerate neutralizing alternations if the product of these processes does not unduly increase semantic ambiguity in the speech signal, in the form of deriving excessive homophony, excessive NEUTRALIZATION. In Chapter 13, we considered the domains over which an anti-homophonic pressure on language change might exert its force. In this final chapter of Part I, RHYME, we focus on the potential functional consequences of speech variation itself. We consider several unusual cases of alternation that reinforce the proposal that variation in speech – even phonetically unnatural variation – may naturally evolve in a language, provided the *phonetic* distinctions have immaterial consequences for *semantic* distinctions.

Instead, as we'll see, "distinctions are drawn that matter"; we'll unpack this somewhat opaque Wittgenstein-esque aphorism by exploring three cases in detail. We first we consider a peculiar case of phonetic variation that was purportedly present in the history of Austronesian (Blevins 2004). We move on to consider the s-to-h change in Eastern Andalusian Spanish (Gerfen 2001). Finally, we discuss a very perplexing pattern of genuinely neutralizing variation in Pirahã (Everett 2008).

AUSTRONESIAN

Consider a superficially curious pattern found in a number of Austronesian languages (Blust 1990, Blevins 2004): historic **t** has evolved into modern **k**. This is an unusual sound change, because the phonetic distinction between **t** and **k** is quite robust, whereas most diachronic neighbors tend to be phonetically similar. The issue, then, is how and why **t** and **k** presumably entered into a relationship of variation that culminated in the observed sound change. The answers, I propose, may be found in the title of this chapter: "distinctions are drawn that matter".

Blevins makes two important observations about the **t**-to-**k** change: (1) it was non-neutralizing, since **k** had already moved (or was in the process of moving) towards **ʔ**; and (2) the languages undergoing this change had small consonant inventories. Now, why are these two observations important to our understanding the **t**-to-**k** change?

In languages that possess a full array of stop place distinctions – canonically, **p t k** – not only are these values robustly distinct in terms of their phonetic properties, but also, they are robustly distinct in terms of their functional properties, in the sense of typically being responsible for a non-trivial number of minimal pairs. Consequently, in a comparatively crowded phonetic space such as this, there is likely to be a passive curtailment of variation, for if one value strays too close to another, there is a risk of inducing semantic confusion among listeners. More specifically, if a certain number of words are minimally distinct along the very dimension on which variation is observed, then, if this variation proceeds uncurtailed, it is likely to induce homophony, hence, on occasion, listener confusion. Instead, since semantically ambiguous speech signals are less likely to be reproduced and conventionalized than are semantically unambiguous ones, then, as a natural consequence, the very sorts of variation that might induce such confusion may be passively curtailed. The result is a system with well-separated values in the phonetic *and* functional spaces. Thus, in a system with a full **p t k** array – and with these three values crucially responsible for a significant number of minimal pairs – there is likely to be a passive curtailment of phonetic variation here, such that the three values maintain functionally efficacious phonetic buffer regions amongst themselves.

But now consider the Austronesian systems under scrutiny. Recall: (1) the change was non-neutralizing, since **k** had already moved (or was in the process of moving) to **ʔ**; and (2) the languages undergoing this change had small consonant inventories. These two seemingly disparate facts are, in fact, intimately related. It is exactly because the oral stop inventory consisted of only two members – **p t** – that variation of **t** towards **k** was less likely to be curtailed, since there were no functional pressures acting against such variation.

Now, despite their functional non-distinctness in the languages at hand, recall that **t** and **k** are indeed quite distinct in terms of their phonetic properties. So what might prompt their interaction? Blevins considers certain acoustic properties that isolate the non-labial consonants as a distinct class from labials: non-labials possess longer VOTs and higher burst frequencies than do labials. And given their functional non-distinctness, listeners might naturally attend to the very phonetic properties that properly delineate – or rather, correspond to – the distinctions that *are* functionally relevant, that is, the cues that distinguish labials and non-labials. The result is that some productions of the non-labial stop may be alveolar, but others, on occasion, may be dorsal. A sound change is thus set in motion. Here, raw phonetic similarity – it is uncontroversial to assert that labials and dorsals bear a closer phonetic relationship than do alveolars and dorsals – is insufficient to prompt the alveolars to be perceived as non-distinct from the dorsals. Rather, listeners' language-specific experience clearly prompts the functional override of their phonetic dissimilarity.

Further, it may be *exactly because* the systems in question possessed impoverished consonant inventories that phonetically distinct values could enter into a pattern of mutual variation. Recall, "distinctions are drawn that matter"; if a system possesses a limited number of contrasts along a certain phonetic dimension (say, within their stop consonant systems), there exist few passive pressures against variation here, exactly what Blevins reports in the history of Austronesian.

EASTERN ANDALUSIAN SPANISH

Gerfen (2001) discusses a sound change – rather pervasive across the Spanish-speaking world, actually – in which s is becoming h in an expanding number of contexts. Simplifying, in Eastern Andalusian Spanish (henceforth Andalusian), historic s has become h both word-finally, and, under certain conditions, word-internally as well (accompanied by post-h consonant gemination). For example, historic **ganas** has become Andalusian **ganah** ("desire"), **boske** has become **bohkːe** ("forest"), **eslaβo** has become **ehlːaβo** ("Slavic"). It is the "certain conditions" that we especially focus on herein.

But before doing so, let's consider the word-final context. It is not especially surprising that word-final s should evolve towards h. In running speech, such *word*-final articulatory events will, on occasion, be *utterance*-final as well. Now, utterance-final position is one of the very few contexts in which the otherwise salient cues to the voiceless alveolar fricative – most perspicuously, high-frequency noise – may be jeopardized. This is due to the simple fact that, in utterance-final position, oral airflow often weakens. In the absence of a strong upstream air source, particle excitation at the relevant obstruction sites (the alveolar ridge and the upper teeth) diminishes, perhaps ultimately culminating in a loss of the high-frequency energy that is characteristic of **s**. The result, of course, may be an **h**-like percept. So, first off, we can understand how **s** may evolve towards **h** utterance-finally. This then establishes the presence of an **h–s** alternation: in the relevant words, we find word-final **h** utterance-finally, whereas we find word-final **s** utterance-internally.

Before moving on, notice that the variation inherent in speech that presumably led to the conditioned alternation came at no functional cost: since Andalusian had lacked lexical non-prevocalic **h** at the time the **h–s** alternation entered the language, **h** and **s** were never responsible for minimal pairs, and thus the newly introduced alternation could never induce NEUTRALIZATION. Thus, not only was there an absence of a counter-pressure inhibiting any variation towards utterance-final **h**, but there was also an absence of a functional pressure to inhibit the sound change's expansion into additional contexts.

So, into what contexts might **s**-to-**h** change expand? Well, once certain words engaged in a word-final **h–s** alternation, the pattern may readily generalize towards **h** in *all* word-final contexts, even when not utterance final. Furthermore, concomitant with the progress of this change are the seeds of an additional generalization, one based on raw phonotactics: since word-final **s** is increasingly headed towards **h**, and this **h** is typically followed by a (word-initial) consonant, the pattern may generalize to include comparable word-internal phonotactic contexts: the emerging generalization is that we end up finding **h** – and decreasingly finding **s** – when this value is lexically non-prevocalic. This is the pattern found in Andalusian today.

Gerfen remarks that there is little *phonetic* motivation for an **s**-to-**h** change in word-internal contexts in particular, because, unlike most consonants, **s** does not rely on its context for the salient expression of its cues. Rather, **s** possesses salient "internal" cues that should not be subject to loss, regardless of its context (except, perhaps utterance-finally, as I have suggested herein). Based on this very correct observation, he crucially implicates the role of syllable structure in his account of the Andalusian pattern: quite simply, **s** goes to **h** in syllable coda position.

The alternative I have just proposed, of course, makes no reference to syllable structure at all. Instead, a sound change that has its origins in phonetic naturalness – that of **s**-to-**h** in utterance-final position, may sow the seeds for its own expansion into contexts that are not necessarily phonetically natural, but nonetheless are phonotactically analogous, first at the post-lexical level (that is, word-final **h** is typically followed by a word-initial consonant), and eventually at the lexical level as well (that is, **h** – and, decreasingly, **s** – is found in lexical non-prevocalic positions everywhere). The leniting sound change was tolerated, and able to expand into analogous phonotactic – though phonetically "unnatural" – contexts, exactly because this expansion never encountered a functional counter-pressure: s-to-h was non-neutralizing, and hence by logical necessity, was non-NEUTRALIZING as well.

"Distinctions are drawn that matter": it matters not a whit that **s** changed to **h** in Andalusian, since the phonetic distinction between the two was functionally irrelevant; there were – and there remain – no functional pressures passively militating against the change's pervasion across the lexical phonotactic domain.

PIRAHÃ

The cases of Austronesian and Andalusian involve variation that could never induce semantic confusion on the part of listeners, since variation along the relevant phonetic dimensions – **t** to **k**, **s** to **h** – were non-neutralizing: since s–h and t–k did not contrast, their variation could never induce NEUTRALIZATION. Consequently, the cases of Austronesian and Andalusian may indeed exemplify a pattern of variation with an absence of neutralization (hence, by logical necessity, a trivial absence of NEUTRALIZATION), but do not really exemplify what we're looking for, that is, a system possessing neutralizing variation with a *non-trivial* absence of NEUTRALIZATION. Such a system would involve phonetic variation such that (1) one contrastive value varies with others, and (2) this variation results in neutralization, but results in only a negligible amount of semantic ambiguity in the speech signal; an increase in RHYME without a decrease in REASON.

The Amazonian isolate Pirahã may present exactly such a scenario. We turn to this case now.

Everett (2008:181) relates some of his many remarkable experiences while doing his field studies of Pirahã. I provide here his most relevant vignette:

I sat one day with Kóxoi at the table under my thatched roof in order to learn more about the sound structure of Pirahã words. Keren appeared with a cup of coffee. She gestured at Kóxoi to see if he would also like a cup. Kóxoi smiled and said, "*Tí píai*," which I immediately guessed to mean "Me too." To check this out, I organized a few elicitation sentences to confirm my hunch, acting out and saying, "Kóxoi drinks coffee, Dan *píai*," "Kaixoi drinks coffee, me *píai*," and so on.

I recorded examples and isolated the phrases for *me too*, *you too*, *her too*, and so on.
    Then I asked Kóxoi to repeat them to me so that I could verify their
    pronunciation.
What he gave me was surprising and confusing.
He repeated, "*Tí píai*."
I repeated.
He said, "Right, *kí píai*."
"What did you say?" I asked with frustration and surprise. Why was he changing
    the pronunciation? Was there a more simple expression than I had thought?
"*Kí kíai*," he repeated.
    . . .
"*Kí kíai*?" I asked.
"That's right, *pí píai*" came the exasperating answer.
In other repetitions, Kóxoi then gave additional pronunciations ([. . .] the
    x represents the glottal stop of Pirahã): "*xí píai*," "*xí xíai*."

What had Everett observed here? Well, the first point to emphasize is
that the Pirahã segment inventory – even more so than Austronesian's –
is remarkably impoverished: three vowels and seven consonants for
women; three vowels and eight consonants for men. Instead, tone,
length, and overall word length distinctions bear the functional brunt
here. Thus, given that other sub-systems – tone, vowel length, and
overall word length – bear so much of the functional burden, little
"work" remains for the impoverished consonantal system. Consequently, the functional load of any given consonantal contrast is likely
to be quite low. The idea, then, is that since certain sub-systems bear
a heavy functional burden, other sub-systems may concomitantly be
relieved of this burden. In Pirahã, as we have just noted, it is the
suprasegmental system that bears the brunt of this burden, and so
the segmental system is comparatively free to wander about the phonetic space with, apparently, few function-negative consequences.

With this is mind, let's now consider the variation that Everett
documents. Recall that contrastive consonantal values seem to freely
switch out with no loss of semantic content, at least among certain
words and/or in certain grammatical or real-world contexts. This phenomenon is quite different from that observed in Austronesian and
Andalusian, since the values that are varying in Pirahã are not merely
phonetically distinct, but are *phonologically* distinct as well. That the
language tolerates this variation strongly suggests that the pattern
does not induce semantic confusion for listeners by producing homophones; by hypothesis (or, according to the unsympathetic reader, by
circular reasoning), the language would not tolerate it otherwise!
Thus, the observed phonetic variation in Pirahã is both neutralizing,
and, at least in theory, may be NEUTRALIZING as well; that is, it has the
potential to create homophones. Yet, as noted, it is exactly because the

consonant system bears such a low functional burden – and is likely to be responsible for so few minimal distinctions – that switching out one consonant for another yields so few function-negative consequences. Distinctions are drawn that matter; in Pirahã, consonantal differences, quite simply, don't matter that much.

To set these observations in high relief, consider that Pirahã supra-segments matter a great deal. How do we know this? Everett observes that there exists a number of "channels" in Pirahã – *whistle speech* while men are hunting, *hum speech* in certain intimate situations, and *yell speech* during which vocalism may solely involve **a** – each of which retains suprasegmental values, though forfeits some or all segmental ones. Now, it is apparently *not* the case that these channels may be freely employed in all contexts. Rather, their use is circumscribed such that in particular social contexts, a particular channel may be employed. Everett notes, for example, that the whistle speech employed while hunting is less likely to scare off prey, since the low frequencies – intimating "bigness" – are missing, hence deceptively cueing an absence of danger. It is also likely that hunting groups rely on a fairly limited inventory of rote or at least transparent phrases, in a fairly closed system. Consequently, it is exactly because speech is *situationally* circumscribed that its users are able to eliminate so much of its *phonetic* content with no loss of *semantic* content. Indeed, Everett's interaction with Kóxoi may perhaps be described similarly: in the particular context or situation, the semantic correlates of the forms being investigated were likely to be wholly unambiguous, since, at least from Kóxoi's vantage point, the "answers" to Everett's questions were so patently obvious: distinctions are drawn that matter. Dan Everett tells me that this consonant switch-out is, in fact, observed in any and all situations; not terribly surprising, given the low functional load of Pirahã's consonantism.

Now, while we may marvel at Pirahã's various "channels", in actu-ality, the presence of whistled, hummed, and yelled speech in Pirahã is no more remarkable – and no more exotic – than is something as mundane as whispered speech in English. Whereas we may wonder how in the world these whistle, hum, and yell channels came about in Pirahã, we would certainly find it odd were a Pirahã linguist to marvel at our whispered channel, wondering how we can possibly make ourselves understood without pitch contours; indeed, we might even regard such a reaction as rather "exotic". In the English language, of course, the suprasegments do little work, the functional brunt being bequeathed to the "segmentation". Interestingly, Everett reports that Pirahã is never whispered, since this channel would eliminate pitch distinctions from the speech signal; tone clearly bears a heavy functional load in Pirahã.

Let's briefly consider a comparable case to the "channels" employed in Pirahã, spoken closer to home. My middle brother and I often speak a "secret language" (though really, it's not so secret; I disclose all herein) that I call *rhotto voce*. In *rhotto voce* all vowels are completely rhotacized, while consonants remain unchanged. We New York natives devised this joke language in our childhood, as an absurd extension of the Brooklyn dialects that rhotacize the vowels in words like "oil" (ɹɫ) and "toilet" (tʰɹli?) as a presumed hyper-correction of dialect-specific forms like tʰʌɪɾi- tʰʌɪd ("thirty-third"): ɹt ɹz ɹɹlɹ ɹzɹ tɹ bɹθ spɹk ɹnd ɹndɹstɹnd ɹɹtɹ vɹtʃɹ…ɹʌɹ ɹaɪ ɪ ɹɪ ɹaɹoɹɪ ɛɹ ɹu ɹɪ ɹi ɹʌɹiɹi ɹɔɹ ("It is really easy to both speak and understand *rhotto voce*…but try it with consonants and you will be completely lost"). Clearly, in English the vowels are doing far less work than the consonants are doing, and so *rhotto voce* is a completely plausible distortion of the canonical system.

When I emailed the preceding paragraph to my brother, he wrote back, "*Herler smerks! Derdernt rerlerz er wers berern ser serpherstercerterd ernd scherlerler. Thert er wers jerst ferlern erernd…*"

CONCLUSION

So, "distinctions are drawn that matter": patterns of both variation and alternation may be subject to slow-going and attritive listener-based tendencies – assimilatory or otherwise, many of which may indeed be neutralizing in character – until encountering a completely passive, usage-based counter-pressure that serves to maintain lexical semantic clarity. In other words, phonological RHYME may proceed until adversely affecting phonological REASON.

This, then, concludes Part I, RHYME. We have observed, described, and explained neutralization from many different theoretical vantage points. In Part II, REASON, we come to our most surprising conclusion: far from *decreasing* the semantic clarity of the speech signal, neutralization, instead, is shown to actually *increase* phonological REASON. Thus, we conclude once again that the only function-negative consequence of neutralization occurs in those rare, passively curtailed circumstances when it derives homophony, that is, NEUTRALIZATION. Otherwise though, (traditional) neutralization is not merely function-neutral, but is, rather, function-positive; a "force for good" (if you will).

DISCUSSION QUESTIONS AND FURTHER READING

(1) Consider again the listener-based approaches of **Lindblom (1990)**, **Jun (1995, 2004, 2010)**, **Steriade (2008)**, **Ohala (1981, 1989, 1990, 1992, 1993b)**, **Martinet (1952)**, and **Labov (1994)**. In light of the phonetic variation discussed in this chapter, which of these proposals are more adept at handling these cases, and which proposals less so?

(2) In Chapter 1 I proposed that the inventory of contrastive values in phonology consists of those components of morphemes that alternate, those that don't, and nothing else. In light of subsequent discussion, what would the consequent inventory of contrastive values look like? What problems do you foresee in this approach to phonological inventories? What advantages? To investigate this question, it might be best to consider some particular language(s) in relative detail. Consider also relevant discussion by **Swadesh (1934)**, **Chomsky and Halle (1968)**, **Drescher (2011)**, and papers in the **Lombardi (2001)** volume, which will certainly place the current proposal into high (or low?) relief.

PART II
Reason

PART II

15   Cement

"A sound complex cannot be considered a mechanical juxtaposition of a certain quantity of independent sounds. When combining with one another, sounds – we have in mind here not only their acoustic, but also their physiological aspect – accommodate themselves to one another. This accommodation is the *cement* which transforms several sounds into one integral complex" (Kruszewski 1883:25). This is the first mention of "cement" in Kruszewski's dissertation of 1883. It also serves as fine jumping-off point for our discussion of neutralization and phonological REASON.

As I understand Kruszewski's writing – and I think I do, because his prose is exceedingly clear (at least as translated from the Russian by Gregory M. Aramian) – the basic idea of his "cement" is this: due to the constant repetition of speech motor routines – and the especially frequent repetition of *word-internal* speech motor routines – morphemes within words come to phonetically "accommodate" to one another such that there come to exist phonetic cues to word boundaries. In more modern parlance, word-internal assimilations tend to result in suspension of contrast within some lexical domain, the functional consequences of which may serve as an aid in parsing: the less-frequent phonetic patterns *across* word-boundaries are thus set in high phonetic relief against the suspended background. The result of these word-internal contrast suspensions – these increases in phonological RHYME – may thus be a concomitant increase in phonological REASON: less common phonetic patterns may come to cue word boundaries.

Kruszewski (1883) cultivates these ideas to fruition in his Chapter 7, which is thus the most appropriate chapter of his remarkable study to discuss in relative detail herein: "In any word we can find the cement which binds the individual morphological units into one whole; these are – figuratively speaking – the negligible phonetic concessions which the morphological unit makes to its neighbor" (p. 86). In keeping with his strict non-teleological orientation, Kruszewski states emphatically that such "accommodating" (assimilatory) tendencies do *not* have their origin in functional (parsing) pressures on language evolution, but instead, are simply natural phonetic consequences of the continual repetition of word-internal speech motor routines. Whatever functional value such "cement" might eventually come to possess (in the form of a parsing aid) is merely an emergent and fortuitous consequence of this natural phonetic tendency; in modern evolutionary-biological parlance, an exaptation.

Kruszewski's first illustrative example, not too surprisingly, comes from (Turkic) vowel harmony: "[V]owel harmony plays the role of this cement; only vowel harmony unites the individual and otherwise phonetically fixed morphological units of the . . . [Turkic] . . . word into one whole" (1883:86). Thus, again, the main point is this: word boundaries may be cued due to a word-internal span of speech over which certain contrasts are suspended.

Now, a by-product of this natural – though decidedly passive – tendency for words to accrete cement is the emergence of allomorphy: as morphemes become increasingly cemented to one another due to natural phonetic tendencies, and as this cement tends to take on functional relevance by serving as a cue to word boundaries, the inevitable result is that individual morphemes take on different phonetic configurations, depending, of course, on the phonetic contexts in which they find themselves. Such word-internal cementing thus acts on language structure to inevitably stymie the "ideal" linguistic state, one, according to Kruszewski, in which there would be a perfect one-to-one match-up between sound and meaning. "Thus, *phonetic changes provide the stimulus for a new distribution of sounds among the morphological units of a word*, i.e., they bring about a *morphological process by which a certain morphological unit degenerates into several varieties distinguished from one another by sounds but having the same function*" (1883:121).

These different degrees of imperfection – manifested as different patterns of allomorphy – are thus both a cause and a consequence of continual changes to the linguistic system: "The varieties of a given morphological unit which differ very little can, with time, develop into units which are much more different from one another, while the function which they must fulfill remains the same" (1883:119).

An additional by-product of these inherent states of imbalance (due to these passively derived increases in both phonological RHYME and phonological REASON) is a blurring of morpheme boundaries (which, importantly, does not entail a blurring of semantic function).

In sum, it is the very tug-of-war among pressures on language structure that induces flux. The passive pressure towards a one-to-one pairing of sound and meaning inherently conflicts with the passive pressure towards increased integration of morphological units. The emergent result is that lexical and morphological structure is in part cued by the very product of this conflict: morphological units are "cemented" together into words.

CONCLUSION

Despite a dearth of relevant exemplification, Kruszewski's ideas on the matter of "cement" are clearly explicated: word-internal alternations tend to be assimilatory in nature, because of the frequency with which word-internal speech motor routines are implemented. Such assimilations have no goal in and of themselves; they are merely an emergent by-product of the rote nature of muscle activities. Such assimilative alternations tend to blur any supposed boundaries between neighboring sounds, and between neighboring morphemes. This blurring may be functionally harnessed to act as "cement", acting to bond together word-internal phonetic material, and thus serving as a cue to the absence of a word boundary. Unbonded morpheme sequences – those at word boundaries – may thus serve as an aid in parsing.

In short, Kruszewski proposals are fully consistent with the proposal that increases in phonological RHYME (the product of his cement) oftentimes correlate positively with increases in phonological REASON (the *by*-product of his cement).

In the next three chapters, we explore, in turn, subsequent – twentieth- and twenty-first-century – proposals concerning the inherent relationship between phonological RHYME and phonological REASON, considering, in turn, Trubetzkoy's boundary signals (Chapter 16), Firth's prosodies (Chapter 17), and Saffran's more recent experimental work on the functional relevance of transitional probabilities (Chapter 18).

DISCUSSION QUESTIONS AND FURTHER READING

(1) In this especially brief chapter we have only scratched the surface of Kruszewski's remarkable scholarship. Readers are strongly encouraged to seek out both **Kruszewski** (**1881**; his master's thesis) and **Kruszewski** (**1883**; his dissertation), and lavish upon them the studied attention they so richly merit. Additional works (in English) that focus on Kruszewski's scholarship include Browne's translation of **Baudouin de Courtenay** (**1888–1889**), **Koerner** (**1986**), reworked as **Koerner** (**1995**; the

introduction to the Kruszewski volume), **Adamska-Sałaciak (1996)**, **Radwańska Williams (1996, 2002, 2006)**, and **Silverman (2012a, 2012b)**. Koerner and Silverman in particular (Silverman being me) place Kruszewski's ideas in the context of subsequent linguistic theorizing, Koerner emphasizing scholarship up to the mid twentieth century, Silverman beyond. Consider the prescience of Kruszewski's scholarship specifically with respect to our current focus, that is, neutralization. To what extent do you think that Kruszewski's insights have been taken up by subsequent scholars? How might we employ modern investigative techniques – experimental, corpus-based, etc. – to explore Kruszewski's claims regarding the functional value of "cement"? You might peek ahead to Chapter 18 for some relevant discussion.

(2) The so-called "Kazan School" consisted of a small coterie of linguists working in provincial Kazan, Tatarstan, in the latter years of the nineteenth century, and more or less overseen by Jan Baudouin de Courtenay (though Baudouin himself apparently scoffed at the notion that any such "school" existed). Kazan linguists were some of the first to take seriously the proposal that linguistics in general (and phonology and morphology in particular) must be seen as the intersection of the physiological and the psychological – "anthropophonics" and "psychophonetics" – and placed a special emphasis on the importance of alternations. In addition to the **Koerner (1995)** volume, which collects Kruszewski's major works in English translation, there is also a Stankiewicz-edited collection of works by Baudouin that has been translated into English **(Baudouin 1972)**. The Kazan School has, overall, received short shrift by both linguistic historiographers and linguistic theoreticians. Consider in particular the discussion (or sometimes, mere mention) of Kazan linguists in **Ivić (1965)**, **Leroy (1967)**, **Robins (1967)**, **Fischer-Jørgensen (1975)**, and **Anderson (1985)**.

16   Boundary signals

We've now clearly established that both static and dynamic neutra-lization increase RHYME in phonology by limiting the inventory of phonetic distinctions within words and morphemes. Dynamic neutral-ization may also synchronically shrink the number of phonetic distinc-tions among words and morphemes in particular contexts, in the form of homophone-inducing alternations, or NEUTRALIZATION. At this level of analysis, only homophone-inducing alternations are genuinely function-negative; static suspension of contrast and non-homophone-inducing alternations being heterophone-maintaining, and thus function-neutral.

Nonetheless – and as already preliminarily considered in the con-text of Kruszewski's "cement" – in their role as what Trubetzkoy (1939) calls "boundary signals", the increases in phonological RHYME brought about by neutralization can and do increase phonological REASON as well, by playing a demarcative or syntagmatic role in terms of cueing word or morpheme boundaries. As Trubetzkoy notes: "In addition to the phonological means serving to distinguish individual units of meaning (sememes), each language has a number of means that effect the delimitation of such individual units of meaning ... [E]ach language possesses specific, phonological means that signal the presence or absence of a sentence, word, or mor-pheme boundary at a specific point in the sound continuum" (p. 273). Trubetzkoy continues with a helpful analogy to boundary signals: "They can probably be compared to traffic signals ... It is possible to get along without them: one need only be more careful and more attentive. They therefore are found not on every street corner but only on some. Similarly, linguistic delimitative elements generally do not occur in all positions concerned but are found only now and then. The difference lies only in the fact that traffic signals are always present at 'particularly dangerous' crossings, whereas the distribution of linguistic delimitative elements in most languages seems to be quite accidental. This is probably due to the fact that traffic is artificially and rationally regulated, while language shapes and develops organically" (p. 274).

Thus, whereas both static and dynamic neutralization are function-neutral or, rarely, function-negative at the paradigmatic level, increasing RHYME while, under rare circumstances, decreasing REASON in phonology, many instances of neutralization are indeed functionally efficacious at the syntagmatic level, increasing both RHYME and REASON in phonology.

In all, Trubetzkoy taxonomizes boundary signals by noting that: (1) they may be contrast-expressing or contrast-suspending; (2) they may be positive or negative; (3) they may be phonemic or non-phonemic; (4) they may be individual signals or group signals. Also, (5) they may be between-unit or within-unit. Discussion of these bifurcations follows.

"CONTRAST-EXPRESSING" VERSUS "CONTRAST-SUSPENDING" BOUNDARY SIGNALS

As we'll see, it is not the case that all boundary signals involve a contrast suspension and/or neutralizing alternation. Many such signals, in fact, crucially rely on the *expression* of contrast – rather than its suspension – in order to serve their demarcative function. Nonetheless every role for a contrast-expressing boundary signal implies a role for contrast suspension as well, since it is exactly because a contrast is *suspended* in one context that a contrast-*expressing* boundary signal serves its function.

Let's start with a schematic example to see how this works. Let's consider a language very much like Babelese, which, recall has three vowels (i u a), and six consonants (p t k m n ŋ). Further recall that Babelese roots possess a maximum of two vowels, and also a maximum of two root-internal consonants in sequence. Root shape is thus maximally CVCCVC. Let's now suppose that there are no positions in this language which in contrast is suspended. That is, any vowel may be found in any "V position" within the word, and any consonant may be found in any "C position" within the word. This being the case, there are no values or sequences in pseudo-Babelese that may function as boundary signals, because any consonantal value or sequence at a non-boundary (VC̲V, VCC̲V) may also be found at a boundary (VC+V, V+C̲V, C̲+C, VC̲#V, V#C̲V, C̲#C). That is, the phonological syntagmatic structure is completely uninformative with respect to the semantic syntagmatic structure.

Let's now compare pseudo-Babelese to "real" Babelese. Recall that the lexical system of consonantal oppositions is different before a vowel (__V) versus before a consonant (__C): all six values may be found in prevocalic position (**CV**), but only the nasals may be found in pre-consonantal position (**NC**). That is, consonantal contrasts are partially suspended when a consonant immediately follows within the word. Due exactly to this contrast suspension, certain consonantal sequences now function as boundary signals. Specifically, any consonantal sequence in which the first consonant is not a nasal serves to cue a word boundary.

It is hardly surprising that no real language possesses the pseudo-Babelese pattern in that it wholly lacks boundary signals. (Even in the absence of segmental boundary signals, some form of stress, pitch-accent, or tone would likely come to the rescue, serving as a cue to word boundaries.) Rather, all languages possess some variant of "real" Babelese, in which contrast expression and contrast suspension crucially interact such that boundaries are often signaled.

Now let's consider a straightforward real-world case. As we now know, in many languages certain boundary-straddling contexts possess a larger inventory of contrastive values than that found in non-boundary-straddling contexts. In such cases, the values that are found at boundaries but not in other positions serve as boundary signals: their presence plays a demarcative role by indicating a morpheme, a word, or perhaps a sentence boundary. For example, in Barra Gaelic contrastively aspirated occlusives are found only in word-initial position, and contrastive long vowels, central vowels, and nasalized vowels are found only in word-initial syllables. These are contrast-expressing boundary signals, rather than a contrast-suspending ones, though, again, it must be emphasized that their role as contrast-expressing boundary signals is a consequence of contrast suspension in other positions.

"POSITIVE" VERSUS "NEGATIVE" BOUNDARY SIGNALS

It is further the case that so-called "positive boundary signals" (signals that cue a boundary) are "joined at the hip" to a negative counterpart (signals that cue the absence of a boundary, or "negative boundary signals"): for every boundary signal a language possesses, it necessarily possesses its opposite (though not equal). Given certain phonetic cues that signal a boundary, then the absence of those very cues may serve to signal a non-boundary. Similarly, given certain phonetic cues that signal a non-boundary, the absence of those cues may signal a boundary. The relationship between such "positive" and "negative" boundary signals is not necessarily fully equal-and-opposite. Their inequalities will become clearer as we discuss an example.

In our Barra Gaelic case, the aspirated occlusives, the long vowels, the central vowels, and the nasalized vowels serve to cue a boundary. These contrastive values thus function as "positive boundary signals". Meanwhile, their absence may serve as a "negative boundary signal". That is, when any of these values is encountered in its position of relevance, a word boundary is necessarily present, but in their positions of neutralization (where none of these values is present) a boundary *may* be absent. Extending his traffic analogy, Trubetzkoy (1939:290) likens negative boundary signals to "green lights that indicate to a traveler that all is well at the particular crossing and that he may proceed safely".

"PHONEMIC" VERSUS "NON-PHONEMIC" BOUNDARY SIGNALS

Our Barra Gaelic case is an example of a "phonemic boundary signal", because certain values are contrastive with other values only at a boundary and, as such, serve to signal that boundary. We may further consider what Trubetzkoy calls "non-phonemic boundary signals". Tamil, for example, possesses a distribution involving voiceless aspirates in word-initial position (a positive boundary signal), and spirants in word-medial position (a negative boundary signal). The voiceless aspirates are "non-phonemic positive boundary signals" because they are mere positional variants of the spirants. That is, they are not in contrast with the spirants in the boundary position, but rather, they earn their boundary-signal status by being a boundary-position variant of these spirants. Meanwhile, we may regard the spirants as "non-phonemic negative boundary signals" because they are non-contrastive variants that cue the absence of a boundary. In such cases of non-phonemic boundary signals, both the positive boundary signal and the negative boundary signal are equally reliable in serving their function.

Another example: in Japanese g occurs only word-initially, and ŋ occurs only intervocalically (word-medially). Since the two are not responsible for minimal pairs, we are dealing not with a phonemic boundary signal, but rather with a non-phonemic one, quite comparable to our Tamil example. Such cases can be multiplied any number of times: elements in complementary distribution, one of which is conditioned by proximity to a boundary, always serve this demarcative function.

Note that in cases of non-phonemic boundary signaling, we are not dealing with neutralization at all. As such, non-phonemic boundary signals do not fall strictly within the purview of our current concerns.

"INDIVIDUAL" VERSUS "GROUP" BOUNDARY SIGNALS

We've thus far concerned ourselves with boundary signals involving the span of one phonetic segment. Another bifurcation in boundary signal typology involves such "individual signals" versus "group signals", which are boundary signals involving a span of more than one segment. As we'll soon see, "group signals", too, may be taxonomically bifurcated: certain of these group signals – especially "within-unit signals" as opposed to "between-unit signals" – are especially relevant in the context of contrast suspension. (Trubetzkoy does not make the "within-unit" – "between-unit" group boundary signal distinction, but it turns out to be quite a useful distinction to consider.)

"Phonemic group boundary signals" are sequences that are peculiar to boundaries. Trubetzkoy (1939:280) discusses the sort for which "[t]he first part ... belongs to the end of the preceding unit of meaning, the second to the beginning of the following unit". (This is what we're calling a "between-unit" type.) For example, in German, he reports that a consonant+**h** sequence necessarily straddles a word boundary. Additional examples from German include **nm mch mtz nb np ng nf nw pw pfw fw**, etc.

An example of a "non-phonemic group boundary signal", according to Trubetzkoy, is the vowel–lateral–vowel sequence in English. When a word boundary precedes the lateral, it is **l** ("clear 'l'"), as in "we learn" **wi lə:n**; when a word boundary follows the lateral it is **ł** ("dark 'l'"), as in "we'll earn" **wił ə:n**: in such vowel–lateral–vowel sequences, the non-contrastive clear–dark distinction signals the location of the word boundary.

Another example comes from Russian. The distinction between palatal and velar **k** is non-contrastive: the palatal variant is found before **e** and **i**: ḳi, ḳe, for example, ḳeta ("a Siberian type of fish"), ḳizbi ("would become sour"). However, this distribution is only observed within words. Between words, the velar variant is found, and it is, rather, the vowel that shifts back: **k#ʌ, k#ɯ**, for example, **k#ʌtomu** ("to this"), **k#ɯzbam** ("to the huts"). As Trubetzkoy (1939:284) writes: "The sequences **kʌ, kɯ** are ... group boundary signals that indicate the presence of a word boundary between the phoneme **k** and the following vowel phonemes."

Consider an example of a "contrast-expressing individual phonemic negative boundary signal": in Finnish, the phonemes **d** and **ŋ** belong to this category, since they are only found word- or morpheme-medially. A "contrast-expressing group phonemic negative boundary signal" is found in Finnish as well: "Finnish does not permit any consonant combinations initially and finally. Furthermore, only vowels, and consonants **n, t,** and **s** occur in final position" (Trubetzkoy 1939:291). Consequently, when any of these consonants is not the first member in a consonant cluster, the sequence serves as a group phonemic negative boundary signal, for example, **kahdeksan** ("eight"), **hupsu** ("stupid"), **selkæ** ("back"). Here, the clusters **ks, ps,** and **lk** provide a "green light": the same morphological unit continues.

"BETWEEN-UNIT" VERSUS "WITHIN-UNIT" BOUNDARY SIGNALS

Russian has a palatal element that is contrastive on all consonants (a distinct element from the **ķ** just considered). Trubetzkoy (1939:284): "Before **e** only palatalized consonants are permitted within a morpheme in Russian. The correlation of palatalization is thus neutralized in this position. However, if a morpheme boundary occurs before the the **e** the preceding consonant can also remain unpalatalized. For example: **s+et͡ɪm** ('with this'), **iz+təvə** ('from this'), **v+ɛtəm** ('in this'), **pad+et͡ɪm** ('under this'), **at+ɛtəvə** ('from/of this'). The absence of a palatalization before the phoneme **e** is a non-phonemic group signal for a morpheme boundary." But remember that positive boundary signals are "joined at the hip" to negative boundary signals: the presence of a palatalization before the phoneme **e** is a "non-phonemic group signal" indicating the absence of a morpheme boundary; a "within-unit non-phonemic group negative boundary signal". Got that? If you do, I'm impressed!

The idea here is that in morpheme-internal position, the correlated opposition between palatalized and non-palatalized consonants is suspended when **e** follows. In this particular case, the contrast suspension cues the absence of a boundary in the form of a within-unit non-phonemic group negative boundary signal. That is, a within-unit sound sequence that involves a contrast suspension serves to cue the absence of a boundary.

In other cases, the suspension of contrast within words and morphemes may also serve as a positive boundary signal. Some of the most compelling examples of this effect involve vowel harmony, as also noted by Kruszewski. We turn to such cases now.

In Igbo vowel height harmony (often regarded as ATR harmony), all the vowels within a word agree with respect to their open or close status. Consequently, when vowels in neighboring syllables differ with respect to whether they are open or close, a word boundary is cued. The overall generalization in Igbo (and in countless other cases) is that a contrast is suspended across a span such that, in the speech stream, when a change of status is introduced along the suspended dimension, a boundary is signaled. (Note that, also, the maintenance of vowel height is a negative boundary signal, but not a completely reliable one, since adjacent words may agree in height.) Trubetzkoy wisely refrains from specifying the Igbo case as either a group signal or a non-group signal: while more than one phonetic segment of the speech stream is involved in the close–open contrast, the contrast itself does not pattern paradigmatically at the segmental level. Rather, either the close–open contrast is suspended towards "close" within the word, or the close–open contrast is suspended towards "open" within the word; such spans of specification cannot be localized to one or another segment, but rather are features of larger domains, here, the word.

Vowel harmony is a case *par excellence* of a pattern that at once increases both RHYME *and* REASON in phonology. RHYME is enhanced due to the increase in phonetic similarity among morphemes that is induced by the harmonic feature, but also, REASON is enhanced due to the boundary-signaling function that the harmonic feature serves.

Finnish presents us with a comparable pattern, as it possesses a front–back harmony that takes the word as its domain of expression, thus inducing suffix alternation. When the speech stream contains a shift in vowel backness, a word boundary is cued, for example, **hyvæ poika** ("good boy"), **iso pyssy** ("big can"). Again, although a number of phonetic segments are involved in the contrast suspension here, the relevant feature does not pattern paradigmatically at the segmental level, and thus the suspended feature cannot be called non-group signal (see Chapter 2 of my 2006 book for a full discussion of this aspect of the sort of pattern exemplified by Finnish).

In Tamil, a limited form of vowel harmony raises mid vowels to high when a high front vowel follows within the word. Consequently, when a mid vowel appears before a high front vowel, a word boundary is cued.

The pervasive "synharmonism" in Turkic languages such as Volga, Tatar, Bashkir, Kazakh-Kirghiz, and the Kipchak dialects of Uzbek provides our final (and very clear) case: "[S]ynharmonism consists in that each word in the particular language can contain either only front vowels and palatalized consonants or only back vowels and velarized consonants. Since such synharmonism is only effective within the frame of a word, the sequence 'palatalized consonant or front vowel + velarized consonant or back vowel' and 'velarized consonant and back vowel + palatalized consonant or front vowel' are a sign of the presence of a word boundary between the two constituents of that sequence" (Trubetzkoy 1939:285).

DISCUSSION

In sum, boundary signals may be:

(1) contrast-expressing or contrast-suspending
(2) positive or negative
(3) phonemic or non-phonemic
(4) individual or group
(5) between-unit or within-unit

While neutralization is not, at the conceptual level, an inherent component of a theory of boundary signals, nonetheless, for all practical purposes, one cannot speak of boundary signals without referring to the role of neutralization. All boundary signals are either contrast-expressing or contrast-suspending. Still, for every boundary signal that involves contrast expression, there is a role for contrast suspension as well: when certain contrastive values cue boundaries, it follows that the suspension of these contrastive values may serve as negative boundary signals. For that matter, the presence of contrast-expressing phonemic negative boundary signals implies the functional relevance of contrast-suspending positive boundary signals. Word-final devoicing patterns are excellent examples of this effect. Here, the presence of a voiced value cues the absence of a word-final boundary, and so the absence of a voiced value may serve to cue a word-final boundary, though not in every case. In such systems, voiced values are always "contrast-expressing phonemic individual negative boundary signals".

CONCLUSION

Boundary signals in the form of contrast suspension thus increase RHYME in phonology by limiting the amount of paradigmatic commutation among lexical forms. Nonetheless, they increase REASON in phonology by serving a demarcative syntagmatic function.

In the next chapter we further investigate boundary signals in the context of J. R. Firth and the London School's "prosodic analysis" approach to phonology. In particular, prosodic analysis provides a principled reason for Trubetzkoy's understandable reluctance to label certain cases of vowel harmony either "group" or "individual" in type. As we'll see shortly, within the prosodic school, no such bifurcation is relevant.

DISCUSSION QUESTIONS AND FURTHER READING

(1) Regarding boundary signals, recall that Trubetzkoy writes: "the distribution of linguistic delimitative elements in most languages seems to be quite accidental". We can perhaps phrase this another way: there are no functional pressures that favor the diachronic development of boundary signals. But consider the alternative: perhaps there *are* functional pressures that favor the diachronic development of boundary signals. What sorts of linguistic studies (synchronic, diachronic, corpus-based, experimental, etc.) might be undertaken to investigate this proposal?

(2) Having now considered a few approaches to the function-positive role of neutralization, it is probably time we considered some non-functional characterizations of syntagmatic redundancy within lexical forms. Among these are the aforementioned generative proposals regarding morpheme structure constraints and syntagmatic redundancy rules (for example, **Halle 1959, Stanley 1967**). But perhaps the most intimately related generative sub-theory is that of underspecification. Consider the literature on underspecification, including **Kenstowicz and Kisseberth (1977), Kiparsky (1982, 1985), Mester and Itô (1989), Itô, Mester, and Padgett (1995)**, and **Steriade (1995)**. The underlying assumption of most of these authors seems to be that supposedly underspecified content is not linguistically relevant, but is instead informationally redundant. In light of Trubetzkoy's work on boundary signals, do you think this assumption can be challenged?

17 Prosodies

As Firth does not cite Trubetzkoy's discussion of boundary signals in his 1948 "program paper" on "prosodies" (though he is clearly aware of Trubetzkoy's writings, mentioning them in passing), we may assume he felt his approach to be sufficiently different from Trubetzkoy's that no citation was necessary (in his 1957a paper on prosodies, Robins, however, does indeed refer to Trubetzkoy's pioneering work, as well as to the American construct, "juncture phoneme"). Indeed, Firth's "prosodic analysis" approach is more ambitious than Trubetzkoy's discussion of boundary signals, in that: (1) it calls for a strictly non-segmental approach to the elements that function as boundary signals, and in so doing lays out a game plan for phonological analysis that radically departs from the phonemic analyses earlier employed by Trubetzkoy and concurrently being advanced in a particularly rigid manner by American structuralists; and (2) it argues for the prosodic relevance of components that, in fact, do *not* function as boundary signals (though, as we'll see, in such cases, the notion of "prosody" gets a bit murky at times). In other ways, Firth's presentation is less ambitious than Trubetzkoy's, at least in the sense that its discussion of the supposedly relevant phenomena is at best scattershot and, at worst downright confusing, whereas Trubetzkoy's prodigious organizational skills were operating at their typical full capacity in his remarks on boundary signals.

As Firth's paper is difficult to interpret, what I hope to accomplish in this chapter is to extract what, for our purposes, are its most relevant aspects. For those familiar with the so-called London School that Firth spearheaded, it will become immediately clear that I am sometimes pruning – perhaps censoring – certain elements of the approach. At times, this censorship is employed in order to stay focused on the elements of prosodic analysis that are most relevant to our present concerns: neutralization and its role with respect to phonological REASON. At other times, this censorship is employed in a (perhaps ill-advised and surely risky) attempt to increase the overall coherence of the theory, by ridding it of what might be extraneous elements; from "pruning", to "censorship" to possible "misrepresentation" – wish me luck!

It might be best to begin with a direct quote: "The phonological structure of the sentence and the words which comprise it are to be expressed as a plurality of systems of interrelated phonematic and prosodic categories. Such systems and categories are not necessarily linear and certainly cannot bear direct relations to successive fractions of segments of the time-track of instances of speech. By their very nature they are abstractions from such time-track items. Their order and interrelations are not chronological" (Firth 1948:151).

Crucial to prosodic analysis is the proposal that phonological structure is *polysystemic*: the contrastive values in one context are functionally distinct from the contrastive values in other contexts, regardless of any phonetic similarities among them. Crudely speaking, there is no inherent link among phonetically comparable elements as they are distributed in the speech stream. Thus, for example, a value (of any shape or size) **a** in context **x** should not automatically be treated as non-distinct from a phonetically comparable **a** in context **y**. Notice the strictly functional orientation of this proposal: elements' linguistic relevance is solely a consequence of the role they play within the confines of their (sub-)system. Thus, if **a**, **b**, and **c** function contrastively in context **x**, and **a**, **d**, and **e** function contrastively in context **y**, there is no inherent link between the two systems, and thus viewing the two **a**s as necessarily phonologically non-distinct is unmotivated. Such an approach is clearly a call-to-arms against the strict *monosystemicity* embraced by Bloomfield and the American structuralists: "There is a tendency to use one magic phoneme principle within a monosystemic hypothesis. I am suggesting alternatives to such 'monophysite' doctrine" (Firth 1948:130).

The primary distinction Firth attends to is that between "sounds" and "prosodies". Sounds (or "phonematic units") are components of phonological structure that do not play a syntagmatic role. Sounds occur in "phonematic systems", and possess solely paradigmatic functional relevance, manifested by "sound substitutions", that is, commutation. Employing the cover terms **C** and **V**, a phonematic system of sounds may occupy a **C** or **V** position and, as such, sounds function contrastively, but impart no syntagmatic information (apart from their being limited to either a **C** position or a **V** position). *Prosodies*, by contrast, are exactly those elements that *do* impart syntagmatic information. This is not to say that some phonetic value cannot be both a sound *and* a prosody in the same language. In such cases, instances of this value are still regarded as phonologically distinct from each other in contexts where they play distinct – paradigmatic or syntagmatic – roles; recall the *polysystemic* nature of prosodic analysis.

The syntagmatic orientation of prosodic analysis is another difference between Firth's ideas and Bloomfield's: American structuralists' strict proscription against "mixing of levels" – that is, its disallowing phonological structure to reference morphological, syntactic, or semantic structure – is quite distinct from Firth's embrace of just such a cross-referencing approach to linguistic structure.

In many ways, prosodies are comparable to both Kruszewski's cement and Trubetzkoy's boundary signals, though, as already noted, Trubetzkoy in particular adheres to a segmental (or segment-sequential) notion of boundary signals, whereas Firth's prosodies are not comparably limited in shape: "Looking at language material from a syntagmatic point of view, any phonetic features characteristic of and peculiar to [particular] positions or junctions can just as profitably and perhaps more profitably be stated as prosodies . . . " (Firth 1948:130). Employing conventional terminology for the moment, a prosody may consist of a "segment"-sized element, a "sub-segment"-sized element, or a "supra-segment"-sized element. But it's misleading to relate prosodies (or sounds) to segments at all, as the prosody–sound distinction is based solely on whether the (sub-)system plays a syntagmatic or paradigmatic role; stated simply, *if a value is predictable with respect to its distribution in some domain, it qualifies as a prosody; if a value is not predictable with respect to its distribution in some domain, it is a sound*. And though Firth does indeed talk in terms of consonants and vowels, it is clear from his exposition that these are mere terminological expedients.

Robins (1957a) makes a partially successful attempt to elucidate the sound–prosody distinction:

> Phonematic units refer to those features or aspects of the phonic material which are best regarded as referable to minimal segments, having serial order in relation to each other in structures. In the most general terms such units constitute the consonant and vowel elements or C and V units of a phonological structure. Structures are not, however, completely stated in these terms; a great part, sometimes the greater part, of the phonic material is referable to prosodies, which are, by definition, of more than one segment in scope or domain of relevance, and may in fact belong to structures of any length . . . A structure will thus be stated as a syntagmatic entity comprising phonematic or segmental units and one or more prosodies belonging to the structure as a whole.

Recall from Chapter 2 that Robins emphasizes that the phonetic exponence of prosodies need not pervade their domain of association: as already noted, a prosody may be "segmental", "sub-segmental", or "supra-segmental" in its phonetic exponence, its status as a prosody being a consequence of its predictable distribution within some domain:

> Broadly speaking [prosodies] come about in two ways. (1) In the first case a feature may be spread or realized phonetically over a structure, such as a syllable, as a whole ... (2) In the second case may be mentioned features which are not realized phonetically over the whole or large part of a structure, but which nevertheless serve to delimit it, wholly or partly, from preceding and following structures, thus entering into syntagmatic relations with what goes before or after in the stream of speech. By virtue of their syntagmatic relations in structures, such features may be treated as prosodies of the structures they help to mark or delimit ... (1957a:193 indices added)

Notice Robins' use of the passive voice when mentioning the "spread" of features: unlike segmental approaches to phonology, "spread" prosodies are not regarded as derived structures; "be spread" here is thus employed by Robins as an adjectival passive, not a verbal passive.

It should be emphasized that, at a conceptual level of analysis, sounds and prosodies never overlap, in the sense that they are categorially distinct: sounds participate in paradigmatic systems (contrastive in phonematic contexts), and prosodies participate in syntagmatic systems (predictably distributed in some domain). At a more prosaic level of analysis however, they may appear to be in just such a state of overlap. Thus for example, recall from our discussion of Trubetzkoy's boundary signals that in Barra Gaelic, aspirates are found in word-initial position only. In many approaches, we can say that p^h t^h k^h contrast, or perhaps say that p^h t^h k^h contrast in word-initial position. In a prosodic analysis however, ^{h} is to be treated as a prosody of the word: if a word possesses ^{h}, it is found at the release of an initial voiceless stop. The prosody, though prosaically overlapping (in the relevant sense) with the sounds in the paradigmatic system, belongs to a completely separate functional system, the syntagmatic one. Moreover, the symbols themselves (p, t, k, ^{h}), should probably be treated as terminological expedients only, as no claims are necessarily being made as to whether they represent genuine segment- or feature-like elements of phonological structure; they are merely ways of representing the functional elements of the system.

By functionally separating the prosodies from the sounds with which they may or may not co-occur, we might observe a relationship between Firth's prosodies and the syntagmatic redundancy rules characteristic of generative phonology, though this latter approach, unlike

Firth's, is silent – as a matter of (questionable) principle – on the issue of whether its redundancy rules have functional value. If we can establish a link between Firthian prosodies and generative syntagmatic redundancy rules, this suggests that such so-called "redundant" content may, in fact, be quite relevant indeed at the functional level. As noted by Fischer-Jørgensen in her 1975 book, "[Generative] sequence structure rules ... give information about a great deal of that which in other phonological schools is described by means of phonotactic rules ... or by means of neutralization rules" (1975:238), or, perhaps, by means of prosodies.

Another point before moving on to exemplification: (1) polysystemicity, (2) the sound–prosody distinction, and (3) level-mixing, are not simply unrelated characteristics on a numbered list of attributes of prosodic analysis. Rather, they cohere as necessarily interdependent components of the approach; once we accept the syntagmatic–paradigmatic distinction that Firth emphasizes, it naturally follows that our analysis is polysystemic and level-mixed in orientation. By distinguishing between sounds and prosodies, we are necessarily engaging in a polysystemic treatment, since we are treating different functional groupings of the phonetic elements in the system as independent of one another, phonetic elements that may reference non-phonological information (morphology, syntax, semantics, etc.).

A preliminary example: in his brief mention of Danish stød ("glottal stop"), Firth (1948:144) writes, "The Danish glottal stop ... occurs chiefly with sounds said to be originally long, and in final position only in stressed syllables. If the word in question loses its stress for rhythmical or other reasons, it also loses the glottal stop. It is therefore best considered prosodically as a feature of syllable structure and word formation." That is, regarding the limited distribution of stød to word-final stressed syllables, it may indeed be characterized as a word prosody: a word may possess a stød prosody, and when it does, that stød is present in a stressed, word-final syllable.

With its emphasis on the relevance of phonological syntagmatics, it should not come as a surprise that Firth's showcase example of prosodic analysis is taken from Semitic. As its morphology intertwines with its syllable canon, Semitic strikingly exemplifies the proposed forces at work. In Cairene Arabic, for example, "[t]he principle to be emphasized is the *interrelation of the syllables*, what I have previously referred to as the *syntagmatic relations*, as opposed to the *paradigmatic* or *differential relations* of sounds in vowel and consonant systems ..." (1948:138).

Though only minimally explicated by Firth (for example, he doesn't even provide English glosses, thus virtually defeating his very purpose!), in Cairene, the system of phonematic units is functionally distinct from the system of prosodies, in the sense that the phonematic systems bear root information, while the prosodic systems bear inflectional information. The sounds in the phonematic systems involve "[the] ranges of possible sound substitutions" (1948:141). The prosodies include "(1) the number of syllables, (2) the nature of the syllables – open or closed, (3) the syllabic quantities, (4) radicals and flexional elements separately treated, [including] (4a) the sequence of syllables, (4b) the sequence of consonants, (4c) the sequence of vowels, (5) the position, nature, and quantity of the prominent, and (6) the dark or clear qualities of the syllables [that is, 'emphasis']" (adapted from p. 141). Syllable shapes include (1) open short **CV** (**fihim, nizil**), (2) open medium **CVV** (**faahim, gineenah**), (3) closed medium **CVC** (**ʕafham, duxulhum**), (4) closed long **CVVC** (**naam, kitaab**), and (5) closed long **CVCC** (**ʃadd, bint**).

Though studiously avoided by Firth, the main point of this discussion seems to be that Cairene (and Semitic in general) is best characterized in polysystemic terms, including systems of sounds (the consonants) that express root information, and prosodies (the syllable structures over which the roots are distributed) that express inflectional information. Vocalism too forms its own system. (Such an analysis of Semitic has long been embraced by Semiticists, and has subsequently been taken up in Brame 1970 and McCarthy 1979.) Note that the proposed prosodies of Semitic do not function exclusively as boundary signals in the Trubetzkoyan sense. Rather, it is the syllable types that, by their varying distribution with respect to each other, impart information about morphological structure. It is clearly due to the nature of Semitic word structure that Firth's (more broadly defined) prosodies are better able to handle these facts than are Trubetzkoy's (more narrowly defined) boundary signals.

In Semitic at least, so-called "syllable structure" indeed plays this prominent morphological role. Still, assuming for the moment that we can talk of entities called "syllables", they are rarely relevant to morphological structure (Semitic being the most obvious exception), and are always irrelevant to lexical structure (in that no language encodes lexical contrast in terms of syllable structure distinctions). Indeed, it is far from clear that syllables are genuinely relevant at any functional level of analysis. This has not stopped prosodic analysts from incorporating syllable-based generalizations into their reports of non-Semitic-type systems. For example, Firth himself characterizes the Hunanese Chinese "medial glides" **j** and **w** as "syllable prosodies" and "syllabic features" presumably because they are limited in their distribution to only one per syllable, affecting the phonetic quality of both the initial (the onset) and the final (the rime). Thus, if a syllable possesses a glide, its location is predictable. Given its predictable distribution within the domain of the syllable, we may treat it as a prosody of the syllable, rather than a sound. Firth does just this, and further considers the following components of the Hunanese syllable to be prosodies as well: "tone, voice quality, and other properties of the sonants" (1948:136). He does not include onset consonants in this list, even though, in fact, all consonants except **n** function as prosodies in Hunanese: as Firth and Rogers discuss in their 1937 paper on the topic, all consonants may be found prevocalically, while only **n** may be found post-vocalically. Consequently, a prosodic analyst could plausibly assert that all consonants except **n** function as syllable prosodies, since all these consonants are predictable in their distribution within the syllable. It is difficult to understand the advantages of such an analysis, however.

Now, for Hunanese, one can readily make the argument that the medial glides, as well as the other prosodies Firth lists (and also all the consonants except **n**), function as boundary signals: since the syllable is largely coextensive with the morpheme in Chinese languages, then a syllable boundary signal is also a morpheme boundary signal. It is less clear why we should regard the Hunanese medial glides (etc.) as prosodies simply because they signal syllable boundaries, since, as noted, syllables almost never play a functional role in phonological syntagmatics. Once again: although we may make generalizations about the distribution of elements within the syllable in our role as language analysts (prosodic or otherwise), such generalizations, in and of themselves, do not necessarily possess functional value for language users. As we have just seen though, it is the syllable, rather than the morpheme, on which Firth places his emphasis.

His discussion of English **h** as a prosody prompts similar concerns. English **h** is indeed limited in its distribution as "an *initial signal* in stressed syllables of full words having no weak forms" "though it has phonematic value in such paradigms as *eating, heating; eels, heels; ear hear . . .* " (Firth 1948:146). Still, again, however accurate this characterization of English **h**'s distribution, its syntagmatic patterning plays a very limited functional role in terms of cueing functionally relevant aspects of structure: **h** may be present in any stressed syllable (either primary or secondary stress), regardless of its proximity to, or marking of, a morphological boundary, though it does, on occasion, serve as a word boundary signal if appearing in an unstressed syllable, for example, h̩ɹ'pʰɛɹɪk ("herpetic"). Clearly, Firth is assuming a far larger role for his prosodies than Trubetzkoy does for his boundary signals, but it is not obvious what, in such cases, is being illuminated by this broader application.

Before a fuller discussion of the relevance of prosodic analysis to the issue at hand – that being the role of neutralization in increasing phonological REASON – let's first consider a few additional prosodic analyses, in order to get a better sense of the mechanics of the approach.

SANSKRIT

In his analysis of Sanskrit retroflexion, Allen (1951:82) begins by wisely cautioning against a too-literal interpretation of the term "assimilation" as it relates to phonological and phonetic analysis, "on the ground that the implied change is only metaphorical, having reference to a hypothetical 'basic' form derived from the consideration of other contexts or of earlier stages of the language". His discussion of Sanskrit *nati* or "cerebralization" – long-distance retroflex assimilation – should be viewed in this light. This supposed "action at a distance" ("action à distance", Bloch 1934; Allen distances himself from the term) involves a domain of retroflexion from a "focal point" (ṣ ṭ) to a following coronal nasal within the word, provided a non-coronal consonant does not intervene. (For more detailed discussion, see Whitney 1889, Allen 1953, and Hansson 2001.)

Since its distribution within the domain of the word is predictable, Allen proposes that retroflexion be "abstracted as a prosody". Thus, as we considered in Chapter 2:

$$\text{niṣaṇ-ṇa-} = \text{nisanna-} \qquad \text{aːṭabʲa-maːṇa-} = \text{aːrabʲamaːna-}$$

Here, **R** represents retroflexion, the domain of which is indicated by the graphic notation. Indeed, since it is predictable, specifying the phonetic domain of the prosody may be unnecessary, and may instead be "[left] to study at the proper phonetic level" (Allen 1951:943):

$$\text{niṣaṇ-ṇa-} = \text{nisanna-} \qquad \text{aːṭabʲa-maːṇa-} = \text{aːrabʲamaːna-}$$

Phonetic material within the domain of the retroflex prosody may be assumed to manifest retroflexion in the form of a "word palatogram" that would, perhaps, manifest a low-level amount of retroflexion across the entire span. Clearly, while the presence versus absence of retroflexion is non-neutralizing, that is, it is contrastive, the span that is either retro-flexed or not retroflexed does not contain further distinctions along this dimension, in that any given span lacks contrasts along the retroflex–non-retroflex dimension; a clear instance of contrast suspension.

As stated, this "word palatogram" is additionally delimited by the presence of a coronal that follows focal points ʂ and ʈ. Allen graphic-ally characterizes this pattern in the following way:

Here, r represents the focal point, and T represents a coronal that delimits the domain of the retroflex prosody.

SUNDANESE

Robins (1957b:90) writes that the prosodies of Sundanese are relevant at the word level and at the syllable level. Nasalization, the focus of his study, is a word-level prosody, as its distribution within the word is a fully patterned "structural unity": "[O]nce nasality has been initiated by the articulation of a nasal consonant, whether as syllable initial or as syllable final, it continues irrespective of the syllable boundaries until checked ... Nasality is checked by: (1) a word boundary, (2) a supraglot-tally articulated consonant, i.e. any consonant other than h or ʔ." Furthermore, "[a] second or subsequent nasal in a word may be regarded as the check point of the previously initiated nasality and as initiating subsequent nasality" (p. 90). Again, the word-level prosodic status of nasality is due to the fact that if a word possesses nasality, its distribu-tion is exhaustively predictable within that domain; it is a "structural unity" (even if not a phonetic unity) at the syntagmatic level.

A few example words (using Robins' "structural formula" notation, for which C and V represent phonematic systems, and the additional notation represents the nasal prosody):

| mãɾo | CVCV | "to halve" | ɲiãr | CVVC | "to seek" |
| ɲãhõkɤn | CVCVCVC | "to inform" | bɤŋhãr | CVCCVC | "to be rich" |

It is irrelevant to the prosodic analyst that nasality here is, on occasion, discontinuous in its phonetic realization (as in the under-lined portions of n̪ā̃hõ̃kᵛn̪). The only observation relevant to the pros-odic status of nasality here is that its distribution may be exhaustively characterized in syntagmatic terms.

This aspect of the analysis is made most clear when considering words possessing the verbal infix -ar-/-al- ("the choice being contextually deter-mined"). In words possessing a nasal that precedes the infix, the infix consonant checks the nasal prosody, and the immediately following vowel is oral, though the nasal prosody is again present on following sounds, as if the infix check were absent (for clarity, the prosody here is underlined, and the infix is set off by dashes): n̪ĩʔĩɾ – n̪-āl-iʔĩɾ ("to pierce"), mā̃hā̃l – m-āɾ-ahā̃l ("to be expensive"), n̪ā̃hõ̃ – n̪-āɾ-ahõ̃ ("to know"). Quite interestingly, this patterning introduces the pos-sibility of minimal phonological (though not morphological) pairs, since comparable phonetic forms that lack the infix show no such phonetic discontinuity of the nasal prosody: mā̃rĩos ("to examine"), n̪ū̃liat ("to stretch"), mõ̃lohok ("to stare").

The patterning of the nasal prosody vis-à-vis the -ar-/-al- infix clearly complicates the grammatical statement, requiring mention of the root (and suffix domain) as distinct from the infix domain. The nasal pro-sody within roots is characterized by Robins thus, when the first root consonant is nasal (*n* = nasal prosody; **R** = root):

$$\overset{\textit{n}\!-\!-\!-\!\,-\,-\,-}{\underset{\text{R}\rule{2.4em}{0.4pt}}{\text{CV(C)V(C)...}}}$$

And thus, when the infix is present (**I** = infix):

As already noted, the possibility of minimal phonological (though not morphological) pairs is introduced exactly because the nasal pro-sody is absent on the vowel immediately following the infix, and is present on subsequent lexical material until a check point is present further along within the word (schematically, N-āl-Vh̃Ṽ; again, where the nasal prosody is indicated by underlining); a minimally distinct phonological form lacking the infix would possess the nasal prosody only until the ɾ or l check point (N̄ālVhV).

Schematically, we may imagine a sequence of words of the form $\underline{\text{nṼʔṼ#hV}}$ [...]. In such cases, the cessation of nasality is a word boundary signal, for if this particular sequence were within the confines of a single word, the last two sounds would be nasalized as well: $\underline{\text{nVʔṼh̃Ṽ}}$ [...]. Even with this odd patterning in mind, the nasal prosody does indeed function as a boundary signal under certain conditions, since – just like retroflexion in Sanskrit – its distribution is exhaustively statable in terms of the word level.

Note that one can predict the distribution of nasal consonants within the word due to the presence of the nasal prosody just as readily as one can predict the distribution of the nasal prosody due to the presence of nasal consonants. Thus the prosody begins at the focal point (an oral closure), and ends at the check point (a supra-glottally articulated consonant or a word boundary), but neither the starting point nor the ending point of the prosody should be regarded as segmental in nature. Consequently, it would be a mis-taken analysis to propose that the domain of the prosody can be "read off" its segmental starting and ending points: the starting point is as much a component of the prosody as anything else is, and the check point, exactly because it is a check, imparts syntag-matic information. Thus, the focal point and the check point, despite appearances to the contrary, are not phonematic units at all, but are, rather, the starting point and the ending point of the nasal prosody, respectively.

The exact same argument may be applied to Allen's retroflex prosody: the starting points and endpoints of the prosody – a retroflex consonant; a nasal – are not phonematic units, but are instead inseparable from the prosody.

These aspects of prosodic analysis offer a satisfying explanation for Trubetzkoy's reluctance to specify harmonic vowel features as "group signals" or "non-group signals". The strictly segmental approach in which Trubetzkoy was operating makes it difficult to characterize any harmonic feature as (1) definitively belonging to a single segment that is predictably distributed across a larger domain, or as (2) definitively belonging to each of the segments within its domain of expression. Comparable problems have plagued generative analyses of harmonic features, for which purport-edly predictable information is afforded a different status from purportedly unpredictable information, thus typically requiring some sort of multi-staged or derivational analysis. Prosodic analysis eschews all these unnecessary conundrums due to its strictly *declara-tive* nature.

DISCUSSION

From a functional viewpoint there are many advantageous aspects to prosodic analysis. First, its polysystemic nature succeeds in hugging the functional ground of phonological systems far more effectively than the monosystemic theories devised before and since: the functional roles of comparable phonetic values are wisely treated as bearing no intrinsic relationship to each other simply because of their phonetic similarity.

Second, as a direct consequence of its polysystemic functional nature, prosodic analysis imparts no proscriptions against the "mixing of levels". On the contrary, the relevance of a contrastive value is only expressible in terms of the (sub-)system in which it participates, (sub-)systems that may be functionally relevant at *any* level of linguistic analysis.

Third, its strict non-segmental nature allows for an equally strict declarative characterization of linguistic systems. There are no "before" and "after" stages, there are no "inputs" and "outputs", there is no notion of phonological "operations" such as assimilation or deletion, apart from, perhaps, observing that such patterns have a diachronic origin.

Still, it is important to stay focused on the issues of immediate relevance: neutralization and its effect on phonological RHYME and phonological REASON. Here, prosodic analysis only partially succeeds. Its success is due to the boundary-signaling function of prosodies. Considering only these sorts of prosodies, a Firthian analysis may, in fact, be superior to Trubetzkoy's already tremendously successful treatment. By divorcing boundary signals from any apparent segmental stream, prosodic analysis more effectively zeros in on their functional role. As stated several times now, phonetic elements that signal boundaries may be expressed in varying ways – as "sub-segments", as "segments" or as "supra-segments" – but these phonetically disparate manifestations all serve a comparable linguistic function, a function that is intrinsically wed to neutralization: (1) the presence of a "segmental" or "sub-segmental" prosody serves as a positive boundary signal due to its suspension in non-boundary contexts; (2) the absence of a "segmental" or "sub-segmental" prosody may serve as a negative boundary signal due to this prosody's presence in a boundary context; (3) the presence of a "suprasegmental" prosody suspends contrast within its domain of expression, thus serving as a negative boundary signal (that is, within its domain of expression, there are no further contrasts between the presence and the absence of the prosody, even when the prosody is phonetically discontinuous); and (4) the absence of a "suprasegmental" prosody suspends contrast within the domain of its absence. That is, when absent, there are no contrasts involving the prosody within that span of the speech stream, and thus its absence may sometimes serve as a negative boundary signal.

As noted by Lodge (2009:35), "The very notion of neutralization trades on monosystemicity ... ": if **a** and **b** do not contrast in context **x** (say, only **a** is present in **x**), there is no necessary link between the **a** in positions of relevance and **a** in positions of neutralization. Indeed, it may be said that, by jettisoning monosystemicity, traditional structural approaches to neutralization are rendered indefinable and analytically useless (apart from their boundary-signaling function).

Rather, these **a**s are in different (sub-)systems, and thus bear no phonological relationship to each other. Lodge further observes that Trubetzkoy's archiphonemes constitute a positive step forward from structuralist and generativist thought, because – regardless of phonetic similarity – the values present in positions of relevance are systemically distinct from the values present in positions of neutralization (that is, the archiphonemes), and they are also systemically distinct from the values present in positions of neutralizing alternation (that is, the morphonemes). Thus, just as his boundary signals prefigure Firth's prosodies, Trubetzkoy's archiphonemes and morphonemes prefigure Firth's emphasis on polysystemicity.

It is less clear that prosodic analysis succeeds outside the domain of boundary signals. This issue has already been addressed: phonological elements that pattern syntagmatically do not automatically have functional relevance as a direct consequence of this syntagmatic patterning. For example, the prosodic analyst may observe that certain elements are limited to certain syllable positions, but this observation on the part of the language analyst does not necessarily have functional value for the language user. As discussed earlier in this chapter, so-called syllables, apart from a few exceptional cases like Semitic, do not possess functional value in the sense of imparting linguistic information to listeners (and even for Semitic, of course, there are alternatives to a specifically syllable-based account). In this sense, they are linguistically inert, and thus their very existence as phonological entities may rather readily be called into question.

If we exclude this problematic aspect of the approach, we might eschew certain unpalatable elements of prosodic analysis by limiting the relevance of prosodies to their strictly boundary-signaling function. Whether or not the prosodic analyst strives for a strictly functional grammatical statement – that is, one that plausibly has psychological relevance – remains an open question.

CONCLUSION

By unshackling our phonological analyses from the "phonemic straightjacket", Firth's prosodic analysis takes Trubetzkoy's nascent ideas to far more bountiful fruition: "phonemism" and "alphabetism" (Silverman 2006a) – the sources of Trubetzkoy's hedging in his characterization of harmonic features – may be mercifully deposited on to the junk heap of theoretic history.

In the next chapter we conclude our discussion of neutralization and phonological REASON by considering Saffran's work on "transitional probabilities".

DISCUSSION QUESTIONS AND FURTHER READING

(1) Read the following papers comparing "prosodic analysis" to "autosegmental phonology": **Goldsmith (1992, 1994)**, and **Ogden and Local (1994)**. In both theoretic and rhetorical terms, how effectively do you think the authors defend their respective positions?

(2) The London School endured a rather strident critical analysis by **Langendoen (1968)**. Compare the relevant papers in the volumes edited by **Firth (1957b)** and **Palmer (1970)**, and also consider **Lyons (1962)**. How compelling do you find Langendoen's criticisms of the approach?

18   Transitional probabilities

Kruszewski's, Trubetzkoy's, and Firth's theorizing on the functional value of neutralization – that is, its role in serving as an aid to parsing – has, in recent years, been operationalized by a number of researchers investigating *transitional probabilities*. The work of Saffran and associates is our focus herein. Saffran investigates the utility of transitional probabilities in both adult and infant learning of contrived mini-languages, finding that, indeed, the statistically rare sound sequences found at "word" boundaries (of course, in these experiments they are not real words) serve to cue these boundaries. The necessary flipside to this finding is that statistically more prevalent sound sequences – those involving neutralization within some domain – may function as negative boundary signals.

Before beginning, it should be noted that, in much of the experimental work of Saffran, the functional role of low transitional probabilities in terms of signaling boundaries is a purely statistical calculation over physical objects (speech tokens); there is no role for lexical semantic feedback. As such, the determination of transitional probabilities in these experimental contexts actually serves to factor out the concomitant semantic feedback that is necessarily present in real-world language learning contexts. The information extracted in such studies is purely distributional (harking back in some sense to American structuralist notions of phonological structure and juncture, and perhaps in particular, so-called "monosystemicity"). In real-world contexts, of course, the raw role of transitional probabilities is difficult to accurately gauge, since any statistical calculations engaged in by language learners is necessarily accompanied by lexical semantic feedback, to which language learners become more attuned with experience and maturation (Firth's "level-mixing" properly acknowledges this role for lexical semantic feedback). From my 2006 book (pp. 22–23):

> [Although] we have experimental evidence showing that children are differentially sensitive to the more common and less common sound sequences they encounter in the speech signal, even at the

early pre-linguistic levels of infancy [. . .], children cannot possibly understand that the speech signal might be structured into words and morphemes until they begin to associate these particular sound sequences with particular meanings. It's exactly because certain chunks of the speech signal are semantically relevant and useful to speakers of the language that they are repeated over and over again in particular real-world situations. Because of this repetition, they are constantly encountered by learners, and eventually emerge to these learners as the functional units that they are for speakers. As they learn to associate particular sound chunks with particular meanings, learners are beginning to parse [. . .] the functionally relevant chunks of the speech signal.

Structuring the speech signal into sentences, words, and morphemes emerges as a consequence of patterns of sounds that are heard again and again by language learners, with which they come to associate with a particular meaning, due to what we might call the richness of the stimulus. At the earliest stages of vocabulary building, the more often a particular sound sequence is encountered, the more readily that such a sound–meaning correspondence will be established. And the more often these sound sequences combine and recombine with other sound sequences, indeed, the more likely that learners will take note of these sequences' tendency to combine and recombine in various ways, and so emerge as independent functional units of the language. In this sense, learners' knowledge of the *form* of language is determined to a great extent by the very *function* that language has for speakers.

With this in mind, let's turn to Saffran's work. Saffran, Newport, and Aslin (1996:609) provide a nice cross-modality illustration of what they intend to investigate: "[O]ne might discover words in the linguistic input in much the same way that one discovers objects in the visual environment via motion: the spatial–temporal correlations between the different parts of the moving object will be stronger than those between the moving object and the surrounding visual environment."

To illustrate their proposals, the authors consider the English word "baby", which consists of two parts, each of which is an English word on its own, **beɪ** and **bi**. Moreover, while **beɪ** is followed by **bi** in "baby", **beɪ** may be followed by other speech segments in other words, such as "basic", "baker", "basil", etc. It may also be found in word-final position, such as "obey" and "bay". Given the fixed and stable arrangement of elements within a word however, word-internal sequences involving **beɪ** and some other element should be more frequently encountered than cross-word sequences involving **beɪ** and some other element: "Intuitively, an occurrence of *bay* is more predictive of the following syllable when both syllables belong to the same word than when the pair spans a word boundary" (Saffran, Newport, and Aslin 1996:610).

Formulaically, the transitional probability of **y** given **x** is:

$$\frac{\text{frequency of pair } \mathbf{xy}}{\text{frequency of } \mathbf{x}}$$

If this ratio is high, the presence of **x** is a good predictor of a following **y**; such sequences might thus serve as negative boundary signals – Trubetzkoy's "green light" – indicating that the sequence is word-internal. However, if this ratio is low, then the sequence **xy** may serve as a positive boundary signal.

For example, the likelihood of **beɪ** being followed by **bi** is likely to be comparatively high as compared to the likelihood of **beɪ** being followed by **tʰu**.

$$\frac{\text{frequency of } \mathbf{beɪ\ bi}}{\text{frequency of } \mathbf{beɪ}} \quad \text{is greater than} \quad \frac{\text{frequency of } \mathbf{beɪ\ tʰu}}{\text{frequency of } \mathbf{beɪ}}$$

That is, word-internal sequences such as **beɪbi** are likely to be more prevalent than cross-word-boundary sequences like **beɪ tʰu**, and so if **tʰu** follows **beɪ**, there is a high probability that it belongs to a different word, and thus the low transitional probability signals a word boundary: "A learner, then, might hypothesize word boundaries upon discovering troughs in the transitional probabilities between syllables" (Saffran, Newport, and Aslin 1996:610).

In their first experiment, two sets of adult subjects were taught a contrived mini-language consisting of four consonants (**p b t d**) and three vowels (**a i u**). Twelve CV syllables were constructed, which were strung into trisyllabic sequences constituting the "words" of the language, for example, **bapuba**, **dutaba**, etc.). Transitional probabilities at "word" boundaries were lower than transitional probabilities within "words". The learning phase involved subjects listening to a total of twenty-one minutes of running speech. No information about word length was provided to the subjects.

During the testing phase, half the subjects were asked whether a given three-syllable sound sequence was a word (a sequence they had encountered during the learning phase) or a non-word (a sequence employing a novel combination of "phonemes" [sic]). The other subjects were tested on words versus part-words. Part-words consisted of two syllables that were present in words of the mini-language, and a third syllable that was never found alongside the first two syllables within words.

The non-word condition yielded a 76 percent success rate, and the part-word condition yielded a 65 percent success rate. Both conditions yielded significant results at the p<.01, and moreover, the difference between the two groups was significant at the p<.05 level.

When comparing the word boundary sequences with the highest transitional probability to those with the lowest transitional probability, it was found that subjects identified words significantly better when the transitional probabilities were low: "These data support the hypothesis that the strength of the statistical relationship between pairs of syllables affects subjects' ability to learn word-like units" (Saffran, Newport, and Aslin 1996:614).

Interestingly, subjects confused part-words that resembled the *end* of words more often than part-words that resembled the beginning of words: subjects appeared to pay more attention to word endings than word beginnings. One might speculate that, under normal language conditions, word-endings possess characteristic cues that learners come to associate with this position, cues that thus serve as an aid in parsing. A likely candidate? The common phenomenon of word-final lengthening.

In their second experiment, the researchers added this "prosodic cue" to half the "words". Half the subjects heard words with initial lengthening, the other half with final lengthening. Clearly, this added cue – particularly in the case of final lengthening – better reflects natural language patterns. All else being equal, subjects should perform even better under this condition.

Subjects in the initial lengthening condition performed at 61 percent; subjects in the final lengthening condition performed significantly better, at 80 percent. Thus, final-syllable lengthening indeed facilitated the word-learning task, while initial-syllable lengthening did not. The authors plausibly speculate that, indeed, their subjects were bringing their real-world knowledge of phonological word structure to the task.

In a subsequent study, Saffran (2001) was interested in whether nonsense words are treated differently by infants, depending on whether they are embedded in genuine language contexts, or instead, embedded in nonsense contexts. She trained infants on uninterrupted strings of trisyllabic nonsense sequences, and then embedded these trisyllabic sequences in both actual (English) sentences (for example, "I like my *tibudo*"), and nonsense sentences (for example, "zy fike ny *tibudo*"). Also though, infants heard *part*-"words" embedded in these two contexts, where so-called part-words were trisyllabic nonsense sequences that were low-probability, since they straddled the (nonsense-)word boundary.

Saffran's ultimate question was this: Under what circumstances might infants come to treat the learned nonsense words as legitimate words of the ambient language (in this case, English)? Infants' different reactions to *novel* versus *familiar* stimuli may provide an answer, according to Saffran: novel stimuli tend to evoke a greater response, which begins to wane as familiarity sets in. However, in seemingly contradictory fashion, infants seem to prefer listening to actual examples of their language, rather than novel, unfamiliar sound patterns. So, after being trained in a nonsense language, if both whole-words and part-words are embedded in both English and non-sense sentences, how do these infants react? These four conditions may be tabularly displayed as follows:

| English sentences + whole nonsense words | Nonsense sentences + whole nonsense words |
| English sentences + part nonsense words | Nonsense sentences + part nonsense words |

If infants treat nonsense whole-words differently from nonsense part-words, proposes Saffran (2001:152): "We would expect infants to prefer English sentences containing newly segmented words over English sentences containing part-words." This, indeed, is what she finds: when embedded in real English sentences, infants preferred listening to whole nonsense words rather than part nonsense words. As Saffran concludes: "The pattern of results suggests that the representation emerging from statistical learning may serve as candidate lexical items for infants, available for integration into the native language" (p. 157).

Saffran thus concludes that word-like categories *can* begin to emerge, even without semantic feedback, due to the statistical prevalence of some sound sequences over others, provided these sequences are embedded in a genuine linguistic context. Again, this does not mean – nor *can* it mean – that learners are capable of partitioning such "words" into any smaller functional constituents, but nonetheless, chunks of speech that frequently co-occur may indeed trigger an organic "itch" to seek out a particular *function* – a particular meaning – to associate with the sound chunk, an itch that seems to be quelled in non-language contexts. Does this conclusion contradict my 2006 claim that "children cannot possibly understand that the speech signal might be structured into words … until they begin to associate these particular sound sequences with particular meanings" (2006a:22f.)?

Well, with apologies to Bill Clinton, it depends on what the meaning of the word "word" is …!

CONCLUSION

This discussion of transitional probabilities has been meant to reinforce the overarching proposal that neutralization is typically neither function-negative nor even function-neutral. Rather, the product of neutralization – in the form of cement, boundary signals, prosodies, transitional probabilities – is indeed function-positive, serving as an aid to parsing the speech signal into its linguistically significant semantic/functional components.

DISCUSSION QUESTIONS AND FURTHER READING

(1) Saffran plausibly suggests that final lengthening may serve as a cue to word parsing. Readers may have noted that a related phenomenon – stress – has been largely missing from all discussion up to this late point in the book. While stress may be uncontroversially characterized as providing "rhythmic structure" to spoken language, this role, in and of itself, is functionally irrelevant. Apart from those rare instances of lexical stress, what *genuinely* functional value does stress possess, and how might we account for the existence of those aspects of stress that are not immediately functionally relevant (for example, secondary stress, proposed foot structure, etc.)? Some of the most important works you might consult are **Liberman and Prince (1977)**, **Prince (1983)**, **Halle and Vernaud (1987)**, and **Hayes (1995)**.

(2) If you have found some of the ideas considered herein to be compelling, you might also read the following books: **Sampson (1980)**, **Keller (1994)**, **Bybee (2001)**, **Blevins (2004)**, **Deutscher (2005)**, and **Silverman (2006a)**. These volumes do not necessarily place special emphasis on neutralization, but are nonetheless of a comparable theoretical bent.

And, by all means, please read the papers by Baudouin de Courteney in the 1972 volume, and those by Kruszewski in the 1995 volume.

19   The power of Babelese

We have now considered quite a few approaches to neutralization in phonology, all the while showing accreting arguments in favor of the overarching thesis that: (1) neutralizing alternations almost always maintain heterophony, and hence are usually function-neutral; (2) neutralizing alternations are function-negative only to the extent that they derive homophones; and most surprisingly, (3) neutralization is often function-positive, by serving as an aid to parsing. Employing the specialized terminology used herein, phonological RHYME may readily increase until encountering a counter-pressure inhibiting undue decreases in phonological REASON, in the form of NEUTRALIZATION.

Our first tasks were to observe and describe (traditional) neutralization, the emphasis of Part I, Section A.

In Chapter 2 we characterized neutralization as a topological deformation of the amount of phonetic distinctiveness across the speech stream – in terms of spans, edges, and points – observing that the speech signal consists of time periods with *more* phonologically significant information (the expression of contrastive cues) interwoven with time periods of *less* phonologically significant information (the suspension or loss of contrastive cues).

In Chapter 3 we taxonomized the phenomenon by considering the contexts in which neutralizations – both oral and laryngeal – are more likely to be encountered: lexical non-prevocalic positions, non-initial positions, stressless contexts, and affixes. We also considered contexts in which neutralizations are less likely to be found: lexical prevocalic contexts, initial positions, stressed contexts, and roots.

Following Trubetzkoy, in Chapter 4 we discussed the typology of neutralization with respect to: (1) the sorts of logical/functional relationships that exist among values that are likely to engage in neutralization; and also with respect to (2) the sorts of logical/functional relationships that exist among neutralizing values and their conditioning environments.

Having observed and described patterns of neutralization in these terms, in Section B we temporarily drove off the main highway of our discussion, taking a scenic route that terminated at some "false positive" dead ends.

In Chapter 5 we rejected the superficially tempting proposal that Bloch's "partial phonemic overlap" constitutes a form of neutralization, and, in fact, called into question Bloch's very examples of the (very real) phenomenon.

We discussed in Chapter 6 the fact that many putative cases of neutralization (and merger) are, in fact, merely nearly-neutralized (or nearly-merged), and thus may unproblematically be characterized as contrast-maintaining.

In Section C, we entertained various proposed explanations for the patterns of neutralization we have considered.

In Chapter 7 we considered – and readily rejected – the proposal that neutralization may be rooted in a synchronic pressure or constraint on *speakers* to ease their articulatory efforts.

In Chapter 8 we considered – and also rejected – the proposal that neutralization may sometimes have its origins in speakers' knowledge of the phonetic consequences of their speech activities, such that they might ensure easy perception on the part of their interlocutors.

We then switched our orientation, and considered *listeners'* roles as progenitors of neutralization, in Chapter 9 investigating Ohala's proposals regarding listeners' interpretations – and crucially, their sporadic *mis*interpretations – of the *phonetic intentions* of their interlocutors, finding this account wanting for a number of reasons.

We then switched our emphasis from phonetics to semantics. In Chapter 10 we considered Martinet's proposals regarding the role of "functional load" in patterns of neutralization, that is, that oppositions which are responsible for few minimal pairs are more likely candidates for neutralization, whereas oppositions that are responsible for many minimal pairs are less likely candidates. We took kindly to this proposal, ultimately rejecting King's rejoinder.

In Chapter 11 we expanded our investigation into *semantic misperception* as an important factor in patterns of neutralization, discussing Labov's proposed mechanism by which systems might avoid rampant homophony. We concluded that there exists a sporadic tendency for listeners to misinterpret the lexical semantic content of the speech signal when phonetic variation is sufficiently pronounced so as to make one word sound too similar to another word. The consequent semantic confusion may set in motion an ongoing – and decidedly passive – pressure towards homophone avoidance: successful speech propagates and conventionalizes; unsuccessful speech gets passively filtered out, falling by the wayside.

Having explored explanatory approaches to neutralization, in Section D we moved on to further exemplify the effect.

In Chapter 12 we explored the proposal that an anti-homophonic pressure may passively act on language change, by considering a single case study – neutralization and anti-homophony in Korean – finding that, indeed, a language may tolerate massive amounts of (traditionally characterized) derived neutralization, while simultaneously possessing remarkably limited derived homophony as a consequence of these neutralization alternations.

Now embracing the proposal that anti-homophony is indeed a pressure affecting the diachronic trajectory of linguistic sound systems (whereas a pressure against traditional neutralization – passive or certainly otherwise – seems not to exist), in Chapter 13 we inventoried and exemplified some of the domains over which anti-homophony might manifest itself, including the lexical, the morphological, the phonological, the phonotactic, the paradigmatic, and the pragmatic.

In Chapter 14 we concluded Part I by reiterating the proposal that neutralization – as traditionally characterized – is *not* a function-negative pressure on language evolution, in the sense of serving to decrease the semantic clarity of the speech signal. Indeed, we considered systems that might tolerate downright bizarre patterns of variation that may lead to alternations which, we argued, encountered no counter-pressure inhibiting their conventionalization, exactly because the variation is heterophone-maintaining. We concluded that "distinctions are drawn that matter".

In Part II we came to what is perhaps our most surprising conclusion: far from being a function-negative pressure on language evolution, traditional neutralization actually plays a function-positive role, in the form of serving as an aid to parsing the speech stream into its functional (that is, lexical semantic) constituents; words and morphemes.

We first considered these ideas in the context of Kruszewski's "cement" (Chapter 15), then Trubetzkoy's "boundary signals" (Chapter 16), Firth's "prosodies" (Chapter 17), and finally Saffran's modern experimental approach to "transitional probabilities" (Chapter 18). Far from being a function-negative component of the phonological system, these *decreases in phonetic distinctiveness* were shown to correlate positively with *increases in semantic distinctiveness*; again, a most surprising result.

In this very brief postscript we return to our hypothetical language called Babelese, revisiting the salient characteristics of its sound system in light of all subsequent discussion.

BABELESE AGAIN

Recall that Babelese was initially characterized as possessing nine values – three stops, three nasals, three vowels – with roots of the form **CVCV**, **CVCVC**, **CVCCV**, and **CVCCVC**. Recall further that, within roots, **CC** sequences may only consist of homorganic nasal–stop sequences. This restriction constitutes a suspension of contrast and is thus a *static* property of roots: such nasal–stop sequences are never in alternation such that one of the phonetic events – either the nasal or the stop – may switch out independently. Because of this static or fixed quality of these phonetic events, there is no functional motivation for language learners/users to partition them into smaller linguistically significant units (call these segments if you must).

Indeed, we argued that *any* portion of the speech stream that is static – that is, is *fixed* – in terms of its phonetic content may be treated as an unanalyzed chunk – as a *Gestalt* – due to the simple fact that there is no linguistic evidence suggesting otherwise, since these portions never decompose into smaller units. Any fixed *phonetic* events that possess fixed *functional* status are *Gestalten*. These are, as a first approximation, morphemes, at least to the extent that morphemes do not engage in alternation.

But of course, morphemes typically *do* engage in alternation, such that some sub-morphemic phonetic components switch out under predictable circumstances, that is, as conditioned by some extra-morphemic criteria. In Babelese we encounter just such a scenario in the form of nasal assimilation: nasals assimilate to following (extra-morphemic) stops, such that a phonetic subcomponent of one morpheme predictably co-varies with a phonetic subcomponent of another morpheme.

At this point, it becomes clear that (static) morpheme-internal nasal–stop sequences (**NC**) – despite phonetic appearances to the contrary – bear no linguistic relationship to (dynamic) between-morpheme nasal–stop sequences (**N+C**), or, for that matter, between-word nasal–stop sequences (**N#C**). The morpheme-internal nasal–stop span is embedded in an (unanalyzed) *Gestalt*, while the cross-morpheme nasal–stop span transparently consists of pieces belonging to more than one linguistic chunk. The different statuses of these two phonetically comparable spans (**NC** versus **N+C**) are evident to language users because of the simple fact that they engage in distinct behaviors: **NC** never separates, whereas **N+C** does, such that, under the proper circumstances, one nasal may switch out with another nasal. Under such **N+C** circumstances, the phonetically distinct nasals are underlain by an identical linguistic function: in the **N+C** context, morpheme meaning almost always remains stable upon replacing one nasal with another. No such situation ever arises in the (morpheme-internal) **NC** context.

Thus, phonological *Gestalten* – the elements of phonological contrast – come in only two varieties: alternating and non-alternating portions of morphemes. Remember: the spans of speech within morphemes – despite phonetic appearances to the contrary, and however "recyclable" their attendant motor routines – are *not* necessarily built out of smaller linguistically significant units that combine in various ways. Rather, the spans of the speech stream underlain by a specific linguistic *function* – that is, morphemes – are the genuine building blocks of linguistic structure, blocks that may only be partitioned into smaller units when there is evidence from alternation to do so. It is thus incorrect to claim that Babelese possesses the nine contrastive values inventoried earlier. Rather, Babelese possesses as many contrastive values as there are phonetic components that don't alternate, and phonetic components that do, and that's it. And if some linguists find it unpalatable that the inventory of contrastive values does not consist of temporal and spectral slices that fit so snugly into the nice neat rows and columns that graphically reveal their phonetic properties, well, with all due respect, tough!

Now, whereas most elements in alternation do indeed subserve a single linguistic function by maintaining heterophony, there is, of course, one – and *only* one – exception to this generalization, an exception that has been the (zooming) focus of the present study. These are elements whose alternation derives homophones. It is these sorts of alternations – and, again, *only* these – that may have function-negative linguistic consequences. And it is therefore just these sorts of alternations that Babelese best steer clear of – or at least severely limit – if it wants to effectively maintain its communicative function.

Obviously, we don't need to anthropomorphize Babelese in the sense of its "steering clear" of excessive derived homophony. Rather, there are interlocutionary factors that slowly exert a passive and decidedly self-organizing pressure on linguistic sound patterns such that derived homophony is inevitably limited in its prevalence: the phonetic variation inherent to speech production is a means by which new conventions evolve. Slow-going listener-based *phonetic pressures* towards increases in neutralization inevitably encounter slow-going listener-based *semantic counter-pressures* inhibiting excessive homophony: successful speech propagates – listeners repeat the speech that they understand, and do not repeat the speech that they don't understand, speech that does not carry the requisite semantic clarity. The result is that alternations may readily evolve provided they are heterophone-maintaining; they are unlikely to evolve if they are pervasively homophone-deriving.

Indeed, in Babelese (as elsewhere), traditional neutralization is not merely function-*neutral* because of its typically heterophone-maintaining status. Rather, it is usually function-*positive*. Whenever speakers of Babelese encounter a consonant sequence in which the first is not a homorganic nasal, they are provided with unambiguous information that one word has ended, and another word has begun. Although the jury is still out, it would not be unreasonable to speculate that there exists a function-*positive* pressure *towards* an increase in (traditionally defined) neutralizing alternations, exactly because of their boundary-signaling function.

The power of Babelese, then, is self-generated and self-maintaining. By its very use, it creates, processes, and deploys the raw materials necessary to persist, to evolve, and, indeed, to thrive. Babelese, just as all real languages do, will always – *always* – succeed in fulfilling its communicative function.

Glossary

Alternation: A relationship between or among constellations of phonetic cues such that their context-conditioned commutation either maintains heterophony, or derives homophony; a non-contrastive sound substitution. Alternation results in allomorphy.

Anti-homophony: A proposed passive, usage-based pressure towards the curtailment of homophony.

Archiphoneme: According to Trubetzkoy (1939), those features that are uniquely common to neutralizing values constitute an archiphoneme. Archiphonemes appear in positions of neutralization.

Boundary signal: According to Trubetzkoy (1939), languages possess specific phonological means to signal the presence or absence of a sentence, word, or morpheme boundary at a specific point in the sound continuum.

Cement: According to Kruszewski (1883), the "accommodation" (assimilation) of one vocal tract posture to another that may come to serve a function-positive role by cueing (the absence of) a word boundary.

Centrifugal vowel neutralization: Pertaining to vowel systems, neutralization towards the edges of the vowel space; often i u ɐ.

Centripetal vowel neutralization: Pertaining to vowel systems, neutralization towards the center of the vowel space, often ə.

Commutation: The "switching out" of one value with another, typically (though not exclusively) relevant in minimal pairing situations.

Commutation test: An interview procedure in which subjects/consultants listen to and interpret the speech (or speech patterns) that they have previously been asked to produce.

Contrast: A relationship between or among constellations of phonetic cues (and, often, systematic variants of these constellations of cues; allophones) such that their commutation alters lexical semantic content; an opposition.

Contrast suspension: A static limitation on the distribution of contrastive values.

Contrastive value: A constellation of phonetic cues (and, often, systematic variants of this constellation of cues) whose commutation may alter lexical semantic content. Contrastive values come in two varieties: those that alternate, and those that do not.

Dynamic: Pertaining to two or more phonetic values that alternate with each other, thus inducing allomorphy.

200

Evaluation metric: According to Halle (1962), a grammar is more highly valued to the extent that it involves fewer terms: "Given two alternative descriptions of a particular body of data, the description containing fewer ... symbols will be regarded as simpler and will, therefore, be preferred over the other."

Form/Formal: Relating to the *phonetic* properties of language (as opposed to the *functional*, or *semantic* properties of language).

Function/Functional: Relating to the *semantic* properties of language (as opposed to the *formal*, or *phonetic* properties of language).

Function-neutral: Having no effect on lexical semantic distinctiveness.

Function-negative: Having a detrimental effect on lexical semantic distinctiveness.

Function-positive: Having a beneficial effect on lexical semantic distinctiveness.

Functionalism (in phonology): A theoretical vantage point proposing that both *communicative success* and *communicative failure* are significant factors in the shaping and changing of phonological systems.

Functional load (/yield/burden): According to Martinet (1952), the degree to which an opposition is responsible for lexical distinctness. An opposition that is responsible for few minimal pairs has a low functional load; an opposition responsible for many minimal pairs has a high functional load. All else being equal, an opposition with a high functional load is less likely to neutralize or merge; an opposition with a low functional load is more likely to neutralize or merge.

Garde's Principle: According to Garde (1961): "A merger realized in one language and unknown in another is always the result of an innovation in the language where it exists. Innovations can create mergers, but cannot reverse them. If two words have become identical through a phonetic change, they can never be differentiated by phonetic means."

Gestalt: A configuration or pattern of elements that cannot be described merely as a sum of its parts. In phonology, contrastive values may be characterized as *Gestalten*.

Hyper-articulation: According to Lindblom (1990), speech involving articulatory routines that are greater in magnitude than is typical, tending to be employed in on-line contexts where semantic ambiguity might otherwise result.

Hyper-correction: According to Ohala (1981), hyper-correction involves listeners misinterpreting a context-independent phonetic property as context-dependent.

Hypo-articulation: According to Lindblom (1990), speech involving articulatory routines that are lesser in magnitude than is typical, tending to be employed in on-line contexts where semantic ambiguity is unlikely to result.

Hypo-correction: According to Ohala (1981), hypo-correction involves listeners interpreting a context-dependent phonetic property as context-independent.

Lexical non-prevocalic context: A context in which consonant neutralization is very frequently encountered.

Lexical prevocalic context: A context in which consonant neutralization is very rarely encountered.

Mark: According to Trubetzkoy (1939), the feature(s) that distinguish(es) a set of neutralizing values. Within a relationship of markedness, the marked feature is (by hypothesis or decree) phonologically present, while the unmarked feature is phonologically absent.

Merger: The diachronic product of a collapse of contrast, either context-conditioned or global.

Monosystemicity: According to Firth (1948), an alternative to the polysystemicity he embraces: phonetically similar values are phonologically non-distinct, regardless of their function, their contexts, or their patterning.

Morphoneme: According to Trubetzkoy (1939), a value that alternates.

Near-merger: A diachronic phenomenon whereby two (or more) values come perilously close to each other without genuinely neutralizing, thus potentially allowing the values to engage in a subsequent robust split.

Near-neutralization (also **incomplete neutralization**): A synchronic phenomenon whereby two (or more) contrastive values possess alternants in the same context(s) that come(s) perilously close to each other without genuinely neutralizing.

Neutralization: a conditioned limitation on the distribution of a system's contrastive values.

NEUTRALIZATION: Derived homophony at the morpheme-and/or word-level.

P-map: According to Steriade (2008), a set of statements about the absolute and relative perceptibility of different contrasts across the different contexts where they might occur. Language users may exploit their knowledge of P-maps to determine which allophone (in a theoretically infinite set) is optimal with respect to (1) its acoustic salience, and (2) its degree of phonetic similarity to its "input" value.

Phonetic misperception: According to Ohala (1981), since there does not exist a one-to-one match-up between articulatory states and acoustic signals, listeners sometimes have multiple ways of articulatorily interpreting the acoustic signals they hear. On certain of these occasions, listeners' interpretations do not exactly match speakers' articulatory actions.

Partial phonemic overlap: According to Bloch (1941), two contrastive values **a** and **b** may be in a relationship of partial phonemic overlap if one or both possess(es) a conditioned alternant that eliminates the phonetic distinction between **a** and **b**, though **a** and **b** may still be phonologically differentiated by virtue of their distinct contexts.

Polysystemicity: According to Firth (1948), the contrastive values in one context may be functionally distinct from the contrastive values in other contexts, regardless of any phonetic similarities among them; multiple language-internal systems may exploit phonetically comparable values. Crudely speaking, there is no inherent link among phonetically comparable elements as they are distributed in the speech stream.

Positions of neutralization: According to Trubetzkoy (1939), the context(s) where archiphonemes appear.

Positions of relevance: According to Trubetzkoy (1939), the context(s) where neutralizable oppositions are not neutralized.

Probability matching: The capacity among animals (including humans) to replicate observed frequencies of events in terms of their behavioral responses.

Production hypothesis: According to Jun (1995), speakers may exert more energy in their production of sounds that possess more salient acoustic cues, and may exert less energy in their production of sounds that possess less salient cues.

Prosody: According to Firth (1948), loosely, if a value is predictable with respect to its distribution in some syntagmatic domain, it qualifies as a prosody. In general, a prosody serves a demarcative or boundary-signaling function as a consequence of this predictable distribution.

REASON: The degree of lexical semantic distinctness in the speech signal.

RHYME: The degree of phonetic similarity among lexical forms. RHYME increases upon contrast suspension and neutralization.

Semantic misperception: A misinterpretation of the (lexical) semantic content of the speech stream which, by hypothesis, may passively act to decrease the likelihood of NEUTRALIZATION taking hold in a system.

Sounds: According to Firth (1948), phonological values that possess solely paradigmatic functional relevance. In general, if a value is not predictable with respect to its distribution in some domain, it is a sound. Sounds do not serve a demarcative function, only a contrastive one.

Static: Pertaining to an element that does not alternate.

Taxonomy (of neutralization): For present purposes, a characterization of the amount of linguistic content in the speech stream in terms of common versus uncommon patterns of neutralization, and any implicational hierarchies that might be established between or among these patterns.

Topology (of neutralization): For present purposes, a characterization of the amount of linguistically significant content in the speech stream in terms of contrastive cues' manifestation across spans, or at edges or points, in a morpho-phonological string.

Transitional probabilities: Word and morpheme boundaries may be cued by the statistical likelihood of one phonetic event being followed by another. Less frequently encountered phonetic sequences may cue word boundaries; more frequently encountered phonetic sequences are more likely to be word-internal.

Typology (of neutralization): For present purposes, a characterization of the amount of linguistic content in the speech stream in terms of the inventory of relationships between or among (1) opposition members and their neutralized alternants, and (2) neutralized alternants and their conditioning environments.

Uniformitarianism (in linguistics): The proposal that pressures acting on linguistic phenomena (especially with respect to language change) are equally valid across all space and time.

References

Adamska-Sałaciak, Arleta. 1996. *Language Change in the Works of Kruszewski, Baudouin de Courtenay, and Rozwadowski*. Poznan: Motivex.

Akamatsu, Tsutomo. 1988. *The Theory of Neutralization and the Archiphoneme in Functional Phonology*. Current Issues in Linguistic Theory 43. Amsterdam: John Benjamins.

Allen, W. Sydney. 1951. Some prosodic aspects of retroflexion and aspiration in Sanskrit. *Bulletin of the School of Oriental and African Studies* 13: 939–946.

1953. Phonetics in Ancient India. *London Oriental Series* 1. Reprinted in Palmer, 1970: 82–90.

Anderson, Stephen R. 1985. *Phonology in the Twentieth Century*. University of Chicago Press.

Aronoff, Mark. 1976. *Word Formation in Generative Grammar*. Cambridge, MA: MIT Press.

Barnes, Jonathan. 2006. *Strength and Weakness at the Interface: Positional Neutralization in Phonetics and Phonology*. Berlin/New York: Mouton de Gruyter.

Battistella, Edwin L. 1990. *Markedness: The Evaluative Superstructure of Language*. Albany: State University of New York Press.

1996. *The Logic of Markedness*. New York: Oxford University Press.

Baudouin de Courtenay, Jan Niecisław. 1888–1889 (2005). *Mikołaj Kruszewski, His Life & Scholarly Work*. Trans. Wayles Browne. Krakow: Analecta Indoeuropaea Cracoviensia.

1972. A Baudouin de Courtenay Reader. In Edward Stankiewicz, ed. Bloomington: Indiana University Press.

Beckman, Jill. 1997. Positional faithfulness, positional neutralisation, and Shona vowel harmony. *Phonology* 14: 1–46.

2004. Positional faithfulness In John McCarthy, ed., *Optimality Theory in Phonology: A Reader*. 310–342.

Beddor, Patrice S., James D. Harnsberger, and Stephanie Lindemann. 2002. Acoustic and perceptual characteristics of vowel-to-vowel coarticulation in Shona and English. *Journal of Phonetics* 30: 591–627.

Beddor, Patrice S. and Rena A. Krakow. 1999. Perception of coarticulatory nasalization by speakers of English and Thai: evidence for partial compensation. *Journal of the Acoustical Society of America* **106**: 2868–2887.

Beddor, Patrice S., Rena A. Krakow, and Louis M. Goldstein. 1986. Perceptual constraints and phonological change. *Phonology* 3: 197–217.

Bell, Alan and Joan B. Hooper, eds. 1978. *Syllables and Segments*. Amsterdam: North Holland.

Benediktsson, Hreinn. 1959. The vowel system of Icelandic: a survey of its history. *Word* **15**: 282–312.

Bermúdez-Otero, Ricardo. 2006. Phonological change in optimality theory. In Keith Brown, ed., *Encyclopedia of Language and Linguistics*, 2nd edn. Oxford: Elsevier. 497–505.

Bishop, Jason. 2007. Incomplete neutralization in Eastern Andalusian Spanish: perceptual consequences of durational differences involved in s-aspiration. *International Congress of Phonetic Sciences XVI*: 1765–1768.

Bladon, A. 1986. Phonetics for hearers. In G. McGregor, ed., *Language for Hearers*. Oxford: Pergamon Press. 1–24.

Blevins, Juliette. 1995. The syllable in phonological theory. In Goldsmith. 206–244.

2004. *Evolutionary Phonology*. Cambridge University Press.

Blevins, Juliette and Andrew Wedel. 2009. Inhibited sound change: an evolutionary approach to Lexical Competition. *Diachronica* **26**: 143–183.

Bloch, Bernard. 1941. Phonemic overlapping. *American Speech* **16**: 278–284.

Bloch, Bernard and George L. Trager. 1942. *Outline of Linguistic Analysis*. Baltimore: Waverly Press.

Bloch, Jules. 1934. *L'indo-aryen du veda aux temps modernes*. Paris: Adrien-Maisonneuve.

Bloomfield, Leonard. 1933. *Language*. London: George Allen and Unwin.

Blust, Robert. 1990. Three recurrent changes in Oceanic languages. In J. H. C. S. Davidson, ed., *Pacific Island Languages: Essays in Honour of G. B. Milner*. London: University of London and School of Oriental and African Studies. 7–28.

Boersma, Paul. 2008. Emergent ranking of faithfulness explains markedness and licensing by cue. Unpublished manuscript, available at www.fon.hum.uva.nl/paul/papers/EmergeFaith.pdf.

Brame, Michael. 1970. Arabic phonology: implications for phonological theory and general Semitic. Doctoral dissertation, Massachusetts Institute of Technology.

Browman, Catherine P. and Louis Goldstein. 1986. Towards an articulatory phonology. *Phonology Yearbook 3*. Cambridge University Press. 219–252.

1989. Articulatory gestures as phonological units. *Phonology* 6: 201–251.

1992. Articulatory phonology: an overview. *Phonetica* **49**: 155–180.

Bybee, Joan. 2001. *Phonology and Language Use*. Cambridge University Press.

2005. Restrictions on phonemes in affixes: a crosslinguistic test of a popular hypothesis. *Linguistic Typology* **9**: 165–222.

Byrd, Dani. 1994. Articulatory timing in English consonant sequences. Doctoral dissertation, UCLA.

Cameron, Richard. 1992. Pronominal and null subject variation in Spanish: constraints, dialects, and functional compensation. Doctoral dissertation, University of Pennsylvania.

Charles-Luce, J. 1993. The effects of semantic context on voicing neutralization. *Phonetica* **50**: 28–43.

Chitoran, Ilona, Louis Goldstein, and Dani Byrd. 2002. Gestural overlap and recoverability: articulatory evidence from Georgian. In Carlos Gussenhoven and Natasha Warner, eds., *Laboratory Phonology 7*. Berlin/New York: Mouton de Gruyter. 419–447.

Chomsky, Noam and Morris Halle. 1968. *The Sound Pattern of English*. New York: Harper & Row.

Clark, Eve V. and Herbert H. Clark. 1979. When nouns surface as verbs. *Language* **55**: 767–811.

Clayton, Mary L. 1976. The redundancy of underlying morpheme-structure conditions. *Language* **52**: 295–313.

Clements, G. Nick and Rachid Ridouane, eds. 2011. *Where Do Phonological Features Come From?* Amsterdam: John Benjamins.

Clumeck, Harold. 1976. Patterns of soft palate movements in six languages. *Journal of Phonetics* **4**: 337–351.

Cohn, Abby. 1993. Nasalisation in English: phonology or phonetics. *Phonology* **10**: 43–81.

     2011. Features, segments, and the sources of phonological primitives. In Clements and Ridouane. 15–41.

Collins, Beverly and Inger M. Mees. 1990. The phonetics of Cardiff English. In Nikolas Coupland, ed., *English in Wales: Diversity Conflict, and Change*. 87–103.

Crosswhite, Katherine. 1999. Intra-paradigmatic homophony avoidance in two dialects of Slavic. In Matthew K. Gordon, ed., *Papers in Phonology 2*, vol. 1 of *UCLA Working Papers in Linguistics*. Los Angeles: UCLA. 48–67.

Davidsen-Nielson, Niels. 1978. *Neutralization and Archiphoneme – Two Phonological Concepts and their History*. Copenhagen: Akademisk Forlag/Wilhelm Fink Verlag.

de Boer, Bart. 2001. *The Origins of Vowel Systems*. Oxford University Press.

Derwing, Bruce L. 1992. Orthographic aspects of linguistic competence. In P. Downing, S. D. Lima, and M. Noonan, eds., *The Linguistics of Literacy*. Amsterdam/Philadelphia: John Benjamins: 193–210.

Deutscher, Guy. 2005. *The Unfolding of Language*. New York: Henry Holt and Company.

Diver, William. 1979. Phonology as human behavior. In D. Aaronson and R. Rieber, eds., *Psycholinguistic Research: Implications and Applications*. Hillsdale, NJ: Lawrence Erlbaum Associates. 161–182.

Drescher, B. Elan. 2011. The phoneme. In Van Oostendorp *et al.* 241–266.

Ernestus, Mirjam. 2006. Statistically gradient generalizations in phonology. *The Linguistic Review* **23**: 217–234.

2011. Gradience and categoricality in phonological theory. In Van Oostendorp *et al.* 2115–2136.

Ernestus, Mirjam and R. Harald Baayen. 2011. Corpora and exemplars in phonology. In Goldsmith *et al.* 374–400.

Everett, Daniel L. 2008. *Don't Sleep, There Are Snakes: Life and Language in the Amazonian Jungle*. New York: Pantheon.

Faber, Alice. 1992. Phonemic segmentation as epiphenomenon: evidence from the history of alphabetic writing. In P. Downing, S. Lima, and M. Noonan, eds., *The Linguistics of Literacy*. Amsterdam: John Benjamins. 111–134.

Faneslow, Gisbert, Caroline Féry, Matthias Schlesewsky, and Ralf Vogel, eds. 2006. *Gradience in Grammar: Generative Perspectives*. Oxford University Press.

Féry, Caroline and Ruben van de Vijver, eds. 2003. *The Syllable in Optimality Theory*. Cambridge University Press.

Firth, John Rupert, 1948. Sounds and prosodies. *Transactions of the Philological Society*. 127–52.

1957a. *Papers in Linguistics*. London: Oxford University Press.

ed. 1957b. *Studies in Linguistic Analysis*. Special volume of the Philological Society. Oxford: Basil Blackwell.

Firth, John Rupert and B. Rogers. 1937. The structure of the Chinese monosyllable in a Hunanese dialect Changsha. *Bulletin of the School of Oriental Studies* **8**: 1055–1074

Fischer-Jørgensen, Eli. 1952. On the definition of phoneme categories on a distributional basis. *Acta Linguistica* **7**: 8–39.

1975. *Trends in Phonological Theory*. Copenhagen: Akademisk Forlag.

Flemming, Edward. 1995. Auditory representations in phonology. Doctoral dissertation, University of California, Los Angeles.

2009. The phonetics of schwa vowels. In Donka Minova, ed., *Phonological Weakness in English*. Palgrave. 78–95.

Flores, Luis, John Myhill, and Fernando Tarallo. 1983. Competing plural markers in Puerto Rican Spanish. *Linguistics* **21**: 897–906.

Fowler, Carol. 1988. Differential shortening of repeated content words produced in various communicative contexts. *Language and Speech* **31**: 307–319.

Fujimura, Osamu. 1962. Analysis of nasal consonants. *The Journal of the Acoustical Society of America* **34**: 1865–1875.

Gahl, Susanne. 2008. Time and thyme are not homophones: the effect of lemma frequency on word durations in spontaneous speech. *Language* **84**: 474–496.

Gallistel, Randy. 1990. *The Organization of Learning*. Cambridge, MA: MIT Press.

Garde, Paul. 1961. Réflexions sur les différences phonétiques entre les langues slaves. *Word* **17**: 34–62.

Gerfen, Chip. 2001. A critical view of licensing by cue: the case of Andalusian Spanish. In Lombardi. 183–205.

Gessner, Suzanne and Gunnar Hansson. 2004. Anti-homophony effects in Dakelh (Carrier) valence morphology. In Marc Ettlinger, Nicholas

Fleischer, and Mischa Park-Doob, eds., *Proceedings of the 30th Annual Meeting of the Berkeley Linguistics Society*. 93–104.

Gilliéron, Jules. 1910. Études de géographie linguistique XII – mots et collision. A. Le coq et le chat. *Revue de philologie française* 4: 278–288.

Goldsmith, John 1976. Autosegmental phonology. Doctoral dissertation, Massachusetts Institute of Technology.

1992. A note on the genealogy of research traditions in modern phonology. *Journal of Linguistics* 28: 149–163.

1994. Disentangling autosegments: a response. *Journal of Linguistics* 30: 499–507.

ed. 1995. *The Handbook of Phonological Theory*. Cambridge: Blackwell.

2011. The syllable. In Goldsmith *et al.* 164–196.

Goldsmith, John, Jason Riggle, and Alan Yu, eds. 2011. *The Handbook of Phonological Theory*, vol. 2 Oxford: Blackwell.

Gurevich, Naomi. 2001. A critique of markedness-based theories in phonology. *Studies in the Linguistic Sciences* 31: 89–114.

2004. *Lenition and Contrast: Functional Consequences of Certain Phonetically Conditioned Sound Changes*. Outstanding Dissertations in Linguistics series, Routledge: New York.

Hall, Nancy. 2009. Long-distance /r/-dissimilation in American English. Unpublished manuscript, California State University at Long Beach.

Halle, Morris. 1959. *The Sound Pattern of Russian*. The Hague: Mouton.

1962. Phonology in generative grammar. *Word* 18: 54–72.

Halle, Morris and Jean-Roger Vergnaud. 1987. *An Essay on Stress*. Cambridge, MA: MIT Press.

Hansson, Gunnar. 2001. Remains of a submerged continent: preaspiration in the languages of Northwest Europe. In L. Brinton, ed., *Historical Linguistics*. Amsterdam: John Benjamins. 157–173.

2003. Laryngeal licensing and laryngeal neutralization in Faroese and Icelandic. *Nordic Journal of Linguistics* 26: 45–79.

Harris, Zellig. 1944. Simultaneous components in phonology. *Language* 20: 181–205.

1951. *Methods in Structural Linguistics*. University of Chicago Press.

Haspelmath, Martin. 2006. Against markedness (and what to replace it with). *Journal of Linguistics* 42: 25–70.

Hayes, Bruce. 1995. *Metrical Stress Theory*: Principles and Case Studies. University of Chicago Press.

Hayes Bruce, Robert Kirchner, and Donca Steriade, eds. 2004. *Phonetically Based Phonology*. Cambridge University Press.

Henderson, Eugenie J. A. 1985. Feature shuffling in Southeast Asian languages. In Suriya Ratanakul, David D. Thomas, and Suwilai Premsrirat, eds., *Southeast Asian Linguistic Studies Presented to André-G. Haudricourt*. Institute of Language and Culture for Rural Development, Mahidol University. 1–22.

Herzog, Marvin I. 1965. *The Yiddish Language in Northern Poland: Its Geography and History*. The Hague: Mouton.

Hochberg, Judith G. 1986a. Functional compensation for /s/ deletion in Puerto Rican Spanish. *Language* **62**: 609–621.

1986b. /s/ deletion and pronoun usage in Puerto Rican Spanish. In David Sankoff, ed., *Diversity and Diachrony*. Amsterdam: Benjamins. 199–210.

Hockett, Charles F. 1955. *A Manual of Phonology*. Indiana University Publications in Anthropology and Linguistics 11.

1967. The quantification of functional load. *Word* **23**: 301–320.

Hoenigswald, Henry M. 1960. *Language Change and Linguistic Reconstruction*. University of Chicago Press.

Houston, Ann. 1985. Continuity and change in English morphology: the variable (ING). Doctoral dissertation, University of Pennsylvania.

Hulst, Harry G. van der. 1980. Towards a lexical theory of phonological change. In Wim Zonneveld and Fred Weerman, eds., *Linguistics in the Netherlands 1977–79*. Dordrecht: Foris, 170–182.

Hume, Elizabeth. 2011. Markedness. In Van Oostendorp *et al.* 79–107.

2012. *Phonological Markedness*. Cambridge University Press.

Ichimura, Larry. 2006. Anti-homophony blocking and its productivity in transparadigmatic relations. Doctoral dissertation, Boston University.

Itô, Junko. 1986 (1988). *Syllable Theory in Prosodic Phonology*. Doctoral dissertation, University of Massachusetts at Amherst. Outstanding Dissertations in Linguistics series. New York: Garland.

1989. A prosodic theory of epenthesis. *Natural Language and Linguistic Theory* **7**: 217–260.

Itô, Junko and Armin Mester. 2004. Morphological contrast and merger: ranuki in Japanese. *Journal of Japanese Linguistics* **20**: 1–18.

Itô, Junko, Armin Mester, and Jaye Padgett. 1995. Licensing and underspecification in optimality theory. *Linguistic Inquiry* **26**: 571–613.

Ivić, Milka. 1965. *Trends in Linguistics*. The Hague/Paris: Mouton.

Jakobson, Roman. 1965. Quest for the essence of language. *Diogenes* **13**: 21–37.

Jakobson, Roman, Gunnar Fant, and Morris Halle. 1952. *Preliminaries to Speech Analysis*. Cambridge, MA: MIT Press.

Jones, Daniel. 1950. *The Phoneme – Its Nature and Use*. Cambridge: W. Heffer and Sons.

Jun, Jongho. 1995. Perceptual and articulatory factors in place assimilation: an optimality theoretic approach. Doctoral dissertation, University of California, Los Angeles.

2002. Positional faithfulness, sympathy and inferred input. Unpublished manuscript, available at http://ling.snu.ac.kr/jun/work/inferred.pdf.

2004. Place assimilation. In Hayes *et al.* 58–86.

2010. Stem-final obstruent variation in Korean. *Journal of East Asian Linguistics* **19**: 137–179.

Kahn, Daniel. 1976. Syllable-based generalizations in English phonology. Doctoral dissertation, Massachusetts Institute of Technology.

Kaplan, Abby. 2011a. How much homophony is normal? *Journal of Linguistics* **48**(2): 1–41.

2011b. Perceptual pressures on lenition. *Language and Speech* **54**: 285–305.

Keating, Patricia. 1985. Universal phonetics and the organization of grammars. In Victoria Fromkin, ed., *Phonetic Linguistic Essays in Honor of Peter Ladefoged*. Orlando: Academic Press. 115–132.

Keller, Rudi. 1994. *On Language Change – The Invisible Hand in Language*. London/New York: Routledge.

Kelly, John and John Local. 1989. *Doing Phonology*. Manchester University Press.

Kenstowicz, Michael. 2005. Paradigmatic uniformity and contrast. In Laura Downing, T. Alan Hall, and Renate Raffelsiefen, eds., *Paradigms in Phonological Theory*. 145–169.

Kenstowicz, Michael and Charles Kisseberth. 1977. *Topics in Phonological Theory*. New York: Academic Press.

King, Robert. 1967. Functional load and sound change. *Language* **43**: 831–852.

1969. *Historical Linguistics and Generative Grammar*. Englewood Cliffs, NJ: Prentice-Hall.

Kiparsky, Paul. 1973. Abstractness, opacity, and global rules. In Osamu Fujimura, ed., *Three Dimensions of Linguistic Theory*. Tokyo Institute for Advanced Studies of Language. 57–86.

1978. Rule reordering. In Philip Baldi and Ronald N. Werth, eds., *Readings in Historical Phonology*. Pennsylvania State University Press. 218–235.

1982. Lexical phonology and morphology. In I.-S. Yang, ed., *Linguistics in the Morning Calm*. Seoul: Hanshin. 3–91.

1985. Some consequences of lexical phonology. *Phonology Yearbook* 2. 82–138.

Kirchner, Robert. 1996. Synchronic chain shifts in optimality theory. *Linguistic Inquiry* **27**: 341–349.

1998 (2001). *An Effort-Based Approach to Consonant Lenition*. Doctoral dissertation, University of California, Los Angeles. Outstanding Dissertations in Linguistics series. New York: Garland.

2004. Consonant lenition. In Hayes *et al.* 313–345.

Kisseberth, Charles. 1970. On the functional unity of phonological rules. *Linguistic Inquiry* **1**: 291–306.

Kochetov, Alexei. 2006. Testing licensing by cue: a case of Russian palatalized coronals. *Phonetica* **63**: 113–148.

Koerner, Konrad. 1986. Mikołaj Kruszewski's contribution to general linguistic theory. In Dieter Kastovsky and Alexander Szwedek, eds., *Linguistics Across Geographical Boundaries*. Berlin/New York: Walter de Gruyter. 53–75.

ed. 1995. *Writings in General Linguistics*. Amsterdam: John Benjamins.

Kruszewski, Mikołaj. 1881 (1995). On sound alternation. In Koerner. 1–34.

1883 (1995). Očerk Nauki O Jazyke [An Outline of Linguistic Science]. In Koerner. 35–178.

Kula, Nancy C., Bert Botma, and Kuniya Nasukawa, eds. 2011. *The Continuum Companion to Phonology*. London: Continuum.

Kurowski, Kathleen and Sheila Blumstein. 1984. Perceptual integration of the murmur and formant transitions for place of articulation in nasal consonants. *Journal of the Acoustical Society of America* **76**: 383–390.

1987. Acoustic properties for place of articulation in nasal consonants. *Journal of the Acoustical Society of America* **81**: 1917–1927.

Labov, William. 1994. *Principles of Linguistic Change: Internal Factors*. Oxford: Blackwell.

Ladefoged, Peter. 2005. *Vowels and Consonants*. Wiley-Blackwell.

Langendoen, D. Terence. 1968. *The London School of Linguistics: The Linguistic Theories of B. Malinowski and J. R. Firth*. Cambridge, MA: The MIT Press.

Lavoie, Lisa M. 2001. *Consonant Strength: Phonological Patterns and Phonetic Manifestations*. Outstanding Dissertations in Linguistics Series. New York: Garland.

Leben, William. 1973. Suprasegmental phonology. Doctoral dissertation, Massachusetts Institute of Technology.

Leroy, Maurice. 1967. *Main Trends in Modern Linguistics*. University of California Press.

Liberman, Mark and Alan Prince. 1977. On stress and linguistic rhythm. *Linguistic Inquiry* **8**: 249–336.

Liljencrants, Johan and Bjorn Lindblom. 1972. Numerical simulation of vowel quality systems: the role of perceptual contrast. *Language* **48**: 839–862.

Lincoln, Peter. 1976. Describing Banoni, an Austronesian language of Southwest Bougainville. Doctoral dissertation, University of Hawaii.

Lindblom, Bjorn. 1990. Explaining phonetic variation: a sketch of the H and H theory. In W. J. Hardcastle and A. Marchal, eds., *Speech Production and Speech Modeling*. Dordrecht: Kluwer Academic Publishers. 403–439.

Lindblom, Björn, Randy Diehl, Sang-Hoon Park, and Giampiero Salvi. 2011. Sound systems are shaped by their users: the recombination of phonetic substance. In Clements and Ridouane. 65–98.

Linell, Per. 1982. The written language bias in linguistics. Studies in Communication. Linköping: Department of Communication Studies.

2005. *The Written Language Bias in Linguistics – Its Nature, Origins, and Transformations*. London: Routledge.

Lodge, Ken. 2009. *Fundamental Concepts in Phonology: Sameness and Difference*. Edinburgh University Press.

Lombardi Linda, ed. 2001. *Segmental Phonology in Optimality Theory*. Cambridge University Press.

Lyons, John. 1962. Phonemic and non-phonemic phonology. *International Journal of American Linguistics* 28: 127–133.

Malmberg, Bertil. 1963. *Structural Linguistics and Human Communication.* Berlin: Springer-Verlag.

Manuel, Sharon. 1990. The role of contrast in limiting vowel-to-vowel coarticulation in different languages. *Journal of the Acoustical Society of America* 88: 1286–1298.

1999. Cross-language studies: relating language-particular coarticulation patterns to other language-particular facts. In William J. Hardcastle and Nigel Hewlett, eds., *Coarticulation.* Cambridge University Press. 179–199.

Manuel, Sharon and Rena Krakow. 1984. Universal and language particular aspects of vowel-to-vowel coarticulation. Haskins Laboratories Status Report on Speech Research, SR77/78: 69–78.

Martin, Samuel E. 1992. *A Reference Grammar of Korean.* Rutland, VT: Charles E. Tuttle.

Martinet, André. 1952. Function, structure, and sound change. *Word* 8(2): 1–32.

1955. *Économie des changements phonétiques.* Traité de phonologie diachronique. Berne: Francke.

1975 (1988). The internal conditioning of phonological changes. *La Linguistique* 24: 17–26.

Mattingly, Ignatius G. 1981. Phonetic representations and speech synthesis by rule. In Terry Myers, John Laver, and John Mathieson Anderson, eds., *The Cognitive Representation of Speech.* Amsterdam: North Holland Publishing Company. 415–419.

McCarthy, John J. 1979. Formal problems in semitic phonology and morphology. Doctoral dissertation, Massachusetts Institute of Technology.

1998. Morpheme structure constraints and paradigm occultation. In M. Catherine Gruber, Derrick Higgins, Kenneth Olson, and Tamra Wysocki, eds., *Chicago Linguistics Society 32, Part 2: The Panels.* Chicago Linguistic Society. 123–150.

1999. Sympathy and phonological opacity. *Phonology* 16: 331–399.

2007. *Hidden Generalizations: Phonological Opacity in Optimality Theory.* London: Equinox.

McCarthy, John J. and Alan Prince. 1995. Faithfulness and reduplicative identity. In Jill Beckman, Laura Walsh Dickey, and Suzanne Urbanczyk, eds., *Papers in Optimality Theory.* University of Massachusetts Occasional Papers 18. Amherst, MA: Graduate Linguistic Student Association. 249–384.

1996. Prosodic morphology. Technical Report #32, Rutgers University Center for Cognitive Science.

Mester, Armin and Junko Ito. 1989. Feature predictability and underspecification. *Language* 65: 258–293.

Mondon, Jean-François. 2009. The nature of homophony and its effects on diachrony and synchrony. Doctoral dissertation, University of Pennsylvania.

Newmeyer, Frederick J. 2006. On Gahl and Garnsey on grammar and usage. *Language* **82**: 399–404.

Nooteboom, Sieb. 1981. Lexical retrieval from fragments of spoken words: beginnings versus endings. *Journal of Phonetics* **9**: 407–424.

Ogden, Richard and John Local. 1994. Disentangling autosegments from prosodies: a note on the misrepresentation of a research tradition in phonology. *Journal of Linguistics* **30**: 477–498.

Ohala, John J. 1975. Phonetic explanations for nasal sound patterns. In Charles A. Ferguson, Larry M. Hyman, and John J. Ohala, eds., *Nasálfest: Papers from a Symposium on Nasals and Nasalization*. Language Universals Project, Stanford University. 289–316.

1981. The listener as a source of sound change. In Carrie S. Masek, Roberta A. Hendrick, and Mary F. Miller, eds., *Papers from the Parasession on Language and Behavior*. Chicago Linguistics Society. 178–203.

1989. Sound change is drawn from a pool of synchronic variation. In Leiv Egil Breivik and Ernst Håkon Jahr, eds., *Language Change: Contributions to the Study of its Causes*. Berlin: Mouton de Gruyter. 173–198.

1990. The phonetics and phonology of aspects of assimilation. In J. Kingston and M. Beckman, eds., *Papers in Laboratory Phonology I: Between the Grammar and the Physics of Speech*. Cambridge University Press. 258–275.

1992. What's cognitive, what's not, in sound change. In Guenter Kellermann and Michael D. Morrissey, eds., *Diachrony Within Synchrony: Language History and Cognition*. Frankfurt/M: Peter Lang Verlag. 309–355.

1993a. Coarticulation and phonology. *Language and Speech* **36**: 155–170.

1993b. The phonetics of sound change. In Charles Jones, ed., *Historical Linguistics: Problems and Perspectives*. London: Longman. 237–278.

Ohala, John J., Harowuki Kawasaki, Carol Riordan, and Michelle Caisse. (no date). The influence of consonant environment upon the perception of vowel quality. Unpublished manuscript, cited in Ohala (1981).

Öhman, Sven E. G. 1966. Coarticulation in VCV utterances: spectrographic measurements. *Journal of the Acoustical Society of America* **39**: 151–168.

Palmer, F. R. 1970. *Prosodic Analysis*. London: Oxford University Press.

Pike, Kenneth L. 1952. Operational phonemics in reference to linguistic relativity. *Journal of the Acoustical Society of America* **24**: 618–625.

Port, Robert. 2006. The graphical basis of phones and phonemes. In Murray Munro and Ocke-Schwen Bohn, eds., *Second Language Speech Learning: The Role of Language Experience in Speech Perception and Production*. Amsterdam: Benjamins. 349–365.

Port, Robert and Penny Crawford. 1989. Incomplete neutralization and pragmatics in German. *Journal of Phonetics* **17**: 257–282.

Port, Robert and Adam Leary. 2005. Against formal phonology. *Language* **85**: 927–964.

Port, Robert and Michael L. O'Dell. 1985. Neutralization of syllable-final voicing in German. *Journal of Phonetics* **13**: 455–471.

Prince, Alan. 1983. Relating to the grid. *Linguistic Inquiry* **14**: 19–100.

Prince, Alan and Paul Smolensky. 2004. *Optimality Theory: Constraint Interaction in Generative Grammar*. Oxford: Blackwell.

Pye, Susan. 1986. Word-final devoicing of obstruents in Russian. *Cambridge Papers in Phonetics and Experimental Linguistics* **5**: 1–10.

Radwańska Williams, Joanna. 1996. Kruszewski's semiotics. In Kurt R. Jankowsky, ed., *Multiple Perspectives of the Historical Development of Language*. Münster: Nodus.

    2002. The Polish tradition in linguistics. *Historiographica Linguistica* **29**(3): 391–430.

    2006. Examining our patrimony. *Historiographica Linguistica* **33**(3): 357–390.

Read, Charles, Zhang Yun-fei, Nie Hong-yin, and Ding Bao-qing. 1997. The ability to manipulate speech sounds depends on knowing alphabetic writing. *Cognition* **24**: 31–44.

Recasens, Daniel, 1983. Place cues for nasals with special reference to Catalan. *Journal of the Acoustical Society of America* **70**: 329–339.

Recasens, Daniel, M. D., Pallarès and J. Fontdevila. 1998. An electropalatographic and acoustic study of temporal coarticulation for Catalan dark /l/ and German clear /l/. *Phonetica* **55**: 53–79.

Robins, R. H. 1957a. Aspects of prosodic analysis. *Proceedings of the University of Durham Philosophical Society* 1:1–12. Reprinted in Palmer, 1970: 188–200.

    1957b. Vowel nasality in Sundanese: a phonological and grammatical study. In J. R. Firth, ed., *Studies in Linguistic Analysis*. Oxford: Blackwell. 87–103.

    1967. *A Short History of Linguistics*. London/New York: Longman.

Rice, Keren. 1999. Featural markedness in phonology: variation. *GLOT International* **4**(7): 3–6; **4**(8): 3–7.

Saffran, Jenny R. 2001. Words in a sea of sounds: the output of infant statistical learning. *Cognition* **81**: 149–169.

Saffran, Jenny R., Elissa L. Newport, and Richard N. Aslin. 1996. Word segmentation: the role of distributional cues. *Journal of Memory and Language* **35**: 606–621.

Sampson, Geoffrey. 1980. *Schools of Linguistics*. Stanford University Press.

Sapir, Edward. 1933. La réalité psychologique des phonèmes. *Journal de Psychologie Normale et Pathalogique* **30**: 247–265.

Scobbie, James M. 2007. Interface and overlap in phonetics and phonology. In Gillian Ramchand and Charles Reiss, eds., *Oxford Handbook of Linguistic Interfaces*. Oxford University Press. 17–52.

Scobbie, James M. and Koen Sebregts. 2011. Acoustic, articulatory, and phonological perspectives on rhoticity and /r/ in Dutch. In Rafaella Folli and Christiane Ulbrich, eds., *Interfaces in Linguistics: New Research Perspectives*. Oxford Studies in Theoretical Linguistics. Oxford University Press. 257–277.

Scobbie, James M. and Jane Stuart-Smith. 2008. Quasi-phonemic contrast and the fuzzy inventory: examples from Scottish English. In Peter Avery, Elan B. Dresher, and Keren Rice, eds., *Contrast: Perception and Acquisition: Selected papers from the Second International Conference on Contrast in Phonology*. Berlin: Mouton de Gruyter. 87–113.

Serniclaes, Willy. 2011. Features are phonological transforms of natural boundaries. In Clements and Ridouane. 237–258.

Silverman, Daniel. 1995 (1997). Phasing and Recoverability. Doctoral dissertation, University of California, Los Angeles. Outstanding Dissertations in Linguistics series. New York: Garland.

2000. Hypotheses concerning the phonetic and functional origins of tone displacement in Zulu. *Studies in African Linguistics* **29**(2): 3–32.

2002. Dynamic versus static phonotactic conditions in prosodic morphology. *Linguistics* **40**: 28–58.

2004. On the phonetic and cognitive nature of alveolar stop allophony in American English. *Cognitive Linguistics* **15**: 69–93.

2006a. *A Critical Introduction to Phonology: of Sound, Mind, and Body*. London/New York: Continuum Books.

2006b. The diachrony of labiality in Trique, and the functional relevance of gradience and variation. In Louis M. Goldstein, Douglas H. Whalen, and Catherine T. Best, eds., *Papers in Laboratory Phonology VIII*. Mouton de Gruyter. 133–154.

2010. Neutralization and anti-homophony in Korean. *Journal of Linguistics* **46**: 453–482.

2011. Schwa. In Van Oostendorp *et al.* 628–642.

2012a. Mikołaj Kruszewski: theory and vision, Part 1. *Language and Linguistics Compass*.

2012b. Mikołaj Kruszewski: theory and vision, Part 2. *Language and Linguistics Compass*.

Slowiaczek, Louisa M. and Daniel Dinnsen. 1985. On the neutralizing status of Polish word-final devoicing. *Journal of Phonetics* **13**: 325–334.

Sohn, Ho-Minh. 1999. *The Korean Language*. Cambridge University Press.

Stampe, David. 1969. *The acquisition of phonetic representation. Papers from the Fifth Regional Meeting, Chicago Linguistics Society*. Chicago Linguistic Society. 443–454.

1973a. How I spent my summer vacation. Doctoral dissertation, University of Chicago.

1973b. On chapter nine. In Michael Kenstowicz and Charles Kisseberth, eds., *Issues in Phonological Theory*. The Hague: Mouton. 44–52.

Stanley, Richard. 1967. Redundancy rules in phonology. *Language* **43**: 393–436.

Steriade, Donca. 1988. Reduplication and syllable transfer in Sanskrit and elsewhere. *Phonology* **5**: 73–155.

1995. Underspecification and markedness. In Goldsmith. 114–174.

1999. Alternatives to the syllabic interpretation of consonantal phonotactics. In Osamu Fujimura, Brian Joseph, and Bohumil Palek, eds., *Proceedings of the 1998 Linguistics and Phonetics Conference*. The Karolinum Press. 205–242.

2001. Directional asymmetries in place assimilation: a perceptual account. In Elizabeth Hume and Keith Johnson, eds., *Perception in Phonology*. San Diego: Academic Press. 219–250.

2008. The phonology of perceptibility effects: the P-map and its consequences for constraint organization. In Sharon Inkelas and Kristin Hanson, eds., *The Nature of the Word*. Cambridge, MA: The MIT Press. 151–180.

Stockwell, Robert Paul and Ronald K. S. Macaulay, eds. 1972. *Linguistic Change and Generative Theory* (Study in History & Theory of Linguistics). Indiana University Press.

Surendran, Dinoj and Partha Niyogi. 2003. Measuring the usefulness (functional load) of phonological contrasts. Technical Report TR-2003–12. Department of Computer Science, University of Chicago.

2006. Quantifying the functional load of phonemic oppositions, distinctive features, and suprasegmentals. In Ole Nedergaard Thomsen, ed., *Competing Models of Linguistic Change: Evolution and Beyond*. Amsterdam/Philadelphia: John Benjamins. 43–58.

Swadesh, Morris. 1934. The phonemic principle. *Language* **10**: 117–129.

Szigetvari, Peter. 2011. Syllables. In Kula *et al.* 64–94.

Takeuchi, S., H. Kasuya, and K. Kido. 1975. On the acoustic correlate of nasality. *Journal of the Acoustical Society of Japan* **31**: 298–309.

Tobin, Yishai. 1997. *Phonology as Human Behavior: Theoretical Implications and Clinical Applications*. Durham, NC/London: Duke University Press, 55–800.

Trubetzkoy, Nikolaj S. 1939 (1969). *Principles of Phonology*, Berkeley: University of California Press.

Twaddell, William Freeman. 1935 (1957). On defining the phoneme. In Martin Joos, ed., *Readings in Linguistics I*. University of Chicago Press. 55–80.

Urbanczyk, Suzanne. 2006. Reduplicative form and the root-affix asymmetry. *Natural Language and Linguistic Theory* **24**: 179–240.

2007. Reduplication. In Paul de Lacy, ed., *Cambridge Handbook of Phonology*. Cambridge University Press. 473–493.

2011. Root-affix asymmetries. In Van Oostendorp *et al.* 473–493.

Van Oostendorp, Marc, Colin J. Ewen, Elizabeth Hume, and Keren Rice, eds. 2011. *The Blackwell Companion to Phonology*. Wiley-Blackwell.

Vennemann, Theo. 1972. Sound change and markedness theory: on the history of the German consonant system. In Stockwell and Macaulay. 230–274.

1988. *Preference Laws for Syllable Structure and the Explanation of Sound Change: With Special Reference to German, Germanic, Italian, and Latin*. Berlin: Mouton de Gruyter.

Warner, Natasha, Allard Jongman, Joan Sereno, and Rachèl Kemps. 2004. Incomplete neutralization and other sub-phonemic durational differences in production and perception: evidence from Dutch. *Journal of Phonetics* **32**: 251–276.

Whitney, William D. 1889. *Sanskrit Grammar*. Cambridge, MA: Harvard University Press.

Wilson, Colin. 2001. Consonant cluster neutralisation and targeted constraints. *Phonology* **18**: 147–197.

Wright, Richard. 2004. A review of perceptual cues and cue robustness. In Hayes *et al.* 34–57.

Yu, Alan C. L. 2004. Explaining final obstruent voicing in Lezgian: phonetics and history. *Language* **80**: 73–97.

  2007. Understanding near mergers: the case of morphological tone in Cantonese. *Phonology* **24**: 187–214.

  2011. Mergers and neutralization. In Van Oostendorp *et al.* 1892–1918.

Zipf, G. K. 1949. *Human Behavior and the Principle of Least Effort*. Cambridge, MA: Addison-Wesley Press.

Zsiga, Elizabeth C. 1993. Features, gestures, and the temporal aspects of phonological organization. Doctoral dissertation, Yale University.

  1997. Features, gestures, and Igbo vowels: an approach to the phonology/phonetics interface. *Language* **73**: 227–274.

Language index

Abipon, 37
Aghul, 48
Akan, 37
Amele, 59
Amharic, 37
Arabic (*see also* Semitic), 32, 178–179
Artshi, 48
Austronesian, 145, 149–151, 153, 154

Banoni, 141, 145
Bantu, 38
Bashkir, 171
Bulgarian, 45, 49, 50, 51, 141, 144, 145

Cantonese (*see also* Chinese), 28, 33, 69, 142–143
Catalan, 29, 32, 33, 69, 71–72
Caucasian, 48
Ch'ak'ur, 48
Cheremis, 48
Chinese (*see also* Cantonese, Hunanese, Mandarin), 134–135, 138, 139, 141, 142–143, 179–180
Corsican, 59
Czech, 49

Danish, 44, 178
Darghinian, 48
Diola Fogny, 32
Dutch, 16, 32, 33, 69–70, 80

English, 16, 18, 44, 53–57, 58–59, 63–69, 79, 106–107, 111–112, 122–123, 127, 142, 155–156, 169, 180, 189–193

Finnish, 104, 170, 171
French, 44, 46, 104, 112, 120, 141, 142

Gaelic, 49, 167, 168, 177
German, 28, 34, 43, 46, 69, 115–116, 169
Greek, 33, 45, 51, 84, 93

Hindi, 125–126, 141, 143–144
Hunanese (*see also* Chinese), 179–180
Hungarian, 32

Icelandic, 115–116
Igbo, 171

Japanese, 33, 84, 104, 168

Kanuri, 37
Kazakh-Kirghiz, 171
Korean, 12, 34, 118, 129, 130–139, 140, 141, 143, 196
Kubachi, 48

Latin, 93, 102, 104, 106, 113
Lezghian, 48
Lithuanian, 32

Malay, 33
Malayalam, 59, 95
Mandarin (*see also* Chinese), 45, 142–143
Mongolian, 49

Nilotic, 39
Nootka, 21

Old Saxon, 115
Otomanguean, 39

Pirahã, xiv, 149, 153–156
Polish, 28, 32, 49, 69
Ponapean, 34

Quechua, 37

Romance, 29, 104
Romanian, 32
Russian, 16–18, 48, 49, 69, 127, 161,
    169, 170
Rutulian, 48

Salish, 37, 38, 39
Sanskrit, 19, 32, 38, 40, 95, 181–182
Semitic, 39, 178–179, 186
Serbo-Croatian, 32, 48, 49
Shona, 104, 127
Slave, 33, 34
Slavic, 48, 49, 50
Slovak, 48
Slovenian, 49
Songkhla, 23
Spanish, 33, 69, 84, 120–121, 149,
    151–153

Sundanese, 182–184
Swahili, 127
Swedish, 127

Tamil, 168, 171
Tatar, 171
Thai, 28
Toba Batak, 34
Tohono-O'odam, 37
Turkic, 50, 162, 171

Ukrainian, 32
Uzbek, 171

Volga, 171

Warndarang, 59–60

Yakut, 32
Yiddish, 32, 115, 116

Subject index

alternation, 12, 118, 119, 130–139, 140–148

anti-homophony (*see also* homophony), 119, 131–139, 140–148

archiphonemes, 42–51, 186

articulatory anticipation, 20, 78, 80–85

articulatory undershoot, 78–80, 85

assimilation, 2, 5, 9, 10, 15, 16, 22, 28, 31–35, 38, 72, 78–85, 87–91, 93–96, 101, 103–106, 123–125, 133, 136, 137, 139, 146, 147, 156, 161, 163, 181, 185, 197

Babelese, 1–12, 123–125, 166–167, 197–199

boundary signals, 165–173, 174, 176, 177, 179–180, 185, 186, 188, 190, 193

cement, 161–164, 165, 176, 193

centrifugal vowel neutralization, 16, 29, 35–36

centripetal vowel neutralization, 16, 29, 35

chain shifting, 59, 60, 68–69, 110

coarticulation, 7, 9–11, 16, 84, 87, 102, 103, 127–128, 133, 146, 147

commutation (of contrastive values), 1, 3, 5, 7, 16, 175

commutation test, 64, 69, 73–75

devoicing, 28, 33, 58–59, 69–73, 92–93, 97, 123, 172

distinctive feature theory, 7, 8, 11, 21, 22, 92, 93

evaluation metric, 91, 93, 96

frequency (in phonology), 39, 66, 73–76, 112, 113, 114–116, 128, 131–137, 161–163, 187–193

functional load, 110–118, 154–156

Garde's Principle, 62, 63, 64, 65, 66, 67

generative theory, 39–40, 105–106, 128, 177–178, 184

Gestalten, 6–7, 197–198

H&H hypothesis, 86–87, 96–99

heterophony, 4, 11, 72, 125, 137, 165, 194, 196, 198, 199

homophony (*see also* anti-homophony), 3, 4, 7, 8, 10, 11, 58, 71, 72, 76, 77, 112, 115, 117, 120, 123, 124, 125, 126, 128, 130–139, 140–148, 149, 150, 154, 156, 165, 194, 195, 196, 198, 199

hyper-articulation, 86–87, 91

hyper-correction, 102–103, 105, 156

hypo-articulation, 86–87, 91

hypo-correction, 102–103, 105

laryngeal neutralization, 15, 28, 31–35, 130, 132, 134

markedness, 45, 46–48, 88

monosystemicity, 175, 185, 186, 188

morphonemes, 42, 50–51, 186

near-merger, 62–69, 70, 71, 76

near-neutralization, 35, 36, 52, 62–77, 137, 145, 146

optimality theory, 28, 39, 87, 88, 92, 145

partial phonemic overlap, 53–61
phonemic theory, 18–19, 22, 37, 42–52, 53–61, 71, 106–107, 111–117, 168–169, 174, 175, 187, 190
phonetic misperception, 75, 101–109
P-map hypothesis, 86, 91–99
polysystemicity, 175, 176, 178, 179, 185, 186
probability matching, 73, 74, 76, 121–123, 125, 146, 147
production hypothesis, 86, 87–91, 96–99
prosodic analysis, 19, 172, 174–187
prosodic licensing, 89, 95

REASON, 3, 4, 9, 10, 11, 124, 125, 133, 139, 140, 146, 153, 156, 161, 162, 165, 166, 171, 172, 174, 181, 185, 187, 194
redundancy (in phonology), 27, 106–107, 177–178
RHYME, 3, 4, 10, 11, 124, 125, 133, 139, 140, 141, 146, 153, 156, 161, 162, 163, 172, 185, 194

semantic misperception, 110–118, 119–129, 140

spans, 5, 7, 15, 16–27, 28, 29, 102, 103, 107, 171, 198
speaker-control, 89–90
stress, 10, 16, 29, 31, 35–36, 45, 49, 50, 51, 53, 54, 56–57, 79, 144, 167, 178, 180
structuralist theory, 106, 174, 175, 176, 186, 188
syllable theory, 7, 19, 140, 151–153, 179–180, 186

teleology (in phonology), 87, 90, 92–93, 117, 123, 138, 140, 141, 161–162
transitional probabilities, 188–194

underlying representations, 39–40, 91–96, 97, 103, 105–108, 140
uniformitarianism (in phonology), 64, 66

variation (in speech), 36, 56, 62–77, 87, 107, 108, 110, 117, 119–129, 137, 138, 147, 149–157
vowel harmony, 8, 9, 16, 35–36, 37, 49, 50, 162, 170, 171, 173